Contemporary Art and Anthropology

009

Contemporary Art and Anthropology

Edited by
Arnd Schneider and Christopher Wright

Oxford · New York

English edition
First published in 2006 by
Berg
Editorial offices:
First Floor, Angel Court, 81 St Clements Street, Oxford OX4 1AW, UK
175 Fifth Avenue, New York, NY 10010, USA

Berg is the imprint of Oxford International Publishers Ltd.

Library of Congress Cataloging-in-Publication Data

A catalogue record for this book is available from the Library of Congress.

701·03
SCH

British Library Cataloguing-in-Publication Data

A catalogue record for this book is available from the British Library.

ISBN-13 978 1 84520 102 9 (Cloth)
978 1 84520 103 6 (Paper)

ISBN-10 1 84520 102 7 (Cloth)
1 84520 103 5 (Paper)

Typeset by JS Typesetting Ltd, Porthcawl, Mid Glamorgan
Printed in the United Kingdom by Biddles Ltd, King's Lynn

www.bergpublishers.com

Contents

Figures

Contributors

Claus Biegert, author, radio journalist, occasional film maker, anti-nuclear activist. Several books on indigenous peoples of North America. Contributing writer to *Süddeutsche Zeitung* and *natur & kosmos*. Collaborated with artist Rainer Wittenborn (see below) on the highly acclaimed *James Bay Project: A River Drowned by Water*.

Rimer Cardillo, artist, Full Professor of Printmaking at the State University of New York, New Paltz. In 2004 the Samuel Dorsky Museum at SUNY New Paltz featured a large retrospective of his work, *Impressions (and Other Images of Memory)*, and in 1998 The Bronx Museum of the Arts exhibited a 10-year survey of his work. He was selected to represent Uruguay at the 2001 Venice Biennial with a large installation.

Fernando Calzadilla is a theatre practitioner, visual artist, and scholar with a multicultural background, who weaves hands-on experience with theory to expand the scope of his art. With more than 30 years of experience in cultural production, his interdisciplinary practice includes performance, theatre, ethnography, and art. He is presently a doctoral candidate in performance studies at New York University.

Elizabeth Edwards is Professor and Senior Research Fellow in the Research Department, University of the Arts, London (LCC). Previously, she was Curator of Photographs at the Pitt Rivers Museum, University of Oxford; author of *Raw Histories* (Berg 2001), editor of *Anthropology and Photography* (Yale University Press 1992) and is co-editing a book *Photographs Objects Histories* (Routledge 2004).

Jonathan Friedman is Directeur d'Études at the École des Études Hautes en Sciences Sociales, Paris and Professor of Social Anthropology at the University of Lund, Sweden. His books include *Cultural Identity and Global Process* (Sage 1994), the edited volume *Consumption and Identity* (Harwood 1994), *System, Structure and Contradiction in the Evolution of 'Asiatic' Social Formations* (Altamira 1998), *PC Worlds* (University of California Press, forthcoming), *Globalization, the State and Violence* (Altamira 2003) and together with R. Denemark, B. Gills and G. Modelski, *World System History: The Science of Long-term Change* (Routledge 2000), with Shalini Randeria, *Worlds on the Move: Globalization, Migration and Cultural Security* (Tauris 2004), and with Kajsa Ekholm-Friedman, *Global Anthropology* (Altamira 2004).

Susanne Küchler is Reader in Material Culture within the Department of Anthropology at University College London. She has worked extensively on art and memory with special reference to the Pacific and has recently directed a collaborative ESRC-funded project on clothing and innovation in the Pacific. Her publications include *Malanggan: Art, Memory and Sacrifice* (Berg 2002) and *Pacific Pattern* (Thames & Hudson 2005).

Nikolaus Lang artist and Professor at the Academy of Arts, Munich. His project *Nunga und Goonya/Nunga and Goonya* (1991) was based on 3 years' fieldwork in southern Australia.

Dave Lewis studied photography at the former Polytechnic of Central London (PCL). He has a personal commitment to teaching and has conducted many workshops, in particular in schools, promoting the creative potential of photography. He has exhibited widely both in Britain and internationally, and is a member of Autograph ABP. He is currently working on a photographic project exploring the social uses of architecture.

George E. Marcus is the Joseph D. Jamail Professor and Chair of the Department of Anthropology at Rice University. He is co-author with Michael Fischer of *Anthropology as Cultural Critique* (University of Chicago Press 1986), co-editor with James Clifford of *Writing Culture* (University of California Press 1995), co-editor with Fred Meyers of *The Traffic in Culture: the Refiguration of Art and Anthropology*, and author of *Ethnography Through Thick and Thin* (Princeton University Press 1998).

César Paternosto born in Argentina, César Paternosto is a painter, sculptor and author who lived in New York from 1967 to 2004, and is now in Segovia, Spain. He received a Guggenheim Fellowship in 1972 and his works are included in public collections, such as the Museum of Modern Art and Solomon R. Guggenheim Museum in New York; Albright-Knox Gallery, Buffalo, NY; the Menil Collection, Houston, Texas and the Städtisches Museum Abteiberg Mönchengladbach, Germany. His book *The Stone and the Thread: Andean Roots of Abstract Art* (University of Texas Press) was published in 1996. In 2001 he curated the exhibition *Abstraction: The Amerindian Paradigm*, which opened at the Palais des Beaux-Arts in Brussels and later travelled to the IVAM, Institut Valencia d'Art Modern, Valencia, Spain. He wrote the main essay as well as editing the catalogue.

Christopher Pinney, Professor, Department of Anthropology, University College, London. He is the author of *Camera Indica: The Social Life of Indian Photographs* (Reaktion 1997), *Photos of the Gods* (Reaktion 2004) and co-editor with Nicholas Thomas of *Beyond Aesthetics* (Berg 2001).

Michael Richardson, Visiting Professor at Waseda University, Tokyo. His most recent work is *Surrealism and Cinema* (Berg 2005). He is the author of *The Experience of Culture* (Sage 2001) and *Georges Bataille* (Routledge 1994). He has also written many articles on aspects of surrealism and has edited several collections of surrealist writings, including The *Dedalus Book of Surrealism* (Dedalus, 1993–4), *Refusal of the Shadow: Surrealism and the Caribbean* (Verso 1996) and, with Krzysztof Fijalkowski, *Surrealism Against the Current* (Pluto 2001).

Denise Robinson is an independent writer and curator based in London. She has been the Director of several contemporary arts organizations including the Australian Centre for Photography and Director of International Film Festival, 'Queer Screen', Sydney. In England, she was Head of Artistic Program, Arnolfini, Bristol, visiting fellow at Tate Britain and visiting fellow at Goldsmiths College. She writes regularly on contemporary art and film for international journals, art magazines and exhibition catalogues, and has published several texts on the work of Susan Hiller. She is currently involved in curating an international project based in Nicosia.

Arnd Schneider (editor) Reader in Anthropology, University of East London, Senior Research Fellow, University of Hamburg, and Associate Fellow of the Institute for the Study of the Americas (University of London), Latin America Programme. Arnd Schneider writes on contemporary art and anthropology, migration and ethnographic film. His main publications include *Futures Lost: Identity and Nostalgia among Italian Immigrants in Argentina* (Peter Lang 2000) and *Mafia for Beginners* (with the illustrator Oscar Zárate (Ikon Books 1994). His essays 'The Art Diviners' (1993) 'Uneasy Relationships: Contemporary Artists and Anthropology' (1996), 'On appropriation' (2003), are exploring a new emerging field of art practices and anthropology. He was co-organizer of the international conference, *Fieldworks: Dialogues between Art and Anthropology* at Tate Modern in 2003. His new book, *Appropriation as Practice: Art and Identity in Argentina*, is being published (2006) by Palgrave/ Institute for the Study of the Americas Series.

Nicholas Thomas, Professor, Department of Anthropology, Goldsmiths College, London. His books include *Entangled objects* (Harvard 1989), *Possessions* (Thames & Hudson 1999), and *Beyond Aesthetics* (Berg, 2001), co-edited with Chris Pinney.

Rainer Wittenborn, artist, professor, Technical University, Munich. His *James Bay Project: A River Drowned by Water* (with Claus Biegert, Montreal Museum of Fine Arts 1982) was a major artistic investigation and exhibition project, collaborating with the Cree Indians of Northern Quebec.

Christopher Wright (editor) Lecturer, Department of Anthropology, Goldsmiths College London. Co-curator of *Presence*, Leighton House, London, January–March 2003. His essays include 'The Third Subject' (1998), and 'Supple Bodies' (2003). He was co-organizer of the international conference *Fieldworks: Dialogues between Art and Anthropology* at Tate Modern in 2003.

Acknowledgements

We take the opportunity to thank all contributors to this volume for their work and their keen interest in this project. Anonymous readers of this volume were very supportive of the project and acknowledged its innovative character, and we are grateful for their suggestions which helped to improve the manuscript. Our thanks also go to Kathryn Earle and Hannah Shakespeare, our editors at Berg, for seeing this book through to final publication.

Furthermore, we are grateful to all institutions and private persons who have aided us in our research and who made visual and written materials available to us, often waiving or reducing fees for copyright permissions. It would otherwise have been impossible to publish this richly illustrated volume as we had no separate budget available.

We also wish to thank hosts and audiences at the following institutions and venues to whom we have presented ideas over the years for their stimulating discussion: Goldsmiths College, London (Nicholas Thomas); University College, London (Susanne Küchler, Chris Pinney); St Antony's College, Oxford (Herminho Martins); the University of East London; City and Guilds of London Art School (Helen Wilkes); the University of Manchester (Anna Grimshaw, Amanda Ravetz); the New School for Social Research, New York (Aleksandra Mir, Vera Zolberg); the University of Texas, Austin (Mari Carmen Ramírez); the University of Colorado, Boulder (Donna Goldstein); the State University of New York at New Paltz (Rimer Cardillo); UNAM, Mexico City (Natividad Guitérrez); the Academy of Sciences, Ljubljana (Kristina Toplak), Universidad de Buenos Aires, Argentina (Catalina Saugy); the Universities of Copenhagen and Vienna (EASA Conferences, 2002 and 2004), the University of Bremen (Dorle Dracklé), and the University of Hamburg (Waltraud Kokot).

Every reasonable effort has been made to trace and acknowledge the ownership of the copyrighted material (including illustrations) included in this book. Any errors that may have occurred are inadvertent and will be corrected in subsequent editions, provided notification is sent to the editors.

The Challenge of Practice
Arnd Schneider and Christopher Wright

The aim of this volume is to stimulate new and productive dialogues between the domains of contemporary anthropology and art, and to discern common endeavours that encompass both disciplines. We want to encourage border crossings; our concern is not with establishing contemporary art as an object of anthropological research – 'art worlds' as other cultures to be studied. Nor do we think it is simply a matter of artists being more rigorous in their borrowings from anthropology, although there are many misapprehensions, on both sides, that could usefully be dispelled. Our aim, in exploring certain areas of overlap, is to encourage fertile collaborations and the development of alternative shared strategies of *practice* on both sides of the border.

In this introductory chapter we want to examine some of the similarities and differences between artistic and anthropological methodologies and practices in representing others. In exploring the limits and possibilities of representation and perception within the two disciplines we are concerned with how artistic practices can extend anthropological practices, and vice versa.

In the second chapter, 'Appropriations', Arnd Schneider focuses on some of the previous encounters between art and anthropology, as well as the appropriation of methodologies and subjects between the two disciplines.

In inviting contributions to this edited volume, our aim has been to point towards areas that require further dialogue between artists and anthropologists. Specifically, we wanted anthropologists to engage with artists' work, and artists and critics to explore the relevance of anthropology for contemporary artistic practices.

Thus a number of anthropologists write on contemporary artists: Christopher Pinney critically comments on Francesco Clemente's work in India; Michael Richardson explores the potentials of surrealist painter Josef Šima; Susanne Küchler investigates the work of Brent Collins and John Robinson, which is inspired by mathematics; Elizabeth Edwards considers the work of Mohini Chandra; Jonathan Friedman looks at the work of Carlos Capelán in the context of recent developments in anthropological theory; and Nicholas Thomas writes on the process of representation and difference with reference to tattooing. Denise Robinson explores the work of Susan Hiller, a major international artist, who originally trained as an anthropologist. The artist and art writer César Paternosto investigates how modern abstract art and the abstract art of the pre-Columbian Americas are connected, and the editors explore in a short chapter with interviews the anthropologically informed work of Rimer Cardillo, Rainer Wittenborn, Claus Biegert, and Nikolaus Lang. We also commissioned a visual essay by photographer Dave Lewis, which takes the Anthropology Department of the University of East London as its ethnographic site.

CROSSING BORDERS

The disciplines and some of the units of comparison involved in the border crossings that occupy us in this book are often difficult to grasp securely. The reified concepts 'anthropology' and 'art' have at times an almost nebulous existence, at others they are palpable, concrete worlds in which disciplinary pressures are exercised. Many of the categories involved are unstable and we want to question some of the 'common-sense' assumptions about these two fields that we feel are no longer valid. Art and anthropology are both made up of a range of diverse practices that operate within the context of an equally complex range of expectations and constraints. Ideas and practices of training are one key area of differentiation between the two fields, and we will argue that these need to be creatively refigured.

Although anthropology, from the perspective of art, is often perceived negatively as a 'science' – and it is precisely the confines of a scientific discipline that artists are critical of – both are disciplines in the sense of having canons of practice (however loosely defined), accepted histories (although these are frequently disputed and rewritten), and their own academies and institutions. We recognize that art and anthropology have both been active in criticizing and extending their own boundaries, but they still involve broadly defined ways of working, regular spaces of exhibition, and sets of expectations. In some cases differences between the two have more to do with exhibition sites and strategies – with finished products, rather than intentions or practices. Certainly, these dramatically influence the kinds of dialogues and audiences that are possible. However, despite the fact that one can identify polarizing or centripetal influences at work in each discipline, neither is a static, stable, or unified entity whose borders can be definitively traced. Both contemporary anthropology and art contain centrifugal movements and a diverse range of culturally, regionally, and historically located and inflected practices.

We are concerned with questioning assumptions about 'anthropology' and 'art' – these are labels that can often work to obscure any affinities – in order to highlight some of the correspondences we think exist between the two endeavours. In focusing on the practices of anthropologists and artists, this book may help to point out the disparity between actual ways of working and received notions of contemporary anthropology and art. We are not solely interested in formal similarities between the work of artists and anthro-pologists, but also want to discern 'deeper affinities'. Neither are we suggesting that all anthropologists should necessarily embrace the methodologies of artists, there are aspects of anthropology where such a move is clearly not relevant.[1] But we do believe that some aspects of anthropological theory and practice, and not just 'visual anthropology' or the 'anthropology of art', would benefit from a consideration of art practices and these in turn could learn much from further dialogues with anthropology. Both disciplines share certain questions, areas of investigation and, increasingly, methodologies, and there is growing recognition and acceptance of these areas of overlap.

The borders between anthropology and art have never been completely or rigidly demarcated and, despite much indifference, at specific historical conjunctures (some of which we will review in the second chapter), each has in some sense required the other as a necessary foil to work against. Although this has sometimes been a productive friction, both disciplines at times also feel threatened by the other, or are envious of the other's practices, as suggested by Hal Foster in his influential article 'The Artist as Ethnographer'.[2] Whilst this book is concerned to promote dialogue, there have been occasions when suggesting border crossings of any kind has provoked hostility on both sides, reflecting an anxiety of interdisciplinarity, which is perhaps also a product of the often blurred nature of the borders. In advocating the development of new practices we do not want to gloss over differences between contemporary anthropology and art, as these can in themselves be productive points of departure for work.

Connections between the two disciplines have become more relevant, and problematic, with the so-called 'ethnographic turn' of contemporary art.[3] This has involved, among other things, the adoption of a broad definition of ethnography, and the production of an increasing number of works that directly tackle some of the concerns of anthropology. From the perspective of contemporary anthropology, the development of DVD and other digital technologies has raised the possibility of an enhanced visual practice within anthropology. This would seem to usher in a new period of creative potential for contemporary anthropology, but, if this is to be a reflexive practice transcending any art/science dichotomy and involve more than the production of illustrated multimedia 'texts', there needs to be a new approach to images and creativity in anthropology.

Similarities between contemporary anthropology and art are not weighted equally, and the same is true for the appropriations that have occurred across the borders between them. Artists have incorporated the methodologies of anthropologists in idiosyncratic ways, making inventories, carrying out 'fieldwork', using interviews, and engaging with anthropology's theorizations of cultural difference.[4] Art writing, too, has taken on some of the theoretical concerns of anthropology. But there has been relatively less traffic in the opposite direction. Post-structuralist philosophy, literary theory, ethnopoetics, and experimental writing all heavily influenced the important 'writing culture' debate in anthropology in the 1980s in which the written nature of anthropology was subjected to a self-reflexive critique.[5] Still, as Arnd Schneider pointed out in his article 'The Art Diviners' developments in contemporary art were hardly noticed by these critiques.[6]

Experimentation and creativity are differently conceived, and differently valued, on either side of the border. For example, in terms of anthropological film making 'anthropological content is often defined as precisely that which takes precedence over, and is the polar opposite of aesthetics', as suggested by Chris Wright in his article 'The Third Subject'.[7] The fact is that there remains an ambiguous and at times hostile relation between these two terms within anthropology. In the current situation in Europe and North America, where academic posts in anthropology are relatively scarce in comparison with the numbers of professionals trained, experimentation and creativity walk a fine line between being an asset and a burden. The role of experiment is still largely relegated to a historical pantheon of established 'maverick' anthropologists (such as Michel Leiris, Gregory Bateson, and Jean Rouch), rather than an actively encouraged and valued facet of anthropological training. Some anthropologists, such as Anna Grimshaw,[8] have argued that the discipline's own *avant garde* was effectively stifled in the early decades of the twentieth century, as the new discipline struggled for academic acceptance and a foothold in the universities. Indeed, this period saw certain common agendas and strategies shared by art, anthropology, and art history dissolved through the creation of more rigidly bounded university disciplines. This process of separation has long outlived any usefulness.

EXPLORATIONS

In the following we will consider new possibilities for dialogues between art and anthropology. We will set what we see as an agenda for future collaborations based on examples of radical experiments from contemporary art and anthropology. Our main argument is that anthropology's iconophopia and self-imposed restriction of visual expression to text-based models needs to be overcome by a critical engagement with a range of material and sensual practices in the contemporary arts.

Anselm Kiefer's book work *Cauterization of the District of Buchen*[9] (1974) uses a viscous amalgam of iron oxide and linseed oil to engage our senses of touch and smell in addition to our visual faculties. The book invokes the tactility of vision, something that the reproduction of two of its pages here can only gesture towards. The blackness of this 'burnt' flux gradually overcomes the book – the physicality of the image resisting any attempts to contain it or subsume experience into 'language'. Kiefer imagines military stores of petrol slowly leaking out, igniting and cauterizing the land (perhaps as one would cauterize a wound?), and the work continues his exploration of the processes of burning, silting, and sinking in relation to German history and *Geist* (spirit).[10] The direct sensual experience involved is not one we normally associate with books, although in this case, paradoxically, its status as an

Figure 1.1. Anselm Kiefer, *The Burning of the Rural District of Buchen*, 1974, bound original photographs with ferrous oxide and linseed oil on fibrous wallpaper ($21^3/8 \times 17^{11}/16 \times 1^1/8$ inches; $62 \times 45 \times 3$ cm), 210 pages, private collection. Courtesy of the Gagosian Gallery.

artwork actually prevents us from touching it (there is something perverse about the thought of it being carefully handled in white gloves by gallery staff). Kiefer has made a diverse range of book works, from printed facsimiles of orginal books containing watercolours, photographs, and collages like *Transition from Cool to Warm* (1988), to the sculpture *High Priestess* (1985-9),[11] a monumental metal bookshelf filled with huge books made of lead.[12] These works suggest productive irritations and resonances for thinking through some of the current relations between anthropology and art.

Kiefer's books involve affective intensities; they engage us bodily. Anthropologists have remained largely unconcerned with these processes, or even actively hostile to them, in creating their own visual works, whether films, photographs, or books. Recent proposals have called for anthropologists to focus on the performative aspects of artefacts, and on the agency of images and artworks,[13] but these have been applied to the cultures that anthropologists study, and not to anthropology's own visual practices. Within anthropology, as in other disciplines, there is a history of apprehending objects and actions of all kinds as if they were texts (Clifford Geertz is exemplary of this approach), but this is often a way of avoiding dealing with difficult issues like affects; Kiefer reminds us that texts can also be encountered as objects. The specifics of these encounters can allow us to cross disciplinary borders.

BLINDNESS

Why does anthropology have this lacuna or blind spot when pursuing its own visual practices? In 1914 Bronislaw Malinowski, one of the 'founding fathers' of British social anthropology, was planning to take his long-term friend Stanislaw Witkiewicz as 'photographer and draftsman' on his paradigm-forming fieldwork in the Trobriand Islands.[14] Both took photographs in Sri Lanka en route – although sadly none have survived – but they also argued and, after hearing of the outbreak of war in Europe, Witkiewicz left Malinowski in Australia and returned to join the Tsar's army. Anthropologists have recently speculated about the kind of work Witkiewicz might have produced in the Trobriands had he stayed with Malinowski, posing one as the antithesis of the other:[15]

> Malinowski appears to have resisted the experimental, art nouveau trends indulged by Witkiewicz. If Witkiewicz's photography leaned towards surrealism, then Malinowski would ensure that his own exemplified realism. Whereas Witkiewicz treated photography as an expressive art form to be explored, Malinowski treated it purely as a visual aid to his science.'[16]

Witkiewicz's concern 'to capture the metaphysical face behind the surface appearance' is seen as the polar opposite of Malinowski's concern with 'science'[17] – the latter's photographs are everything that Wikiewicz's 'are *not*'.[18] A whole series of divisions, like those between surface and depth, which are inscribed at this formative stage of modern anthropology, still haunt relations between anthropology and art.

Despite anthropology's increasing concern with understanding the plurality of approaches to images, and the multiplicity of roles they fulfil in other cultures, it has remained within a relatively narrow realist paradigm in its own creation and use of images. Work that crosses the borders of these paradigms is often contentious. With its lack of narrative voiceover or subtitling and its reliance on visual and temporal structures to create meaning, Robert Gardner's 1986 film *Forest of Bliss*, and the arguments it generated, demonstrated that anthropologists frequently find it hard to appreciate the aesthetics and the effects of film in their own right.[19]

POLARIZED

Oppositional models have contributed to what Lucien Taylor has called anthropology's 'iconophobia',[20] and the visual is still too frequently treated by

Figure 1.2. Bronislaw Malinowski, *Zakopane*, c. 1912, photograph: Stanislaw Witkiewicz. Courtesy of Helena Wayne.

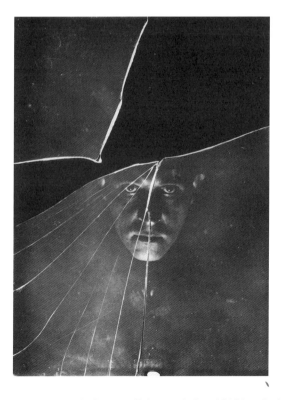

Figure 1.3. *Stanislaw Witkiewicz, Self-portrait*, Zakopane before 1914 (cracked glass negative), collection of E. Franczak and S. Okolowicz. Courtesy of Stefan Okolowicz.

anthropologists as something inherently seductive, illusory, and uncontrollable; Alfred Gell argued that anthropologists should not 'succumb' to the 'enchantment' of art.[21] Christopher Pinney has suggested that film has been the preferred medium of visual anthropologists precisely because it can constrain the visual within temporal and narrative structures, in contrast with still images, which allow 'too many meanings'.[22] And, of course, 'film', in anthropology, usually means single-device recording and projection (with the contemporary use of more than one camera, or multiple projection devices, such as artists use in installations, being virtually unheard of; and this despite recent cautious attempts to incorporate multiple screens into DVD and CD Rom works).[23] Other arguments have revolved around a division, either complementary or antagonistic, between visual works and texts, with the latter retaining a privileged authority.[24] The image bears an impossible burden in visual anthropology; simultaneously a transparent medium of the real (only certain minimal kinds of manipulation are permissible), and yet incapable of producing explanation or understanding in its own right (something that requires diverse forms of manipulation).

The privileged status of the word and the authority of its interpreters, have historically contributed to the proliferation of textual models for the world. Attitudes to mimesis which, in its role as rhetoric, did not attempt to delude an audience into taking an imitation for real, but to incite them to action – to create a reality – were transformed as former connections between textual and visual were severed by a modernism that argued for their radical difference. Anthropologists are increasingly wary of the assumption that text and language are the only paradigms for understanding and explanation, and that meaning can only be discovered by translating or decoding 'texts'. In opposition to suggestions that visual anthropology should adopt the forms and guidelines of text-based anthropology, David MacDougall has persuasively argued for the development of a practice that 'may need to define itself not at all in terms of written anthropology but as an alternative to it, as a quite different way of knowing related phenomena'.[25] MacDougall has described his own recent work as becoming more like 'art practice',[26] and oppositions between art and anthropology are becoming more problematic in the current situation of shared paradigms.

Visual anthropologists and their mainstream counterparts need to develop an approach to images that is aware of what they want, that acknowledges and productively makes use of their affective powers, and develops new ways of using them.[27] The possibilities for new strategies and practices need to be explored without making prior definitions of 'art' and 'anthropology', and automatically excluding certain practices on the basis of this. This has been a long-standing and disabling feature of visual anthropology that needs to be overcome. Recourse to a simple realist paradigm of one kind or another is no longer a guarantee of veracity or integrity, but the implications of this have yet to be embraced by visual anthropology. Although visual anthropologists have repeatedly called for the development of new forms of practice,[28] there is still a reluctance to deal with those aspects that have been relegated to the realm of the aesthetic, and are therefore considered to be the concern of art, art history, or the anthropology of art.[29]

There is little or no attention paid to the possibilities of representing research in the anthropology of art, despite the fact that aesthetics is a well-established research topic within that discipline. Aesthetics is an *object* of study, but the strange lack of connections between theory and practice in this area means that it rarely crosses over to become an actively explored constituent of visual anthropology practice. A whole range of practical concerns are effectively unavailable as valid alternatives for making works.

ART/SCIENCE

The insistence on radical differences between art and science (a rubric under which anthropology is often subsumed) also contributes to anthropological definitions of art practice and to artists' negative conceptions of anthropology as a text-based discipline concerned solely with scientific objectivity and distance. Antony Gormley, writing in 1988, argued that 'the whole history of man since the Enlightenment is one of control: of the world understood as an object out there, of vision requiring distance which promotes knowledge. My work tries to create a place of feeling, which is in contrast to objective rationalism.'[30] His work addresses issues of embodied understanding and questions the idea 'that retinal response is the only channel of communication in art, and the notion that objects are discrete entities',[31] suggesting parallels with Gell's discussion of the efficacy of art works.[32] Polarized models, such as mind/body and objective/subjective, are as likely to be interrogated by artists like Gormley, who studied anthropology, as they are by anthropologists. The scientific world view that Gormley is reacting against is one that many anthropologists would find equally problematic, and his work has much to offer anthropology practice in terms of understanding the image and its affects. We are not suggesting that visual anthropologists necessarily should make sculptures; this would raise productive questions but it would be a transposition of one practice onto another, and we are concerned with the development of new practices that draw on both disciplines.

IMAGE/TEXT

Despite the widespread influence of the 'writing culture' critique, George Marcus laments the fact that experiments with aesthetic issues and textual forms have not become a regular feature of recent anthropological work.[33] Although such explorations are perhaps best conducted by those who already have secure careers,[34] there have always been individual attempts to develop alternatives to the orthodox combination of text and illustration in anthropology. One early example is Edmund Carpenter's 1973 book *Eskimo Realities*,

Figure 1.4. Antony Gormley, *Inside Australia*, 2002/2003. Cast alloy of iron, iridium, vanadium and titanium. The entire work consists of 51 insider sculptures based on 51 inhabitants of Menzies, Western Australia. The image shows Lorraine Williams, who was a model for one of the sculptures, and two children from Menzies. Photo: © Ashley De Prazer. A film, 'Inside Australia', a collaboration between Antony Gormley and the anthropologist Hugh Brody, was also released in 2003, and shown on Channel Five (UK). Courtesy of Antony Gormley.

which uses formal arrangements of text and image in a way that respects Inuit aesthetics and fuses artistic and anthropological sensibilities.[35]

Similarly, the journal *Alcheringa*, started in 1970 by Jerome Rothenberg and Dennis Tedlock, experimented with the visual presentation of texts in its concern with 'ethnopoetics' – although Rothenberg pointed out that 'the visual side (hand and eye) of ethnopoetics has generally been ignored in favour of the oral side (hand and mouth)'.[36] Rarely found on a teaching syllabus, these works cross borders between art and anthropology in exploring some of the possibilities of visual presentation.

One powerful example from the tradition of 'ethnopoetics' is David and Susan McAllester's *Hogans: Navajo Houses and Songs*[37] which presents a collection of ritually sung texts and blessings for Navajo houses ('hogans') alongside photographs from the Navajo reservation. The texts by the Native American ethnomusicologist David McAllester are translations of Navajo 'house songs' that retain the style of the original recordings:

> The aim has been to convey to the reader what the Navajos themselves are say-
> ing rather than to create translations which are comfortable to the ears of

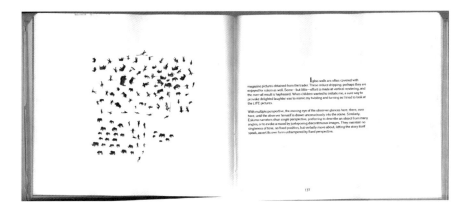

Figure 1.5. From Edmund Carpenter, *Eskimo Realities*, copyright © 1973 by Edmund Carpenter. Used by permission of Bantam Books, a division of Random House, Inc.

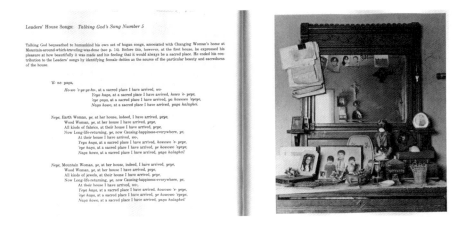

Figure 1.6. David and Susan McAllester, *Hogans: Navajo Houses and Songs*, Middletown CT: Wesleyan University Press, 1980 (2nd edition 1987), pp. 50–1. Courtesy of David McAllester.

non-Navajos, and thus to extend to the reader the privilege of participating further than is usually possible in the beauty and vitality of the Navajo poetic world.[38]

Each house song is presented with one or more photographs by Susan McAllester. These black-and-white images show life on the reservation, including the influence of consumer goods. Few people are shown, and the photographs focus on house interiors (as many songs refer to these) and the architectural layout of settlements on the reservation. Although the general stance appears to be one of detachment rather than 'participation', the images are intimate in their depiction of interiors and objects. Barbara Tedlock has commented on the McAllesters's 're-enactment of Navajo aesthetic':[39]

David McAllester by keeping the original Navajo word order in English . . . forces the English reader who expects smooth literary translations to slow down and puzzle out these syntactically awkward house-blessing texts. Likewise, Susan McAllester, through her startling juxtapostion of photographs which portray with equal reverence Navajo traditionalism and acculturation, shocks and slows down the viewer who desires either social commentary on Navajo poverty or else romantic pictures of strictly traditional hogans . . . Through these dual acts of ethnographic realism, an unusual eye/ear rhythm is set in motion that demands synaesthetic thinking on the part of the hearer/looker.[40]

Critics have argued that, as a result of its lack of contextualization, further narrative direction, or ethnographic explanation, the work may provide ambiguous messages.[41] But, in creating a complex synaesthetic use of image and text a productive tension is created between and within *sung* texts and *silent* images – which would have been lost in a simple explicatory text. Works like these offer a kind of aesthetic resistance to the dominant mode of visual representation found in the majority of anthropological books. The monotonous and incessant flow of text and inset illustrations is interrupted by a visually subtle approach to the aesthetics of others.

Anthropology only appears as a text-dominated discipline if the focus remains firmly fixed on one of its established ways of creating published or publishable works, albeit the overwhelmingly privileged one. In the processes of its making, through fieldwork of many different kinds, anthropology involves, and is concerned with studying, an extremely rich and varied range of sensual experiences.[42]

Steven Feld's recent three-CD *Bosavi: Rainforest Music from Papua New Guinea* combines 'soundscapes' of the forest with Bosavi songs and music in pursuit of aural texture, raising exciting possibilities for the use of sound in anthropological representation.[43] Anthropology must include an active exploration of senses other than vision, which has been considered the restricted domain of visual anthropology. Paul Stoller has argued that 'it is representationally as well as analytically important to consider how perception in non-western societies devolves not simply from vision . . . but also from smell, touch, taste, and hearing.[44] Recent interest in an 'anthropology of the senses' and synaethesia[45] raises many interesting questions but, despite Stoller's point, can end up constituting new anthropological objects of study rather than, as we are advocating here, exploring the implications for anthropological *practices* of representation.

A consideration of other visual cultures can provide challenging insights into the ways in which the ordering of the senses affects our perception of the world. The concept of synaethesia, hearing colours for example, is a well-documented practice among Amazonian cultures.[46] Michael Taussig argued that among the healers of the upper Amazon 'the senses cross over and translate into each other',[47] and Mark Münzel pointed out the corresponding limitations of anthropologists methodological and perceptual tools in asking whether they should be 'allowed to judge the visual art of the Amazon with [their] one-dimensional gaze?'[48] David Howes and Constance Classen suggested that anthropological research should be interrogated to discern 'which senses are emphasised or repressed, and by what means to what ends?'[49] If anthropologists wish to enter into dialogue with the variety of sensual expressions of other cultures they must enlarge their own sensorium. One thing these studies of the senses do reveal is the extent to which the majority of the sensual experiences involved in fieldwork normally disappear from anthropological writing.

The translation – or reduction, depending on your viewpoint – of experience into academic text. The wealth of visual and other sensorial experience frequently remains obscured by the opacity of the written text. Discussing the role of printed words, Bruno Latour asks 'how much explanatory burden can they carry?'[50] He argues that the reduction involved with transforming three-dimensional objects into two-dimensional objects on paper (words) has resulted in similarly two-dimensional thinking. Through the abstraction of writing, objects and the 'world out there' are reduced in dimension and can be dominated in a different way. Our argument is directed against this literally *flat* thinking in the presentation of anthropological research. Hugh Brody comments on his 30 years of living with and writing about Arctic peoples:

> I was left with a deep conviction that I had yet to write about that which is most important. Something lay there that eluded not just me, but many who have experienced another way of life. We write about some facets of it, some surfaces, that we make our business. But the gold we find is transformed by the reverse alchemy of our journey, from there to here, into lead. Not into nothing, not into worthlessness, but into a substance that has more weight than light, more utility than beauty, is malleable rather than of great value . . . Anthropologists are often skilled at crossing divides between peoples in their field work, but clumsy when it comes to writing up their 'findings'. Perhaps the desire for the esteem of peers and critics leads to a tendency to make things unduly complicated or scholarly or heroic – depending on the audience we most need to impress.'[51]

Jean-Francois Lyotard's discussion of 'discourse' and 'figure' provides one productive alternative to models that antagonistically oppose the visual and the textual.[52] The figural is that which discourse cannot contain or explain, 'an alterity within the discursive itself' – in the realm of figure 'things happen . . . intensities are felt'.[53] Lyotard argues for a practice that 'does not transcend the differences between the two realms but insteads inhabits these differences, exhibits them, radicalizes them', and talks of 'the sensible taking shape out of the meaningful, and by doing so, greatly extending its possibilities'.[54] In these terms Malinoswki's diaries, which reveal the inner turmoil of his fieldwork in the Trobriand Islands, are more figural than his photographs.[55] It is not then, a case of persuading anthropologists to abandon discourse, but rather to explore the possibilities of figure in relation to it. The notion that images cannot be adequately subsumed by words is not new to anthropologists; Roy Wagner has

Trees, like palm trees in the distance, fill up the foreground. They hardly move, maybe the tops are swaying a bit, the sky behind is dull and pale blue. A wispy bit of cloud floats across the bottom. A slow rotating sound from somewhere else gets louder but still sounds distant as a heavy looking grey copter moves across the sky in front of the trees. It moves slowly but is gone quickly. Some yellow dust floats up in the wind and follows behind it, then fades back into the green. There's some music, just strobing away, about to get to something. A bit more yellow dust smokes up, leaving a huge silence behind it. Then the music kicks in. Nothing happens but dust. Then the trees behind turn the dust green, you can only see their tops. The rotor sound fades in again, another copter flies higher up this time, you can only see the bottom rails. It's passed, leaving the same misted-out background. So quietly, silently, three fires flare up into the trees. They roll upwards, blinding orange, then three more explode, one, two... three. They roll into one ginormous billowing ball, it's so huge, it's everything. Then it disappears into its own smoke, deep, murky, impenetrable, poisonous green. Just a small fleck of orange flame shows through. The music, it's singing, comes through too, it's all slow and building, "...this is the end...", it's like the first time. It's so deep, all that smoky green. The green copters float past, left to right, right to left, like shadows. The scene sort of slips past, but doesn't change much. The fire gets tugged off in the copters' wind. The picture fades into murky colours, it's impossible to work out what's what. Everything's sort of revealing itself, slowly – it's the slowest. Gradually, in the end, a face comes through. Both eyes stare straight ahead, just looking out at you. I can't tell the face cos it's upside down, but the music's getting hotter and the face is hot too. Something whirrs inconspicuously in in front of it. The eyes blink, and I think they flick left. The background still passes behind, faded out behind the face. More copters, big, faded ones.

Figure 1.7. Fiona Banner, *The Nam*, London: Frith Street Books, 1997, first page (no page numbering).

argued that text is inadequate at glossing certain images and events among the Barok of New Ireland; 'an image can and must be experienced or witnessed, rather than merely described or summed up verbally . . . [it] can never be adequately glossed. It must be experienced in order to be understood, and the experience of its effect is at once its meaning and its power'.[56] Anthropological scepticism about art and its potential is a result of its focus on the textual, and the perceived threat to the authority of the word that images represent.

FIELDWORK

Lothar Baumgarten's 'book work' for the Documenta X exhibition in 1997 consisted of a hundred or so collaged pages of black and white photocopies of his photographs of the Yanomami people of Venezuela, stuck directly on the wall as if they were proofs for an imagined book documenting the year-and-a-half that he spent living with them between 1978 and 1980. The Documenta catalogue referred to the work as 'poetic anthropology', and to Baumgarten's archives as an 'intimate diary' rather than an 'analytic study'.[57] It also suggested that 'his radical shift to an "other space" is also an immersion in the space of the other, and his experience among the Yanomami constitutes a critique of the cultural categories of knowledge and an attempt at shedding the self'.[58] Baumgarten wants to dispense with definitions of 'artist' and 'scientist' and look instead at actions and ways of working, and the duration and rigour of his project with the Yanomami is comparable to anthropological fieldwork, but what differentiates his work from an analytic study? Although his photographs satisfy the empirical demands of anthropologists and represent a broad view of Yanomami life – gardening, canoe making, hunting, drug taking and disputes – their site of display marks them as art. Once this has been effectively established a series of expectations fall into place concerning intention, authority, and the status of the images and their relation to the world.

Artists increasingly engage in fieldwork practices, either in an extended way (like Lothar Baumgarten), or through shorter periods, residencies, or the production of site-specific works. Other examples include Martha Rosler's *The Bowery in Two Inadequate Descriptive Systems* (1974–5), and Renée Green's *Project Unité* (1993).[59] Gillian Wearing's video work *Drunk* (1997–9) shows a group of South London 'street drinkers'; men and women interacting, drinking, arguing, and fighting set against a white studio backdrop. It has the aura of 'authenticity' that is a feature of work included in the 'ethnographic turn' of recent art practice, and her work is frequently discussed as a process of collaboration or collusion with others involving her adoption of 'an apparently anthropological, documentary approach'.[60] Wearing 'researches' her subjects, filming the group on and off over a two year period, and presents the results in the form of photographs, video and text. The work relies on similar

Figure 1.8. Gillian Wearing, *Drunk*, DVD three-screen projection, 23 minutes, 1999. Edition of 3 of 5 + 1 AP (5). Copyright Gillian Wearing. Courtesy of Maureen Paley.

guarantees of duration and intimacy to those that continue to underwrite anthropological fieldwork.[61]

Anthropology has no monopoly on fieldwork and artists appropriate and make use of what are frequently assumed to be anthropological tools to produce a diverse range of works. In the expanded sense of a paradigm that spans both disciplines, fieldwork is an area for radical experimentation. Despite scepticism about threats to 'artistic freedom', these fieldworks by artists demonstrate that a consideration of anthropological issues can be productive. Both artists and anthropologists play with distance and intimacy – an intimacy that is the currency of fieldwork – and both now overtly place themselves between their audiences and the world. Fieldwork based artworks are yet another argument for the replacement of polarised oppositional models with active investigations and dialogues.

ENLARGING VIEWS

Bill Viola's *Nantes Triptych* (1992) inhabits the spaces between discourse and figure and has been described as a 'total installation', an experience which engages all the viewer's faculties of perception.[62] In its incarnation at Tate Modern in London this three-screen video work was projected on a large scale, filling the entire wall of a darkened gallery. The sounds of breathing – that of the woman in labour and that of an elderly woman on a life-support machine; its resonances with medieval altarpieces; its duration – people entering the gallery either watch transfixed until the woman has given birth, or leave quickly. All these elements work together to create a fundamental understanding. For Viola the visual is only a surface overlaying a divine order and he argues that 'art has always been a whole-body, physical experience. This sensuality is the basis of its true conceptual and intellectual nature, and is inseparable from it'.[63] His concern with reconnecting mind and body reaffirms the latter as a key instrument of knowledge, a knowledge that embraces the totality of our sensual perception and experience rather than intellectual activity alone.

Viola does not want to make works that are only visually successful, but works which 'think well'. For him, 'the visual is always subservient to the field, the total system of perception/cognition at work' and this is 'the only whole true image.[64] Art is treated here as a form of knowledge not aesthetics, and the questions his work addresses are not answerable through discursive explanation, they are 'not problems to be solved but, rather, areas to be inhabited, to be encountered through Being'.[65] The relation of experience to understanding is vital. Anthropology, which is fundamentally concerned with experience, not just in the sense of fieldwork, but also in the sense of understanding and representing the experience of others, has generally relied on a separation of body and mind in what it produces; Viola challenges the grounds of this separation. Wanting to return art to a functional relationship with the communities in which it occurs – the artist's role is as a producer of

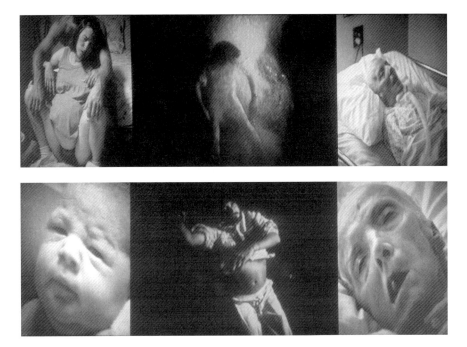

Figure 1.9. Bill Viola, *Nantes Triptych*, 1992. Video/sound installation. Photo: Kira Perov. Musée des Beaux-Arts de Nantes. Courtesy of Bill Viola Studio.

objects to be used – Viola argues that the critical analytic practices 'that dominate our lives as art professionals' should be secondary to this ritualistic function.[66]

Viola's work raises questions about the kinds of information and understanding that anthropology sees itself as concerned with, and directly tackles issues of embodied meaning that visual anthropology avoids. Tensions between the desire to embody the experience of others, and the desire to maintain some form of scientific rigour are as yet unresolved in anthropology. The task is to make them productive tensions.

VISUAL CULTURES

It required the reflexive turn in anthropology and the revision of the founding positivist version of the discipline, including the challenge to the anthropological monograph as text, to prepare the ground for a belated anthropological concern with modern and contemporary art practices. In the wake of Howard Becker's groundbreaking book *Art Worlds* (published in 1982) this produced a number of case studies in which art worlds, in a functionalist sense, were seen as subsystems within late capitalism, albeit with their own social and cultural logic. Furthermore, the role of contemporary Aboriginal and African art forced anthropologists to deal with art markets. However, these studies still dealt with the art of others, and 'art worlds' for anthropologists remain objects of study – they do not imply any methodological dialogue – although there have been occasional collaborations between the two 'worlds'.[67] Art figures largely as a new object of enquiry, without realizing the epistemological potential or critical implications that contemporary art practices have for anthropological representation.

Recent writing in anthropology and art criticism has acknowledged earlier points of contact between the two domains and raised questions that suggest collaborative possibilities and the need to rethink established working practices. Anthropologists George E. Marcus and Fred Myers in their landmark volume *The Traffic in Culture* (1995) emphasize three important points. Firstly, they suggest that 'the concerns of anthropology have been one primary source of innovation for the creation of avant-garde work in the modern art world, a key source of difference on which the engine that powers "art of the new", "creativity", aesthetics, social critique, taste, respectability, desire, and so on, has run', and that figures such as the 'primitive', 'tribal', and 'exotic' have disrupted dominant conventions of modern art at several points. Secondly, aspects of anthropology have been assimilated into the art world only through art discourse and this has resulted in the lack of productive two-way dialogue. Thirdly, the use of anthropology in the art world has depended on the authority and stability of concepts that anthropologists have constructed about the 'primitive'. Since these categories are no longer stable, they can no longer underwrite artistic practices. For Marcus and Myers art needs to accept its loss of autonomy and redefine 'the boundaries and modes of assimilating influence in order to produce art'.[68] This is what a critical ethnographic study of art, and a consideration of ethnographic practices within anthropology, can offer.

The anthropology of art was developed within the categories and practices of Western art worlds themselves. It has traditionally either been critical of Western categories by demonstrating the difficulty of applying them cross-culturally, or it has appropriated Western art's categories to valorize non-Western culture as having aesthetics of equal value to ours. The focus on other ways of seeing has contributed to a reconnection of art to a broader realm of culture. Art is no longer seen as an autonomous aesthetic realm, but is firmly embedded in cultural and historical specifics. The wide-reaching influence of this shift was made apparent by a survey on the rise of the term 'visual culture' that the journal October carried out in the mid-1990s.[69] W. J. Mitchell argued that visual culture involved an

emphasis on the social field of the visual, the everyday processes of looking at others and being looked at. This complex field of visual reciprocity is not merely a by-product of social reality but actively constitutive of it. Vision is as important as language in mediating social relations, and it is not reducible to language, to the 'sign', or to discourse.[70]

The *October* editorial argued that 'the interdisciplinary project of "visual culture" is no longer organised on the model of history (as were the disciplines of art history, architectural history, film history etc.) but on the model of anthropology.'[71] What is required now is an analysis of the image as a social object. Many approaches to visual culture, including those from art history, visual sociology and cultural studies, are now reliant, either explicitly or implicitly, on theories and methodologies derived from anthropology and ethnographic fieldwork, and the interdisciplinary nature of visual culture has meant that boundaries have been increasingly the subject of investigation, rather than denial.

Hal Foster in his seminal article 'The Artist as Ethnographer?' is concerned with recent trends in the traffic between art and anthropology. For Foster, a series of misrecognitions have passed back and forth between art and anthropology. He argues that 'ethnographic surrealism' as discussed by James Clifford (about which more in the second chapter) stands for a kind of 'artist-envy', a form of self-idealization of the anthropologist as an avant-garde collagist or semiologist. A similar kind of 'ethnographer envy' is felt by artists who value anthropology as a 'science of alterity', as a discipline that takes culture as its object (to which it has privileged access), and as a contextualizing, interdisciplinary, and self-critiquing endeavour.[72] Both sides have not only displayed envy at each other's enterprises but also suspicion, and sometimes ignorance, of how methods, paradigms and traditions were established within each field.

Miwon Kwon has also discussed the work of Nikki S. Lee as an example of the 'ethnographic turn' that is a product of 'ethnographer envy'. Kwon argues that it is not just the adoption of an ethnographic methodology that establishes connections between art and anthropology, but a shared concern with the 'politics of representation'. Art practices which have critically examined the 'uneven power relations enacted by and through representations' are relevant to anthropological debates on the production of knowledge. A Korean American, Lee has been involved in several projects in the late 1990s in which she photographs herself, or has herself photographed, disguised as different ethnic and subcultural communities; Hispanic, punk, senior citizen and so forth. The snapshot quality of the photographs of Lee's performances is intended as a guarantee of their 'authenticity' and a sign of her intimate, spontaneous contact with the other. Her own ethnic identity further adds to that aura of 'authenticity'. But for Kwon this 'unstudied informality' effectively masks Lee's status as an outsider who 'in absorbing the identity of the other, will render the other into a prop for the self',[73] and suggests that the work fails to tackle the dynamic relations between experience and interpretation, between participation and observation. What is unacceptable in the name of an objectifying discipline, is equally unacceptable under the name of the 'artist' or the guise of art.

In adopting a pseudo-ethnographic pose the artist can end up assuming ethnographic authority rather than questioning it, and Foster has pointed out three important assumptions that are involved with work such as Lee's. Firstly, artistic transformation is equivalent to political transformation, and that the

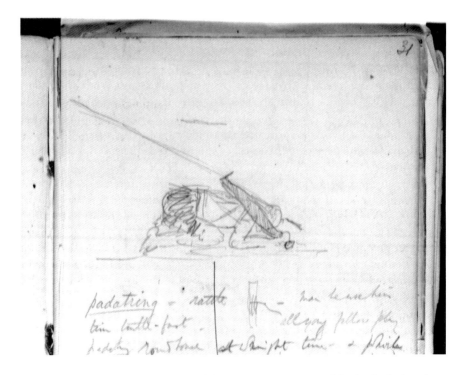

Figure 1.10. Haddon's notebook sketch of the planned re-enactment of the death of culture hero Kwoiam. Courtesy of the Cambridge Museum of Archaeology and Anthropology, Cambridge University Library, Haddon Papers Env. 1053.

site of this is 'always *elsewhere*' in the field of the social or cultural other. Secondly, 'this other is always *outside*' and 'this alterity is the primary point of subversion of dominant culture'; and thirdly, if the artist is '*not* perceived as socially and/or culturally other, he or she has but *limited* access to this transformative alterity, and, more, that if he or she *is* perceived as other, he or she has *automatic* access to it'.[74] These assumptions are obviously highly relevant to current debates around 'multiculturalism', 'post-colonialism', and 'subaltern studies' in relation to contemporary art and anthropology, but this is not our focus here. Neither artists nor anthropologists can now unproblematically claim a privileged position in regard to representing others or even their own cultures.

Anthropological notions of fieldwork and authenticity that underwrite 'ethnographic' contemporary art practices are, and have always been, porous. Fieldwork practices are unstable, changing, and *ad hoc* rather than systematized, despite repeated calls for the latter. Recent critiques within anthropology have shifted the focus to 'multi-sited' ethnography and the impossibility of discerning a discrete separable 'field'. Bruno Latour, for instance, has called for anthropology to abandon the 'territories' it inhabits, and explore 'networks' instead,[75] and there is increasing concern for the complex connectivity between sites – not just between global and local – but in terms of the performative and historical specificity of particular networks of power, translation, and appropriation. Because anthropology is located in changing (modernizing, decolonizing, recolonizing and so forth) cross-cultural domains it has encount-ered crucial problems of authority that are useful paradigms for other fields, and can provide a critical corrective to global-systemic projections of the future. Some of these problems have to do with 'appropriation' – how anthropology (and art) take from and represent others – an issue that will be revisited in the second chapter.

VISUAL ANTHROPOLOGIES

As anthropologists have increasingly had to deal with a mediated world an understanding of representational processes across cultural borders becomes vital to the overall objectives of anthropology. Holly Wardlow discusses the case of the film *Bobby Teardrops*, a popular Turkish melodrama, dubbed into English in Ireland, and shown in the Papua New Guinea highlands where it is popular with women's groups and is used in community training programmes focusing on issues of domestic violence.[76] These are the kind of complex 'texts' that anthropology is now faced with.

In *Rethinking Visual Anthropology* (published in 1997) Marcus Banks and Howard Morphy discuss the dual focus of contemporary visual anthropology; that is the use of visual media in anthropological research, and the study of visual cultures. As self-reflexivity has become a central component of anthropo-logical method anthropologists must be concerned with analysing the visual means of disseminating anthropological knowledge. The presentation and consumption of anthropological knowledge are interdependent with the production of that knowledge. To this end they stress that the properties of the anthropologists own representational and visual systems need to be considered, as well as those of the other cultures studied, and the interrelation-ship between anthropological and indigenous practices needs to be taken into account without collapsing one into the other.

In exploring the extent to which different visual cultures reflect different ways of seeing, anthropologists have become concerned with the properties of visual systems – with how things are seen, and how what is seen is understood – they increasingly have to engage with vision on its own terms. But previous studies of visual culture by, for example Roy Wagner 's work on the role of images among the Usen Barok of New Ireland, have not influenced visual anthropology practice. Why have the insights offered by studying other visual cultures not been applied to anthropology's own practices of representa-tion?

The current relations between the subdiscipline of visual anthropology and anthropology as a whole are to some degree a product of changes that occurred during the latter's academic consolidation in the early 1900s. Anna Grimshaw has suggested parallels between the development of anthropology and cinema in the early twentieth century. Both are modern projects that make a decisive break with existing forms and conventions, but by the 1930s they had become separated into 'scientific ethnography' and 'documentary film'. This division was symptomatic of a larger break between 'objective observation' and 'subjective agency', which anthropology is still struggling with in terms of fieldwork strategies.

Grimshaw argues that both early cinema and anthropology relied on going out into the world to 'discover humanity at first hand'.[77] The Torres Straits expedition organized by Cambridge University in 1898 was one of the founding moments of fieldwork technique in anthropology and Alfred Court Haddon, the leader of the expedition, thought that a movie camera was an indispensable piece of equipment for an anthropologist. He used film and photography in creative ways, not only to record indigenous customs, but also to visualize re-enacted myths.

The technologies of film, photography, and sound recording would seem to be ideal complements to the development of participant observation. But the move towards more abstract subject matter in anthropology contributed to the decline of interest in these media. Although they played a key role in

Figure 1.11. Man imitating the death of culture hero Kwoiam. Mabuiag, 1898 photograph taken on Cambridge Anthropological Expedition to Torres Straits. Courtesy of the Cambridge Museum of Archaeology and Anthropology, P 749 ACH1.

the definition of the evolutionist paradigm of early anthropology, they were largely absent from the development of the 'professional' fieldwork paradigm in the 1930s. The shift away from surfaces and appearances that had been the focus of anthropometric photographs, and an increasing emphasis on interiority, was one factor in the decline in the use of photography.

The development of visual anthropology in the early 1900s was effectively cut short by anthropology's attempts to establish itself as a scientific discipline and the visual was largely abandoned because of its positivist colonial associations with its recent past. 'In the post-evolutionist era photography and film, as tools for the anthropological method, suffered the same fate as did art and material culture as subjects of anthropological research. Tarred by the evolutionists' brush they were left out of the fieldwork revolution that became associated with structural functionalism.'[78]

The 1960s saw a renaissance of interest in visual anthropology which led eventually to its inception as a recognized subdiscipline. Technologically determinist accounts of this process focus on the development of new lightweight movie cameras and their role in supposedly ameliorating any anthropological 'intervention' in events. This new practical visual anthropology, which also saw the emergence of transgressive figures like Jean Rouch whose influence has been felt on both sides of the border, has been largely synonymous with film, either 16 mm or now digital video, and to a lesser extent photography, and is usually taken to involve trained anthropologists learning the technical use of equipment.

David MacDougall has recently argued for a visual anthropology that has more to offer than just auxiliary functions to the ethnographic monograph. If film is to make a contribution to anthropology it has to do so through its own properties, creating a system of meaning parallel to, but different from, that of written ethnographies. 'Visual anthropology can never be either a copy of written anthropology or a substitute for it. For that very reason it must develop alternative objectives and methodologies that will benefit anthropology as a whole.'[79] MacDougall also suggests that 'The more substantive challenge to anthropological thought comes not simply from broadening its purview but from its entering into communicative systems different from the "anthropology of words"'[80] – a point with which we strongly agree.

The potential that digital video offers has recently been put forward by Sarah Pink as 'an opportunity to develop methodologies that are critical of the "inappropriate filmic models" that the market place has offered for both research and film-making uses of moving images in anthropology'.[81] The models for film making in anthropology have mainly been restricted to the documentary, often of the standard 50-minute TV variety, or the 'teaching film'. New technology seems to offer the promise of new practices but how this is to be achieved is less clear. Although these technologies, including digital photography, certainly provide new opportunities for the distribution of work, and to some degree democratize a film-making process that was previously dependent on major funding, if they are to prove capable of fostering alternatives to current practice, then the range of representational and theoretical models needs to be radically rethought. Recent concerns with reconnecting experimental film to ethnographic film suggest that 'ethnography is a means of renewing the avant-gardism of 'experimental film',[82] and these are the kind of productive dialogues that need to be explored. The 'unruliness'[83] of visual anthropology needs to be expanded to embrace practically the possibilities offered by a consideration of art practices.

ARTISTS AS ANTHROPOLOGISTS

With the development of theories of structuralism and semiotics in the 1960s, the artistic appropriation of anthropological concerns took a new turn and both anthropology and art adopted theoretical models from linguistics and semiotics.

Artists like Joseph Kosuth (associated with the influential '*Art and language*' movement) and Susan Hiller talked about the artist *as* anthropologist. Kosuth rejected the distancing, the categories of us and them, typical of anthropology and, building on a functional model of art's role in culture – itself largely taken from anthropological studies of other cultures – argued that 'the artist perpetuates his culture by maintaining certain features of it, by "using" them. The artist is a model of the anthropologist *engaged*.'[84]

Whereas anthropologists studied other cultures, artists were understood as adding something to their own culture. Anthropology's ability to influence the culture it came from was minimal, whereas artists are actively creating culture, as Kosuth argues, 'art is manifested in praxis; it depicts while it alters society'.[85] Artists are 'engaged', as opposed to the 'dis-engagement' of anthropologists who are concerned with maintaining the 'objective' distance of scientists. 'Because the anthropologist is outside of the culture which he studies he is not a part of the community . . . Whereas the artist, as anthropologist, is operating within the same socio-cultural context from which he evolved. He is totally immersed and has a social impact. His activities embody the culture.'[86] This focus on the role of the artist in society was part of art's new self-reflexivity but just as the older models of primitivism provided by anthropology were not stable so the model of anthropology as an objective science was no longer valid. Anthropology itself was developing a self-reflexivity, an assessment of its role in the post-colonial world, and critiques of its own strategies of representation.

Susan Hiller is another key figure in relations between art and anthropology, and her conversion from anthropology to art resonates with some of the earlier encounters between artists and African art. Trained as an anthropologist in the US, and having completed her fieldwork in Central America in the 1960s, Hiller was so moved during a slide show on African sculpture that she decided to give up anthropology for art. For Hiller this meant that she could abandon the writing of a doctoral thesis whose objectification of the contrariness of lived events was destined to become another complicit thread woven into the fabric of 'evidence' that would help anthropology become a 'science'. In contrast, I felt art was, above all, irrational, mysterious, numinous: the images of African sculpture I was looking at stood as a sign for all this.[87]

However, in the 1980s anthropology was becoming critically self-aware of its scientific status, and objective/subjective dichotomies have been subjected to critiques that question the role of anthropologists – and by extension that of artists – as privileged representers of difference. Hiller has said that what she then thought was a matter of abandoning an objectifying discourse in favour of a subjectifying one is complicated by the contradictions of being a subject in culture. Her work deals with the 'seepage' between discourses that are supposed to have clear boundaries[88] and in this volume Denise Robinson explores Hiller's continuing engagement with themes that are directly relevant to anthropological endeavours.

POTENTIALS

Hiller's work is a persuasive example of the potentials for productive new dialogues between art and anthropology, which should be fully and actively pursued. While remaining aware of problems and areas of difference, the contributions to this book suggest some forms these dialogues might take. Our contention is that the ways in which anthropologists and artists work, make, and exhibit should be explored for their productive possibilities in developing new strategies of representation. The works we have discussed by Kiefer, Baumgarten, Viola, the McAllesters, Carpenter, Hiller and others can all, in different ways, provide a stimulus for new dialogues.

For anthropologists to engage with art practices means embracing new ways of seeing and new ways of working with visual materials. This implies taking contemporary art seriously on a practical level and being receptive to its processes of producing works and representing other realities. Doing so raises difficult questions about the status of works produced, about the profession-alism of the discipline, about training, and about audiences. Who is anthropo-logy attempting to address? Calls for the 'popularization' of anthropology have tended to distinguish borders with more serious work, and current strategies of exhibition do much to demarcate and exclude audiences as well as reify distinctions between the disciplines.

As anthropology continues to explore the existence of different visual cultures and ways of seeing it needs to simultaneously explore a wider range of visual strategies in gathering, producing, and exhibiting work. This will only be achieved through the development of new practices. Such a shift takes account of anthropology's exposure to the unforeseen and the unexpected.

Such exposure is central to what anthropology is, and its relative timidity in terms of experimental practices needs to be overcome.

For artists and their commentators – art historians and art critics – crossing the border entails a richer engagement with anthropological methods, including, but not limited to, fieldwork and 'participant observation' in all their shifting complexity. Presumptions about the rigid nature of anthropology, which often surface in interviews with artists, and perceptions of it as a disciplined 'science' (both in the literal and the academic sense), obsessed with classification and proclaiming the truth of its conclusions, can no longer function as a foil to artistic creativity and 'freedom'. Anthropology does not have, and never did have, the internal coherence ascribed to it by either artists or by anthropologists themselves. Border crossings might involve taking anthropological work on perception and cognition, or ideas about how 'locality' is constructed within our 'supermodern' situation, as starting points for producing work. But beyond these approaches, which maintain a certain well-established allocation of tasks – anthropologists produce written theory, artists visual works – artists need to take the creative methodologies and products of anthropologists as potentially useful models. This has already started happening in the realm of film and video and could be extended to other areas of practice where dialogues with anthropology would prove mutually beneficial.

Both disciplines are, to a greater or lesser degree, institutionally inflected and maintained, and training is an area that would certainly benefit from a more active engagement. The practices we are advocating point beyond the textual linearity and rigidity of the anthropological monograph, which attempts to subsume visual material into its narrative structure without exploring its potentials, and beyond those art practices that claim to be 'informed' by anthropological debates but effectively only reference a series of keywords, or invoke an aura, and do not really engage productively with anthropological arguments or methodologies.

Artists and anthropologists are practitioners who appropriate from, and represent, others. Although their representational practices have been different, both books and artworks are creative additions to the world; both are complex translations of other realities. There are no direct one-to-one transferrals of reality and art and anthropology no longer occupy opposing sides of a subjective/objective divide in the same way as they were once assumed to. The status of their respective representational strategies, when compared with each other, has changed, and differences and similarities between ethnographic authority and artistic authorship have similarly been refigured. Rather than continuing to rely on the visual versus the written as a defining opposition in anthropology, a focus on the pursuit of 'texture' might be one way of shifting productively how anthropologists view art practices. Another practice offering creative possibilities of convergence is the 'field diary' of the anthropologist (although there is currently no market for facsimiles of these), and the sketchbook or 'visual diary' of the artist. Although anthropology has employed visual practices, and the border has been porous in this respect, the visual has often been relegated to the margins of the discipline; visual anthropology is a subdiscipline, and the visual, as we have suggested in this introduction, remains largely a way of 'illustrating' textual material. Although this marginality may allow visual anthropology to explore alternatives that would be unacceptable to mainstream anthropology, the fringe status of visual practices needs to be addressed through the encouragement of new work which may well challenge key anthropological assumptions.

Appropriations
Arnd Schneider

Appropriations of cultural otherness are not a new or recent feature of the contemporary art world. The incorporation of cultural difference, historically, has been a feature of art, but it has arguably been one of the central and defining characteristics of twentieth-century art. I shall argue that these encounters between art and cultural others have left a substantial legacy, which continues to cast its shadow on contemporary border crossings.

In this chapter I focus on the nature of appropriation as a defining characteristic of the relationship between contemporary art and anthropology, and of the ways in which they both engage with cultural difference.

'PRIMITIVISM'

The 'primitive', in many different incarnations, has been a central trope of difference for many twentieth-century European and North American art movements, and Primitivism has profoundly influenced the relationship between art and anthropology. Although there are many earlier precedents and examples of artists appropriating from other cultures, including Romanticism, Impressionism and Fauvism (for example, Paul Gauguin and Henri Matisse), and Expressionism (for example, Emil Nolde, Franz Marc, Oskar Kokoschka), the encounter between artists like Pablo Picasso and African sculpture in Parisian museums and collectors' houses around 1905 frequently figures as *the* prototypical encounter between art and anthropology.[1] It has become one of the founding myths of modern art. This turning point was famously presented in the exhibition *'Primitivism' in Twentieth Century Art: Affinity of the Tribal and the Modern* at the Museum of Modern Art in New York in 1984. The show presented audiences with a series of formal affinities, like those between masks from Africa and Oceania – especially Kota reliquary figures – and Picasso's painting *Les Demoiselles d'Avignon* (1907). This encounter is seen not only as one of the key originating moments of modern art, but also as an exemplary case of appropriation from other cultures, highlighting contrasting issues of form and context. Although any formal affinities did not necessarily consist of one-to-one transferrals, as earlier scholars had claimed, a later work by Picasso, the metal *Guitar* sculpture (1912), had been directly inspired by specific Grebo masks.[2] Choices between considerations of form, on the one hand, and those

Figure 2.1. Pablo Picasso, *Guitar* (Paris, winter 1912–13). New York. Digital image, © 2005, The Museum of Modern Art, NewYork/Scala, Florence. Construction of sheet metal and wire, 30$^{1}/_{2}$ x 13$^{3}/_{4}$ x 7$^{5}/_{8}$ inches (77.5 × 35 x 19.3 cm). Gift of the artist.

of a perceived symbolic, ritual or religious content continue to characterize appropriations in contemporary art, as we shall see later on.

The question of whether Picasso was influenced primarily by formal similarities, or whether he was attracted to the 'magic' of African art, is still subject to debate. James Clifford has argued that 'whatever inspirations and affinities may be retrospectively constructed by and for Picasso it seems clear that the exotic objects he collected were tools suited for doing specific jobs'.[3] The appropriation of stylistic elements from the displayed and collected artefacts of other cultures took place in the context of changing ideas about the role of the artist, and about the place of art in society. These ideas were influenced by the work of anthropologists like Lucien Lévy-Bruhl, who discussed the 'primitive mind' and the personae of the artist.[4] In the process the artist became figured as someone with privileged access to the primitive. This was further enhanced through recourse to the new science of psycho-analysis, where the artist was seen as in touch with his/her own psyche and with primitive 'archetypes'. The anthropologist, too, was someone with privi-leged access to the primitive, both practical and theoretical, and the new discipline, in its move towards professionalism in the early decades of the twentieth century, put much effort into differentiating anthropologists as

Figure 2.2. Mask. Grebo. Ivory Coast or Liberia. Painted wood and fibre. Musée Picasso, Paris, 1983–7. Photograph © RMN/ Béatrice Hatala.

having a 'deeper', more intimate contact with the primitive than mere 'travellers' or colonial officials.

Early twentieth-century 'Primitivism' set the tone for artistic appropriations of what anthropology would consider its subject matter for many years to come.[5] For instance, Eduardo Paolozzi's 1985 exhibition *Lost Magic Kingdoms* at the former Museum of Mankind in London combined the artist's work with artefacts chosen by him from the museum's collections. In his introduction, Paolozzi discussed the differences between French and English approaches to the primitive in the 1930s and 1940s, praising 'that French sensibility which could embrace Dogon masks, pre-Columbian stone sculpture and, for example, Baroque churches or modern machinery. But that sort of sensibility does not exist in England even now.'[6] At the time, the exhibition was criticized by anthropologists for its lack of contextualization; display cases were crammed with Paolozzi's own work and artefacts from disparate cultures with no explanatory panels to indicate their role in a cultural continuum. But Paolozzi was concerned with celebrating the enigmatic qualities of artefacts, and his strategy aimed at emphasizing their 'magic' rather than attempting any ethnographic contextualization. The criticism the exhibition generated was symptomatic of the developing anthropological critique of colonial collecting and collections, and the growth of 'museology', whilst also revealing anthropology's uneasiness with contemporary art.[7]

Figure 2.3. Eduardo Paolozzi, *Diana as an Engine*, 1963 (cast aluminium 190 cm). Courtesy of Flowers East Gallery, and © DACS, 2005. Female figure, 1947 (wood, 52 cm). British Museum Af.46.523. Copyright British Museum.

For artists the primitive has offered the possibility of new 'ways of seeing' and for some it provided an idealized vision of a cohesive totality. Daniel Miller has argued that where it proposes models of transcending the fragmented nature of modern existence, all art is reliant on a primitivist model. Indeed, the imagined holism of primitive culture was what allowed the modern to be seen as fragmented in the first place.[8] However, much avant-garde art in the early 1900s was deeply suspicious of stable orders of collective meaning, considering them to be both constructed and ideologically repressive. Early twentieth-century artists valued the *shock* of the primitive, its ability to disrupt the established order and, rather than striving for an imagined totality, were seeking instead to dismember their own. As James Clifford (discussing the work of Georges Bataille) has pointed out, 'the exotic was a primary court of appeal against the rational, the beautiful, the normal of the West'.[9] The primitive was capable of reflecting whatever was projected onto it, but whereas artists often valued the 'savagery' of primitive art, anthropologists became increasingly concerned with understanding it within its own cultural context and as a form of expression that was the equal of Western art.

Notions of the primitive were responsible, along with the adoption of theories from psychoanalysis, for changes in our understanding of what art is and what it does; how it appeals to us, how it affects us, and what we expect from it. For George E. Marcus and Fred Myers, who have advocated the anthropological study of Western 'art worlds', twentieth-century art and anthropology share the same origins, and an affinity exists between them because they are 'rooted in a common tradition, both situated in a critical stance toward the "modernity" of which we are both a part.'[10]

Although other cultures provided a reservoir of forms and beliefs that could be used to challenge Western culture, notions of the primitive were, from the outset, ambiguous and unstable. The primitivism exhibition at MOMA, whilst remaining a seminal achievement, also encountered strong criticism along these lines. In his review of the exhibition, Clifford pointed out that the use of the term 'affinity' implied a shared humanity, a fundamental relationship deeper than any formal similarities. He argued that the exhibition presented modernist art as somehow able to transcend its own cultural and historical context and discern 'elemental expressive modes'; whereas, for him, it demonstrated the 'incoherence' of the primitive as a category, while also revealing its enduring influence. He suggested a series of alternative affinities (such as those between Josephine Baker, a Chokwe wooden figure from Angola, and a costume designed by Fernand Léger) that were not shown at the Museum of Modern Art (MOMA).[11]

The encounter between art and anthropology in the early 1900s initiated a scheme in which objects became classified as either 'primitive art' or 'ethnographic artefacts', and as a result distinctions between the anthropological and the aesthetic became further institutionally reinforced. For Clifford these practices constituted an aesthetic/anthropological 'system' – art works are seen as the products of individuals (art exhibitions), or as the work of cultures (anthropology exhibitions).

A number of exhibitions and publications in the 1980s and 1990s reflected on similar issues to those discussed by Clifford. For example, the museum as the site of the West's appropriation of other cultures, informed by different colonial and postcolonial agendas, was given critical treatment in Ivan Karp and Steven Levine's important volume *Exhibiting Cultures*.[12] However, from the 1960s onwards, artists such as Christian Boltanksi were already questioning the West's obsession with the fictive construction of evidence in museums through various installations, making reference to anthropological exhibition practices. Yet artistic practices and criticisms such as Boltanski's went unnoticed by anthropology for almost two decades.[13]

ART/Artifact, an exhibition at the Center for African Art (now the Museum of African Art) in New York in 1988, further demonstrated the arbitrariness of exhibition displays by showing exhibits in different rooms as, variously, art objects, collectors items, and in their 'ethnographic context'. The show revealed the extent to which the West's gaze and concomitant categorizations determine whether an object is seen as art or artefact.

In 1989 the exhibition *Magiciens de la Terre* at the Centre Pompidou in Paris attempted to redress the imbalance between named European and North American artists and unknown non-Western artists, by juxtaposing work by, for instance, Francesco Clemente and the Chinese magician Huang Yong-Ping. However, critics of the exhibition argued that it did nothing but highlight the disparity between Western artists and others.

Although much has been written about the role of primitivism in modern art,[14] the encounter between artists from other cultures and Western art has received relatively less consideration. The work of reverse appropriation that resulted from this encounter was often dismissed as merely mimicking or copying Western styles, and discussions of it reinforced models of centre and periphery for art, although this is now starting to be addressed.

Nicholas Thomas emphasises that appropriation is better understood as a two-way process, characterized by an inherent 'unstable duality' between rejection and acceptance of both giving to and taking from the other.[15] Similarly, I recently highlighted the hermeneutic nature of appropriation, which presumes an attempt at 'understanding', if not dialogue, with the other.[16]

These double-sided qualities of appropriation are also made clear through the example of the Togolese artist El Loko's student-teacher relationship with Joseph Beuys. The story of El Loko's encounter with Joseph Beuys is a telling case of how a 'hero' of contemporary Western art is perceived from another culture:

> In 1969 my decision had matured to study Fine Arts. Then I was 19 years old and worked as a textile designer in Tema, Ghana. Through the Goethe Institute in Accra I had known about the Art Academy in Düsseldorf and asked for the application forms. A little later, I received the relevant documentation and immediately assembled a portfolio with about 25 works, mainly watercolours, drawings and textile designs. My application was successful in Düsseldorf and I received the confirmation to study in the winter semester 1971 in the class of Prof. Beuys. I was very young then, and also naïve. I didn't know anything concrete about Germany, nothing about studying art at a German academy, and had never heard of Beuys.[17]

In the beginning El Loko hardly met Beuys, who was busy staging his happenings. El Loko, who was looking for a master, a teacher who would guide him in his studies, realized that this was something that Beuys was not going to offer him (although Beuys had paid for his flight after his initial acceptance by the academy). However, with time, they did begin to co-operate and El Loko eventually participated in happenings, commenting that:

Figure 2.4. Experimenta, Darmstadt 1971. Joseph Beuys and El Loko. Plenary Discussion. Photograph © by Inge Werth.

> Much of what Beuys showed in his actions and happenings was not difficult to comprehend for me. His actions were close to some African thought and ritual, for example, the rites of the witch doctors, where places or objects are declared taboo or sacred. For many Beuys experts this is still an alien thought.[18]

Questions of respective otherness between (largely colonized) cultures and the West had been already considered in 1937 by Julius Lips in his landmark volume *The Savage Hits Back*, which investigated representations of 'white' colonizers in indigenous art – or in other words appropriations of the West in non-Western art.

Bronislaw Malinowski, in his introduction to the book, points out that 'Lips works out one of the most fruitful approaches to anthropology. He inquires into the vision of white humanity as held by the native.'[19] However, Lips' approach was too revolutionary for its time and did not find followers (not even in the United States, where he had come on the invitation of Franz Boas to teach at Columbia University after being forced by the Nazis to resign as director of the Cologne Museum of Anthropology). It was only much later in the 1980s and 1990s, with reappreciations of the work of Ernst Auerbach by Fritz Kramer, and of Walter Benjamin by Michael Taussig, that an interest in mimetic processes involved in the visual representation of European others resurfaced in anthropology.[20]

THE POTENTIAL OF APPROPRIATION FOR CONTEMPORARY ART AND ANTHROPOLOGY

I am concerned here with mimetic encounters between, borrowing from, even 'stealing' from other cultures in the widest sense of these terms. Extending on the points made in the introductory chapter by Chris Wright and myself, I want to highlight some of these processes as experimental avenues for future collaborations between art and anthropology.

Strategies of appropriation are, of course, highly problematic (politically and ethically) but I suggest that they are a principal characteristic not only of art which engages with anthropological subject matters, but also of anthropology itself.

Appropriation is usually charged with the implication of some 'inappropriate' action in taking something from one context and placing it into another. I want to propose a new approach to appropriation, which, whilst not doing away with the implied imbalances, puts the stress on learning and transformation.

It is in this sense that I suggest that appropriation works in the mediation of cultural differences and becomes operative in the work of artists and anthropologists. Both share appropriation as a creative technique, and whilst there are differences as to the choice of appropriating strategies, some fundamental characteristics are common to both.

In the following, I will critically revisit the concept of appropriation and evaluate its usefulness for visual practices at the borders of art and anthropology. I suggest that appropriation should be re-evaluated as a hermeneutic procedure – an act of dialogical understanding – by which artists and anthropologists negotiate access to, and traffic in, cultural differences.

Definitions of appropriation have stressed its transformative character in duplicating, copying, or incorporating an image into a new context, thus sometimes completely changing its meaning and questioning its originality and authenticity.

Appropriation is sometimes characterized as a practice by which 'an artist may "steal" another pre-existing image and sign it as his/her own', whereas 'reappropriation connotes "stealing" an image, symbol, or statement from outside the realm of art'.[21] With the Western notion of property belonging to the individual, artistic appropriation, in legal terms, implies an infringement of copyright, as Coombe points out.[22]

Museum anthropologists, in particular, appropriated widely from native people outside Europe during colonial times and after. The absurdity of the Western obsession with dissociating objects from their original owners and then exhibiting them, has been poignantly shown in installations by Christian Boltanski since the late 1960s, long before anthropologists criticised museum practice.[23]

Appropriation, copying,[24] or even citation and reference to the work of previous artists, is an established practice throughout the history of art (with obviously changing connotations according to the historical period), but it has become particularly salient to '(post)modern' art practices, which, as Rosalind Krauss highlights, challenge traditional (Western) notions of exclusive authorship

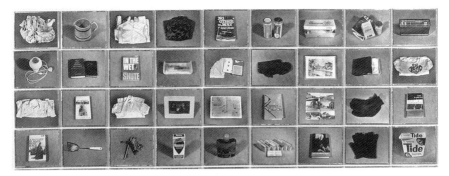

Figure 2.5. Christian Boltanski, *Inventory of Objects Belonging to an inhabitant of Oxford*, 1973, coll, detail. CAPC Musée d'art contemporain de Bordeaux. Photograph © F. Delpech.

and any accepted supremacy of the original (high) over its copy (low).[25] In contrast, Benjamin Buchloh has characterized the strategies of appropriation and montage in twentieth-century modern art as 'allegorical procedures',[26] implying obvious changes of meaning in the process. On the other hand, appropriation for many 'Third World' artists prolongs and extends the experience of the original, whilst also investing it with new meaning and using it as a strategy for identity construction. César Paternosto makes the more general point, following George Kubler's important essay *The Shape of Time*, that artists across different cultures and different historical periods, can retrieve and recreate meaning through appropriation.[27]

As Luis Camnitzer commented on Cuban practices of appropriation, they consist of . . . the use of imported elements without being used by them.'[28]

I want to suggest an extended definition of cultural appropriation 'as the taking – from a culture that is not one's own – of intellectual property, cultural expressions or artefacts, history and ways of knowledge.'[29] The problem with such a definition for many Third World artists is that they appropriate from cultures which at the same time are, and are *not*, regarded as their own. For example, the construction of new identities by these artists often evokes ancestral ties and claims to represent 'indigenous culture', either by presumed biological and/or cultural descent and belonging (even in those cases where artists descend from Europeans), as well as ties to the international, still largely Westernised art canon mediated by the 'art world'. For instance, Rimer Cardillo (whose work is featured in this volume) makes installations of large ant heaps covered with armadillo shell moulds, evoking reference to the earth mounds of the Charrúa Indians of Uruguay, who were completely wiped out in military campaigns in the mid-nineteenth century.[30] Unequal power relations also apply depending on whether it is a 'Westerner 'or someone claiming to be indigenous doing the appropriating.

The Canadian Métis film-maker Loretta Todd put the issues at stake this way:

While making a presentation on cultural autonomy and appropriation at the Independent Film and Video Alliance meeting in Halifax last June I quoted Walter

Figure 2.6. José Angel Toirac, untitled, 1988, *Cuban Mona Lisa*, pencil on printed page, 20 × 30 cm, private collection, photographer: Luis Camnitzer.

Benjamin. Someone challenged my use of Benjamin as an appropriation of Western culture. My response was that I am part of Western as well as Native culture, Benjamin is of my culture. 'Aha', say the appropriators, 'then our use of Native images and stories is analogous to your use of Benjamin, since Native images and stories have become part of contemporary culture'. Was this clever reasoning or just specious argument? What was this cultural crossover of which they spoke?'[31]

I have recently discussed the dilemmas involved in defining and applying the concept of appropriation to contemporary art practices, asking if it is possible to develop a concept of appropriation which takes into account the processes linking artists, artifacts (and their original producers), and the new artworks resulting from the appropriation process.[32]

APPROPRIATION AS CHOICE AND PROCESS

A useful starting point is the distinction between 'soft' and 'hard' primitivists, introduced by Rosalind Krauss. Soft primitivists are those artists who are inspired by the forms and symbols of indigenous cultures, that is their surface *visual appearance* (as Lynne Cooke calls it).[33] Such appropriation often takes place from books and artefacts, with varying degrees of investigation into their

Figure 2.7. Edward Poitras, *Saskatoon Pie*, 1994, digital image with Coyote © Edward Poitras. Courtesy of the artist.

cultural context. Here the ethnographic sources are appreciated primarily for their aesthetic qualities, not for their ethnographically specific symbolic and religious content. An example would be the work of Eduardo Paolozzi, and the way he conceived the exhibition *Lost Magic Kingdoms*, discussed earlier in this chapter. Although interested in a general notion of magic, it looks for the formal affinities, and not the ethnographic specifics of the artefacts.

Hard primitivists, on the other hand, become involved in the recreation of indigenous rituals, assume the indigenous on a more personal level, and show a greater interest in the cultural context. Obviously, artists can combine the two strands, but a good example of a 'hard primitivist' (in Cooke's terms) is Joseph Beuys, who compared his work to that of shamans in traditional cultures. Among the most influential artists after World War Two, Beuys's approach to non-Western cultures is complex and cannot be subsumed within the remit of this book. His engagement with the 'other' became the foundation myth for his art and life, ever since his reported close encounter with the Tartars who saved his life after he had crashed his Stuka plane in the Crimea during World War Two. Beuys conceived of his art practices as similar to those of a shaman (or healer) and of his works as 'social sculpture'.[34]

Whilst the term 'primitivist' inevitably implies an exoticist attitude by the artist, the distinction between 'soft' and 'hard' could serve, nevertheless, as a preliminary guideline for building a typology of appropriations. It seems, then, that distinctions between different types of 'primitivism' would allow us to discern in the work of artists the degree of empirical work, or of *practice*, one of the main concerns in this book. It is very tempting to build a typology along such lines, but this formal approach would not solve the question of original intentions and transformation in the work of the artist, nor does it address the relationship he or she establishes with the other. Ultimately, we have to ask what happens in the process of appropriation?

For this, as I have suggested above, it is best to consider the work of appropriation as a hermeneutic practice. Admittedly, there might also be those artists for whom understanding the other is not an issue at all, and who just deliberately play with form, devoid of ethnographically specific meaning. Criticisms of superficiality and aestheticism have been rightly levelled against such approaches. This book is an invitation for artists to engage more profoundly with other cultures though they might not apply the same criteria to ethnography as anthropologists do.

Similarly, in terms of practice, there are a variety of approaches, ranging from those artists who get inspiration from illustrations and museum collections, to those who investigate the specialized literature and who seek contact with and sometimes the collaboration of professional archaeologists and anthropologists. In the present book a number of such artists are featured, including Carlos Capelán, Mohini Chandra, Rainer Wittenborn, Nikolaus Lang and Rimer Cardillo.

Another example is the Argentine artist Alfredo Portillos, who during his exile in Brazil in the 1970s became a member of a Candomblé cult. The spiritual and magical experiences with the 'other' resulted in works such as *Serie del Vudú a los Conquistadores latinomamericanos.*

José Bedia's work, on the other hand, is based on his experiences of Cuban *santería* as well as references to other indigenous traditions, such a hide paintings by Plains Indians. Maya Deren's involvement with Haitian Voodoo, which resulted in her book *Divine Horsemen*, led to her abandoning the initial project of shooting an artist's film (although unedited rushes, as well as a film edited posthumously by Cheryl Ito exist), and try her hand at an ethnographic account. However, given Deren's sensibilities and close encounter with Vodoo, *Divine Horsemen* goes beyond a standard ethnography (which would abstract from the experience of the ethnographer and purport an 'objective' presentation of facts), and shows precisely what can be achieved by transgressing disciplinary frontiers.[35]

The more austere and cerebral work of César Paternosto is based on an appreciation of Pre-Columbian art and architecture, as original forms of abstract art (see his contribution to this volume and illustrations of his artistic work). Paternosto is one of the rare examples of artist-scholars; Linda Schele, who started out in the 1960s as a painter influenced by the work of Arshile Gorky, Joan Miró, and Paul Klee, and whose later work was crucial in deciphering the Maya glyphs[36] – is another example of somebody applying artistic sensibilities to archaeological and anthropological research.

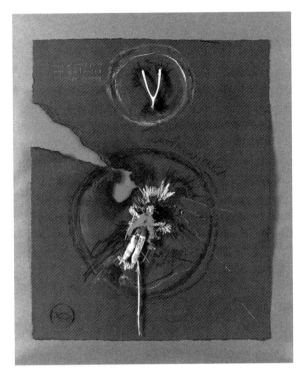

Figure 2.8. Alfredo Portillos, *Serie del Vudú a los conquistadores latinomamericanos*, 1997, 60 × 50 cm. Courtesy of the artist and Fundación Andreani, Buenos Aires.

Collaborations between archaeologists and/or anthropologists and artists have been another possibility for approaching the other, which has at times yielded truly interdisciplinary work – some of which, by Rainer Wittenborn and Claus Biegert, Nikolaus Lang, and Rimer Cardillo, is presented in Chapter 9, 'Dialogues'. For instance, Osvaldo Viteri in Ecuador, during the early stages of his career as an architect, worked as a draughtsman on the surveys of the Brazilian anthropologist Paulo de Carvalho-Neto. These investigations had a twofold premise. On the one hand it aimed to research and survey the popular arts of Ecuador in different regions, and on the other hand it sought to compile, concurrently, a visual register of these arts, which could be used as inspiration by popular artists, and thus promote the development of these artistic crafts in Ecuador. A distinction between simple crafts and the more artistic popular arts was therefore felt necessary in these early folkloric researches in the 1960s, and a restriction to the visual popular arts and material culture (in contrast with other popular arts such as music, story-telling etc.).[37] Although later Viteri would overcome the art/craft divide when, in 1969/1970, he started to use rag dolls he bought in Quito's old town, incorporating them into his paintings and charging them with the spirit-like presence of 'people' from the realm of popular culture. He then commissioned one woman artisan to make these dolls for him in large quantities. For the next 10 years, Viteri produced a large number

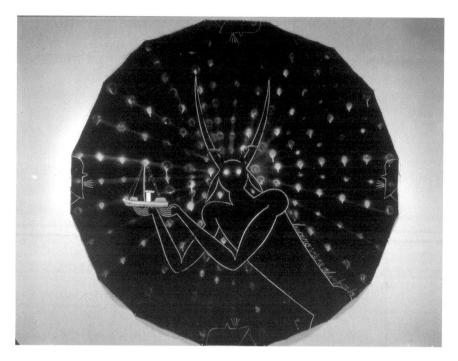

Figure 2.9. José Bedia, *Star Comes to Light the Way,* 1992, acrylic on canvas, found objects, collection of Carlos and Rosa de la Cruz, Key Biscayne, Florida. Image courtesy of George Adams Gallery, New York.

of these *ensemblajes* (assemblages), and with titles often referring to indigenous topics, the Andes, Pre-Columbian cultures (such as the Inca), the conquest, and to *mestizaje*, the 'cultural' and 'biological' mixture of peoples.

This is how Viteri commented on the process of appropriation in his art, when interviewed by Arnd Schneider in Quito in 1998:[38]

> I am starting from the utilisation of symbolic objects. Every object has significa-tion, connotation, roots, an origin of birth. For example, the dolls are of Pre-Columbian origin, and they are used till the present. So I took this element as something inherited from the indigenous people, part of the indigenous popular culture. On the other hand, I have used the old brocades, and other ritual objects, which signify the weight of Catholic religion over indigenous cultures, European design patterns which mix with indigenous ones.
>
> But this is the reality of Latin America, especially Andean America. I consider my work basically as Andean, a reflection of the mountains, the well marked terri-tory, . . . and the heaviness of the landscape. I use sackcloth or hempen cloth to symbolise the marginalisation, the poverty of Latin America, mixed sometimes with the other elements, showing the dramatic reality of the Andean countries.
>
> Whilst being strongly rooted, at the same time my work has a universal mes-sage, which can be understood anywhere, in New York, Tokyo or Buenos Aires.

Figure 2.10. Osvaldo Viteri, *Eye of Light*, 1987, collage on wood, 160 × 160 cm, collection of the artist, Quito. Courtesy of Galería Viteri, Quito.

How has your research activity, working with Paulo Carvalho-Neto, influenced your art?

I wanted to know who are my people, who are we?

I found great difficulty at the beginning to understand what was 'objective' when we made the drawings of folkloric objects. I had to change my psychological structure, the mental structure, in order to assimilate and to understand completely what objective meant. Because as an artists I was in the area of subjectivity, of emotions, and of sensations. I found it very difficult to assume an 'objective' position, but I think, eventually, I achieved it. It was a very important experience, which allowed me to see reality differently. We had to eliminate emotions, we did not invent anything, but there is always an abstraction from reality.

Travelling is another part of the process of appropriation, and a number of artists enter into direct contact with indigenous communities, carrying out fieldwork and using anthropological techniques, including interviews and photographic documentation. For instance, the Argentine artist, Teresa Pereda, in her work *Bajo el nombre de Juan* (Under the Name of John) compared the celebrations for St Johns (24 June) in the Catalan Pyrenees with those in Jujuy province in the Argentine Andes.

Figure 2.11. Teresa Pereda, interviewing Don Víctor in Cochinoca in June 2000 (Province of Jujuy, Argentina) during research for artist book *Bajo el nombre de Juan (Under the Name of John)*, Bogotá: Arte Dos Gráfico Press, 2001. Photo: Arnd Schneider.

Her work focuses both on the indigenous connotation of the winter solstice in the Andes (linked to the Inti Raymi ceremony of the Inca period) and the syncretic elements that are a result of Spanish colonisation. For the Argentine part of the work she travelled several times to the Andes to the small village of Cochinoca, eventually to observe the firewalking rituals for for St John's day and to interview the participants, and also frequented gatherings of *Kolla* people from Jujuy province in Buenos Aires.

In an interview with Arnd Schneider in Buenos Aires in 2000, Teresa Pereda explained the motivations for her work in this way:

> For a long time, I grew up far away from here, not in the cities. I have now lived for twenty years in Lincoln [in the Province of Buenos Aires], and when I was little I lived in the Andes of Neuquén Province in Patagonia. My life has always been marked by travel, because one had to go to the cities to study. I always had inside of me this dichotomy: land vs. city . . . I was always preoccupied, in this coming and going to the city, with how little conscience or knowledge people had in the big city of Buenos Aires of the rest of the country . . .
>
> The other dichotomy was produced by this enormous European migration we experienced relatively recently. Because this migration was numerically much

larger than the original population it created really a different country, imposing itself on the existing one . . . I think a great fissure was created. Argentina is different from the rest of Latin America, and the Argentines feel different within Latin America. Take, for example, 'race': my ancestors were Italian, French, and Spanish. I don't have one drop of Indian blood. My family arrived in 1860 and I have relatives in Europe. My reality is a typically Argentine reality. But the indigenous reality, and the reality of *mestizaje* since the 16th century, remained somehow hidden on the other side.

Therefore, I was interested to amalgamate these two worlds in my work, because I am a little bit a daughter of both. I grew up among Mapuche, an indigenous people in Patagonia. When one grew up on a farm (*campo*), the people of the area were indigenous, and during childhood one lived this very naturally. I learned a lot from them.

However, the approximation to one's subject of artistic investigation and representation is not necessarily measured by physical proximity, in fact, conceptual closeness might avoid fieldwork altogether. For instance, Elaine Reichek's series 'Tierra del Fuego' is based entirely on the photographs taken by turn of the century anthropologist Martin Gusinde. Reichek rejects fieldwork as a device and works on representations which already mediate their subject. Also, by knitting the subjects of the photographs, she restitutes a body, or corporality to the Other which had been lost through the photographic process.[39] Jimmy Durham pointed out that Elaine Reichek's work is not appropriating the other, but is about how the Western system has appropriated the other through images:

Yet the wools, the knitting, the photographs of 'natives', can trick us into the momentary complacency of thinking we are seeing what we expect to see. It is for this reason, combined with an understandable but overly defensive sensitivity to appropriation, that some 'minority' artists have felt that Reichek is improperly messing with 'our stuff'. These artists must think she is talking about *us*; when in fact she is using the systems of her own culture, the 'dominant' culture, to confront hidden oppressions in its systems.[40]

Another form of appropriation involves ritual and performance art. The understanding and theorization of ritual has been at the core of the discipline of anthropology, and Emile Durkheim, Alfred Reginald Radcliffe-Brown and others have been fundamental in clarifying the ritual process. One of anthropology's great students of ritual symbolism, Victor Turner, collaborated with Richard Schechner, to develop an anthropological practice which included performances based on indigenous rituals and non-Western theatre. Eugenio Barba, too, with what he termed 'theatre anthropology', advocated a theatrical practice based on non-Western theatres and performance.[41]

When artists perform rituals they are often concerned with the inventive and creative character of the ritual process. An example is 'The River Pierce',

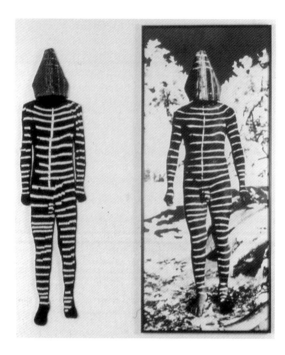

Figure 2.12. Elaine Reichek, *Tierra del Fuego*, 1991. Courtesy of the artist.

a staged procession which was performed on Good Friday of 1990, by artists, art critics and local inhabitants, along an imaginary *via sacra* in the border region between Texas and Mexico.[42] Other artists, such as Alfredo Portillos or José Bedia transform spaces of the art world (museums, galleries) into ritual or religious spaces, pointing both to the inherently religious character of these spaces (or 'temples') in a secularized society, and to the porous borders between some artistic and religious practices.[43]

Certainly, the 'types' we have discussed above might not be represented in pure form, and in fact, artists frequently combine various approaches in their work.

It is important to point out that one can 'learn' to appropriate (as César Paternosto argued repeatedly, see also Chapter 11 in this volume), and consequently 'teach' appropriation. Yet a more general issue arises with how such knowledge is transmitted and whether an attempt is made to learn about how cultures classify themselves, or to understand art in their own terms. Esther Pasztory, for instance, has argued that Pre-Columbian cultures had their own categories of style, often based on specific ethnic groups and polities, which cannot be subsumed under Western concepts.[44]

The challenge of how to do justice to cultures who have produced such designs in the first recorded instance, is faced in many Latin American countries by a wide variety of urban graphic designers, potters, and textile designers who appropriate indigenous imagery.

Figure 2.13. Brother Dunstan Bowles, CSC, flanked by the actress Karen Kuykendall (right) and a student, Hannah McCann, at one of the Stations of the Cross, Michael Tracy, Eugenia Vargas Daniels and Eloy Tarcisio, *The River Pierce: Sacrifice II, 13.4.90.*, Houston TX: Rice University Press, 1990, p. 35, By courtesy of the River Pierce Foundation, Houston. Photograph: Keith Carter.

These practitioners of appropriation often provide a critique of archaeo-logical and anthropological research, which they find is based on abstract notions of artistic production in non-Western societies, neglecting the material practices themselves. Their criticism is not only based on the disapproval of Western stylistic categories, but informed by *practical experience* in working with and producing material artefacts. One instance are the inadequate technical descriptions and visual depictions of Pre-Columbian pottery in archaeological publications. A simple example of the difficulties or rather inadequacies implied, are the 'transcriptions' (as drawings) of ceramic patterns. As Alejandro Fiadone, a graphic designer and researcher into Pre-Columbian pottery, pointed out recently,[45] such patterns are presented as plane in books and articles and thus are necessarily distorted (nor can the volume of ceramics be represented adequately), whereas in fact the surfaces of many ceramics are curved.

The above examples show very clearly how artistic practice, in the process of appropriation, and appreciating more faithfully the creations of other cultures, can contribute to anthropological knowledge. It should also be clear by now that there is no suggestion here to subscribe to the antiquated distinctions between low and high art, or arts and crafts. A perspective which, as César Paternosto pointed out, until recently prevented the appreciation of abstract art in the architecture and textiles of Pre-Columbian as well as contemporary indigenous cultures in the Americas. In arguing that these arts should not be relegated to the categories of 'ornament' and 'decoration', Paternosto polemically asks: 'Would anybody dare to call a Renaissance painting or a Van Gogh a "canvas decorated with colours"?'[46]

CONCLUSION

The process of appropriation is fundamental to exchanges between cultures and to cultural change. This is because a recognition of otherness, as the late George Kubler termed it,[47] lies at the bottom of any appropriation, anthropological or artistic. For if we were unable to discern what is not ours or other, we could not transform it into what is ours, in the most fundamental philosophical sense – even if its otherness is respected in a new context. Of course, the issues at hand are not only of a cognitive order but also involve an ethical dimension. After all, others represent themselves towards us (artists or anthropologists) not just as an inanimate objects but as living subjects or communities of subjects who will voice political, economic and cultural claims over their symbolic heritage. In that sense, appropriations are always 'two-sided'.[48] Current discussions about cultural property are a reflection of these ongoing claims or struggles over representation and power.[49]

The adaptation of anthropological information and methods in the practice of artistic appropriation does not occur in a vacuum but is always situated in an historical context of different economic, social, and cultural power relations. Many appropriations occur from the vantage point of the Western art world, so-called 'Third World' artists also appropriate both from indigenous cultures and from the West, and often see their practice as a form of resistance to globalization and a strategy to construct new identities. Anthropologists have shown many times over how identities are multiple, constructed, and shift with historical context. As there are no 'originals' in art, so there are no fixed ethnic, racial, or national categories – but only different claims to these by groups and individuals.[50]

In some instances 'roots' might be constructed quite independently from geneaological descent, and be informed instead by an insistence on cultural heritage.

This is how Cecilia Vicuña, a Chilean artist and poet, sees her relation with indigenous roots:

> On the one hand, I come from a long line of descendants of a Basque family that came to Chile many generations ago. And on my Mother's side, the Ramirez family was probably from Andalusia. In these two families, rather, there was probably a hidden indigenous presence even though they claim there was *no* indigenous ancestry at all; but I think that is extremely unlikely. There is a presence of indigenous blood that is not acknowledged. And that is what I sense, feel . . .
>
> There is a dimension that is at work here which involves the gradual Americanization of my family through the influence of Andean culture. Furthermore, the transmission of this connection with the American continent came through the women of my family . . .
>
> When I was in Europe for three years,[51] I found that I was searching for a connection to the earth. I could not find it but when I returned to South America, to Bogotá, I threw myself face down on the earth and kissed it. The earth has an energy, a vitality, in the Americas that I don't feel elsewhere.[52]

It is not my intention to arbitrate on who can appropriate or not (the question of legitimacy) or to judge individual practices of appropriation. Writing as an anthropologist, I am acutely aware that anthropology, of course, is the discipline *par excellence* which appropriates from others – even when recent anthropological writing has become more reflexive about the process.

Figure 2.14. Cecilia Vicuña, Bogotá (photo), 1981. Courtesy of the artist.

The history of anthropology provides countless examples of how the discipline appropriated from others not only their artefacts (to be sold on and shown in museums), myths, rituals and kinship systems (to be represented in books for a Western audience), but even living people for anthropological research.

Ishi, the last of the Yahi Indians in California, would serve the anthropologist Alfred Kroeber for his research – the story has been told by Kroeber's wife Theodora.[53] Claire Pentecost send out questionnaires to Native Americans and made an installation with their answers in 1990, entitled *Ishi in Two Worlds*. This is how she introduced her project in the letter which was also exhibited as part of the artwork;

> I am a non-Indian artist currently making a series of works about my own and my culture's historical relations to Native Americans. One of the concepts I'm interested in is the contradiction of the colonial culture's tendency to romanticize Native Americans while simultaneously operating to destroy their culture and land. The pieces partly focus on the story of Ishi, a Yahi Indian whose life was documented in a book by Theodora Kroeber. Ishi died in 1911 and was indeed the last of his own tribe. However, since the idea of American Indians as a 'vanishing people' is a complex part of the romanticizing fiction, I am eager to make reference in some way to contemporary, living Native American Communities and their concerns.
>
> I am writing to ask you to respond briefly to a couple of questions. I would like to include your answers in the documentation of the piece.
>
> Have you heard of Ishi or Theodora Kroeber's book, *Ishi in Two Worlds*?
>
> What would you say are the primary concerns of your community right now? . . .[54]

As will be clear by now, I do not want to reiterate what is swiftly becoming an artificial division between Western and non-Western artists, implicated in practices of appropriation. However, I do acknowledge the historical differences between the two. It is still the North American and European art world that powerfully appropriates the other, not only at a distance but through travel or fieldwork, and also through its all-encompassing tendency to incorporate (literally, to make of its own body) non-Western artists who come to study and work in the metropolitan art centres (such as New York, London, Paris, or Berlin). Yet it seems in the present climate of 'globalization' that non-Western artists – despite their differing agendas – will have to ask themselves similar ethical questions when dealing with the arts and artefacts of other cultures.

The attempt here, of course, is not to judge or compare artists' investigations by the standards of anthropology, which are themselves the outcome of a particular disciplinary history and are now frequently questioned in their scientific pretensions. Rather, it is the degree of respect for the other, which must be at the heart of any evaluation, for both artists and anthropologists. Respect, as well as sincerity and seriousness in one's work, are difficult and value-loaded concepts to apply, which is why we are brought back to the

Figure 2.15. Claire Pentecost, *Ishi in Two Worlds*, 1990, drawings on handmade mirror, wood, trash, letters, 15 lecterns, New York, general view. Courtesy of the artist.

dialogical principle. In this sense, an artist's work will have to show an engagement and dialogue with the other.

There is no prescription as to what form this dialogue might take; whether it is primarily interested in form, cultural content, or whether its sources are direct or mediated – and many of these distinctions are blurred as we have shown. Nor is there any idea of this dialogue happening necessarily contemporaneously (the cultures from which artists appropriate might have vanished), or in any balanced way in terms of power – in fact, in most cases it is not.

Dialogue is conceived here as a rhetorical device – it is for the partners in this exchange to fill the dialogue with content.

Moon and Mother: Francesco Clemente's Orient

Christopher Pinney

At a recent Sydney Biennale, Francesco Clemente exhibited the *Story of My Country*, a work that included many small paintings depicting the history of Rome. These images, in the conventional *patta* style of Orissa,[1] were the work of Orissan artists but collectively bore the signature of Clemente. Another series, of twenty-four powerfully intriguing Indian miniatures (known by their title page inscription) *Francesco Clemente Pinxit* 1980–1, reflect a collaboration between Clemente and craftsmen in Jaipur workshops dedicated to the production of simulacra of miniature paintings for the tourist market.[2]

This co-operative bringing into being (which his publishing collaborator Raymond Foye describes as 'allowing his creativity to flow through another person')[3] had its origins in Clemente's 'apprenticeship' with Alighero Boetti's employment of local embroiders to execute his designs in Afghanistan in 1974.[4]

Such appropriation, familiar from Renaissance *ateliers*, and 'confrontationally' deployed by Sherrie Levine in her rephotography of the American photographic canon, unavoidably – in Clemente's case – inhabits a new political/cultural space in a postcolonial age. Recent declarations by First Nation/Fourth World peoples have dramatically demonstrated the complexities of cultural 'borrowing'. In 1995, the Inter-Apache Summit – a consortium of Apache tribes – issued a demand that it should have exclusive control over all Apache 'cultural property' in which category it included 'all images, texts, ceremonies, music, songs, stories, symbols, beliefs, customs, ideas and other physical and spiritual objects and concepts.'[5] In India cultural patrimony has not yet become this hotly contested, but Clemente's act of collaboration/appropriation remains equally political.

Perhaps Clemente's strategy of 'allowing his creativity to flow through other people' should invoke a space of mutual construction that is also the space that is India's history. In this account, India might be seen not as some primal entity that has emerged 'unscathed' through its colonial encounter, but rather as a new hybrid form reconfigured in many of its core social practices and institutions. 'Fuzzy' precolonial forms of identity have become entrenched, made rigid and problematic through the intervention of a colonial bureaucracy that insisted on static zones of belonging.[6]

We might also situate Clemente's strategy in the broader context of an ongoing process of hybrization and partialization in the Indian artworld. Indian 'folk arts' have not endured in a state of isolated purity but have, on the contrary, been actively constituted through a long history of state intervention. In this sense the 'traditionalism' of Orissan patta painters has a similar status to Gandhi's *khadi* – it was a return to an imaginary originary state.

Discussions around these issues have become central to debates within the anthropology and historiography of South Asia since Bernard Cohn started to publish his seminal essays in the 1960s, and have emerged as a key concern of the Indian 'subalternist' school of historigraphy. Perhaps Clemente should be understood as a sophisticated figural pathfinder in this new world of deterri-torialized cultures. As Lyotard has suggested 'there is always something happening in the arts that incandesces the embers of society'. Where academics only prattle, trapped forever within the dessicated groves of linguistic-philosophical closure, perhaps artists inhabit that vanguard where 'intensities are felt'. Clemente's strategy has been glossed as a radical attempt to reconfigure self/other dichotomies. Raymond Foye has suggested that Clemente is 'seeking to participate in the sensibility of another' and realize Rimbaud's slogan that 'I am an Other'.

It is extremely hard to support this argument in any way that respects what we know of Clemente's actions and thoughts. What we know of these suggest that there is 'something happening [in Clemente's art] that incandesces the embers' of an enduring Orientalism. However, it is a complex and, in parts, benign version of Orientalism, and one that despite its limitations bears with it the seeds of a certain kind of liberation.

Clemente was incalcated as a child in the Roman Catholic aesthetic, a preparation that made him fully susceptible to popular Hinduism's 'succulent realism'. In 1977, following several earlier trips to India, Clemente established a studio in Madras and it was here that he started to engage most fully with India's everday visual culture: 'movie placards, painted plaster statuettes of Hindu deities, postcards and souvenir books sold at temples and shrines, greeting cards depicting stars of soap operas or B-Movies, comic books that retell the great epics of the lives of holy men.'[7]

While Clemente's engagement with this material has been that of an admirer, the discourse that has arisen around this engagement is disturbing, invoking an unreconstructed primitivism. Clemente himself invokes India as a space of desirable alterity. Interviewed by Michael McClure, Clemente allied himself with Twombly's and Beuys' 'fascination for the Mediterranean' and for 'the feminine posssibility of the Western world'. He continued, somewhat cryptically:

> My interest in India is based on the fact that we are the Hindus; that is, the Hindus are Americans who instead of going to California went to India. They are the same people. They just chose the mother instead of choosing the father and chose to turn their back on the sun instead of following the sun as Americans did. We are desperately following the father. The Indians are following the moon.[8]

Clemente vacillates, in a fruitful manner, between a self identity that follows the mother, and one that 'desperately' follows the father. Despite this blurring of the line of identity, Clemente's general stance (and this could be argued more strongly with respect to his suppporters and commentators) is Orientalist in the sense used by both Edward Said and Ronald Inden. In his application of Said's seminal ideas to the study of India, Inden juxtaposes two sorts of Orientalism which have developed around India: what he calls the 'positivist' and the 'romantic'. He notes that these two approaches would appear, on the face of it, to be utterly different because the romantics find those very features of Indian civilization that positivists critique, praiseworthy.[9] Unlike positivists, the romantics 'place high value on the myths and symbolic forms which the positivists denigrate or ignore',[10] and emerge in romantic accounts as elements of a spiritual infrastructure that modern Western man lacks, but needs. Both, however, have an equal investment in sustaining the Otherness of India. Romantic Orientalism, Inden argues, is merely a 'loyal opposition', one that while appearing to challenge the positivist version, merely affirms its epistemological foundation. Both versions are Occidental misconstructions that fail to engage with the Indians own reality; they are both ways of (to recall Trinh T. Minh-ha) 'talking about', rather than attempts to 'speak nearby'.

A key element of both positivist and romantic Orientalism, Inden continues, is what Johannes Fabian has characterized as the 'denial of coevality': the assumption that the 'Orient' inhabits an earlier different time from that of the observing/speaking Western subject.[11] Linda Nochlin has shown how nineteenth-century Orientalist painters such as Jean-Léon Gérôme conjured visions of an imaginary Orient that vigorously excluded all signs of the convulsive political and economic transformation with which it was riven.

Clemente is explicit about the ways in which India embodies a temporal anteriority: 'The gods who left us thousands of years ago in Naples are still in India.'[12] India emerges as the repository of a meaning that has eroded and decayed in the historically more advanced (and more desolate) West. It is a storehouse filled with the 'means to reanimate art with the philosophical, religious, and hermetic import that had existed in centuries past'.[12] Here Clemente's faith mirrors that of the Australian curator Vivienne Johnson for whom Aboriginal art offers the possibility of reviving and resanctifying a spiritually, ethically, and symbolically depleted European colonial culture.

Consonant with this is the promotion of Clemente's recurrent visits to India as a form of 'fieldwork' conceptualized in an anthropologically archaic manner. India is where he collects his raw data, the place where he can inhabit the 'ethnographic present' characterized by its non-coevality. It is also a place of hardship and suffering. Despite the fact that Clemente spends half his time in the Connemara Hotel ('A' class with 'splendid art deco features, extremely comfortable, excellent location' says a recent guide),[14] Foye asserts 'both the quality and quantity of his art often seem to be inextricably equated with the degree of physical discomfort that must be endured during its creation'.[15] This recalls C. G. Seligman's observation that 'fieldwork is to anthropology what the blood of martyrs is to the church'.

THE GANGES AND THE PO

These strategies, and the accompanying idea that this temporal return consti-tutes a 'coming home'[16] resonate closely with the core doxa of 'romantic' Orientalism. Set within a historical (colonial frame), Clemente's position appears curiously familiar.

After 1786, when William Jones proclaimed the unity of Sanskrit and Greek, India's location within an Indo-European philological space positioned it within a collective colonial memory. Such a continuity is expressed geographically in George Birdwood's *Handbook to the British Indian Section* of the Paris Universal Exhibition of 1878.[17] Here he wrote of the 'Indo-Germanic shore', which suggests a unity fractured by the 'arbitrary'[18] division of Europe and Asia into two continents. Further, in one of the most remarkable similies of imperial literature, Birdwood suggests a mirroring in the topography of East and West:

It is a remarkable coincidence that Europe should repeat on a smaller scale the main features of the coast line of Asia. The peninsula of Arabia is repeated in the Iberian peninsular; Asia Minor and Persia in France; India in Italy; Burma, Siam, Anam, and the eastern Archipelago in Turkey, Greece and the Grecian Archipelego; and the Chinese Empire in Russia; while Japan is placed on the east of the Euro-Asian continent symmetrically with the British Isles on the west. The parallelism between India and Italy is very striking; the Himalayas are repeated in the Alps; the Indus and Ganges in the Rhone and the Po; Karachi is Genoa or Marseilles; Calcutta, Venice; Delhi, Milan; Bombay, Naples; Ceylon, Sicily; and the Laccadive and Maldive Islands are the mountain peaks of a submerged Corsica and Sardinia.[19]

The theme of continuity and rediscovery receives its most explicit and most romantic statement in Max Muller's[20] lecture 'What can India teach us?' delivered to candidates for the Indian Civil Service in Cambridge in 1882. To once again find India, Muller argues, is 'to do what the French call *s'orienter*, that is, "to find his East," "his true East"'. This would allow one to: 'determine his real place in the world; to know, in fact, the port whence man started, the course he has followed, and the port towards which he has to steer'.[21]

The navigational course here is provided by a common Indo-European language family whose recent rediscovery allows the tracing of originary lines. Muller draws a striking analogy:

Suppose the Americans, owing to some cataclysmal events, had forgotten their English origin, and after two or three thousand years found themselves in posses-sion of a language and of ideas which they could trace back historically to a certain date, but which, at that date, seemed as it were, fallen from the sky, without any explanation of their origin and previous growth, what would they say if suddenly the existence of an English language and literature were revealed to them, such as they existed in the seventeenth century – explaining all that seemed before most miraculous, and solving almost every question that could be asked![22]

It is precisely this that the discovery of Sanskrit has done for Europe, he continues. It demonstrates philologically and unquestionably that 'we have all come from the East'[23] and with the benefit of this knowledge the voyager to India 'ought to feel that he is going to his "old home," full of memories, if only he can read them'. Foye has suggested that Clemente's sense of India as 'like going home' is 'striking' since it 'conveys an entirely unexpected jolt of recognition, a firsthand discovery that ours is an Indo-European tradition'.[24] Unexpected perhaps, but eminently predictable.

'STRANGE FORMS AND MARVELLOUS DISGUISES'

During his first visit to India in 1973, Clemente started to accumulate what Raymond Foye intriguingly describes as 'a vast body of ideogrammatic images, symbols, and emblems'. These fragmented graphemes ('persistent enough to force themselves onto paper') underscored, as Foye perceptively observes the 'notational' as opposed to 'representational' nature of Clemente's work.

Clemente's rejection of a 'representational' approach might be understood as a move away from a positivist Orientalism: the delusion that a totalised reality of India might be captured in an image and transported from India to an audience elsewhere. Perhaps the work of the photographer Hannah Collins might be seen in this sense as 'representational'. Her large format colour images (including series made in the year 2000 on Indian cities) seem in the process of enlargement to representationally unravel a detailed stillness not available to the embodied eye at the moment of exposing the photographic negative.[25] Clemente's approach is quite different and presumes fragmentary points of potent intersection between parallel cultural cryptographies.

In this respect Clemente's preoccupations have extensive historical precedents. In 1924 the retired colonial educationalist Oswald J. Couldrey[26] provided an elaborate exploration of an Indian (sub)lunar identity articulated through poetically potent ideographs. South India, he suggested, is a 'new world' where 'nothing is as we have known it', and yet beneath this exterior difference there are familiar patterns to be rediscovered:

If we have brought with us any formed preference into this new world, and 'our loves remain' in a sublunar after-life, we may still pursue the same in essence, but under strange forms and marvellous disguises . . . you may find here . . . among palm-thatched cow-sheds, or under the shadow of some horned pagoda, the same poetic meaning, but uttered in another language; only you must put aside the old symbols and acquire new, curious and beautiful in themselves, and able to voice old messages with enriched significance.

The perusal may at first appear monotonous, for the scholar has not yet learned to read. Among the confusion of moving ideographs before him, men, garments, gauds, coiffures, caste-marks . . . he is able to recognise the name as it were and visual cipher of this and that . . . When [this language] is learned, life speaks to us as it spoke before, often as it never spoke before.[27]

But South India, for Couldrey, also allows the attainment of a transcendental state in which an innate 'recognition' triumphs over mere 'reading'. This recognition suggests the:

> reflection from pictures seen in childhood, or memories copied from once-familiar books . . . the revisiting of a former state of existence. Now South India, for all its strangeness, has preeminently this appeal to the imaginative memory, and as it were a kind of metaphysical recognition . . . long ago as in dreams we saw, and thought we had forgotten, the 'palms and temples of the South' . . . all this recognized, all this we found to have somehow grown familiar, before we saw it with the bodily eye.[28]

Within Inden's paradigm such parallels would be a proof of an Orientalist guilt. However, there are good reasons to reject Inden's straightforward ellision of (bad) positivist Orientlism and (good) romantic Orientalism. Although both may share certain certain epistemological assumptions, their political trajectory is quite different. The positivist variant is predicated on the inferiority of India, the romantic variant is predicated on its superiority. Much the same point might be made about theosophy, the spiritualist movement with which Clemente became distantly associated in the late 1970s.[29]

Like the theosophists, Clemente is interested in India not as a 'special case', but rather as somewhere capable of powerfully revealing universal and elemental commonalities. His technique is thus, in a limited sense, anthropo-logical for it affirms the Rousseauian platitude of distantiation – the need to study from afar if one is to understand 'man' (rather than 'men'). His commen-tators certainly wish us to believe that Clemente's goal is this abstract universal 'man'. But his method is distinctly unlike (a certain form of) anthropology in that it completely spurns any engagement with context or polythetic complex-ity. Clemente is not interested in Indian ideograms insofar as they can be explicated via a grounded understanding of Indian philosophy, cultural practice, social structure and such like. Rather, his is a hit and run in the name of the universal, an engagement with mudras, or potent signs in popular Hindu art, as illuminators of (to quote Foye for the last time) 'the wonder and awe of creation', and 'consciousness itself'.[30]

But if there is a limitation imposed by this approach, there is also a clear benefit. One of Clemente's twenty-four Miniatures depicts a hand posed in a complex *mudra*. The index finger points to the sky against an involuted foliage background. The little finger has been severed and the tip lies seeping blood into a river at the bottom of the image while the stump gives vent to three fountains of spurting blood (Figure 3.1). Clemente here draws on common Tantric depictions of hands that have formed the subject matter of other of his works, and the spurting blood takes its cue from images of the goddeses Tara and Chinnamusta who beheads herself (Figure 3.2; see also Figures 3.3 and 3.4).

An 'anthropological' account would seek to establish these connections, striving to embed Clemente's image in a wider Hindu worldview. This might

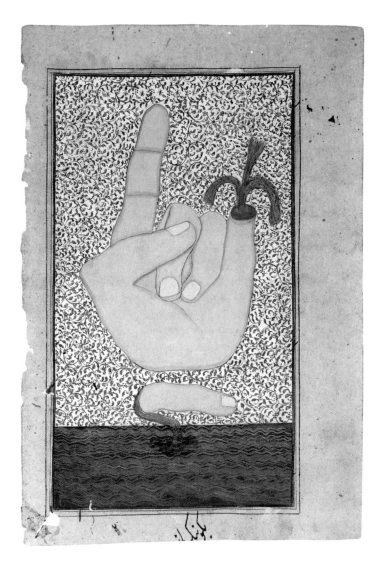

Figure 3.1. Francesco Clemente, *Pinxit*, 1980–1. Gouache on antique paper. From a series of twelve gouaches. 8¾ × 6 inches (22.2 × 15.2 cm). Courtesy of the Gagosian Gallery.

be seen to enhance the image – 'context' tells us 'more' about the image – we could for instance learn about its tantric origins, its history of mass reproduction from the 1880s onwards. But it might also serve to diminish it, diverting attention from the resonant mystery and power of the image into analytic culs-de-sac. This is of course the eternally replayed debate around the construction of 'art' and 'artefact', between the putatively autonomous object which demands our attention for what it claims to be in itself, and the empty signifier of some more potent force located elsewhere.

Figure 3.2. Chromolithograph depicting the Goddess Chinnamusta. Calcutta Art Sudio, c. 1880. Private collection.

Figure 3.3. Francesco Clemente, *Head*, 1988–90, oil on canvas, 24 × 24 inches (61 × 61 cm). Courtesy of the Gagosian Gallery.

Figure 3.4. Chromolithograph depicting the Goddess Kali and Ramakrishna. Calcutta *c.* 1950. Artist and publisher unknown.

ALT.EVERYTHING/ I AM AN OTHER PLC

Finally, a broader political frame requires brief notation. The meaning of texts, and of images, as Barthes suggested, is to be found 'at the point of destination' – through readers' and consumers' interpretations – rather than in the 'theological' effect of authors' intentions. What can we learn from the 'destination' of Clemente's work?

Jostling alongside Clemente in what Naomi Klein calls 'alt.everything' is the image of Che Guevara on every bottle of 'Revolution Soda' and Apple computer's use of Gandhi in their 'think different' campaign.[31] Regardless of Clemente's intentions, it is difficult to see how, in this wider context of alt.everything, Clemente's work is able to do anything to undermine the cultural certainties of the art world that now celebrates him. It is very easy to turn one's discourses in towards Clemente in celebration of his benificence! But this is merely to reproduce the William Rubin view of an agentive European art generously acknowledging its others.

To read the list of Clemente's shows and his selected bibliography is to realise what powerful forces of affirmation are made available to those who redeem otherness. Alongside this catalogue of prestigous gallery space, of engaged critical response by those cultural brokers that mediate success to the dominant class and the corporate world, and the acres of newsprint and tonnes of glossy catlogues that sediment this recognition, we must place the silence and void that greet South Asian artists with an equal claim to our attention.

Clemente's alterity is a Disney version, one reprocessed so that the audience can face it with the assurance that there will never be anything fully confrontational in it. Its championing erases the necessity for its audience to confront the alterity that Indians make themselves. Raymond Foye advances Clemente as the Rimbaud of our age, the living synthesis of the self as an other but this is a 'circumventing [of] the habits of one's impulses'[32] made possible only through the appeal to a dehistoricized, depoliticized and non-agentive fantasy of the 'other'. Clemente's vision is that of cultural 'diversity' rather than of a grounded political awareness of cultural 'difference' in the manner that Homi Bhabha invokes these terms.

The position outlined by the editors of this volume is challenging and urgent. Visual culture practitioners *can* provide one of the possible escape routes from the what Michel Foucault termed the 'absolute eye that cadaverizes'. However, Clemente appears – to this writer at least – a weak case on which to advance this argument. In our haste to embrace those who offer a creative exit from the dry and dusty linguistic-philosophical closure of academic analysis, we run the risk of erasing the possibility of 'speaking nearby', from a position of skilled engagement.

If anthropology is to take seriously the 'counter' in the 'counterscience' that Foucault took it to be, then it must do more than simply affirm Clemente's contribution to 'alt.everything'.

Where Green Grass Comes to Meet Blue Sky: A Trajectory of Josef Šíma
Michael Richardson

When Gaston Bachelard wrote *The Psychoanalysis of Fire*, he was challenging usual modes of investigation. Instead of establishing an object of study in itself, he was positing an active principle as the locus for an enquiry with philosophical, anthropological and psychological implications. What does it mean to 'psychoanalyse' fire? Psychoanalysis establishes its legitimacy as a treatment for neurosis. By extension, it aims to use its methods to contribute to a generalized science of the mind that we call psychology. How, then, can an active principle like fire be subject to psychoanalytical investigation?

With his study, Bachelard was bringing attention to the fact that reality as we understand it is not constituted simply by its material components but also by the perception that we as humans have of it. But if it is possible to 'psychoanalyse' fire, is it not also possible to extend anthropological analysis to the study of elemental phenomena?

In considering the crossover between art and anthropology, we could perhaps bear this question in mind as we try to focus on the possibilities that may be raised for a plastic exploration of anthropological themes. I intend here to focus on the Czech painter Josef Šíma, whose work is concerned precisely with the existence of boundaries, with the question of what it means to cross a border, and with how otherness is inscribed in the very structures of the world. When we speak of a border crossing in this case, we are also speaking of an engagement with those structures: we may, doubtless provisionally, describe this as a kind of 'ethnography' of infinity, an extension of investigation into the realm of the unseen.

Born in Bohemia in 1891, Šíma moved to Paris in 1921, just three years after the establishment of the Republic of Czechoslovakia. In 1926 he became a French citizen, but continued to maintain links and participate in the cultural politics of his native land. A member of the Devevtsil, the major Czech *avant garde* movement of the 1920s, Šíma was cultural advisor to the Czechoslovak ambassador in Paris from 1945–50, and provided a vital link in cultural communication between Prague and Paris.

The crossing of boundaries this displacement involved – his identity as a Frenchman who wasn't really French, or a Czech who wasn't entirely Czech, allied to the fact that to be Czech during the period in which he lived was to

Figure 4.1. Josef Šíma, *Portrait of Nadine Šíma*, 1928, oil on canvas, 155.5 × 105 cm, Gallery of the City of Prague. Reproduced by kind permission of Aline Sima-Brumlik.

live with an identity frequently under threat as a result of political realities – gave his work a particular charge. A people dominated, at different periods of his lifetime, by Austria, Germany and Russia, shamefully betrayed by Britain and France in 1938, the Czechs have cause to reflect ruefully on what a border means and a concern with the theme of boundary crossing, combined with a will to explore elemental, cosmological themes, which is present in the work of precursors such as František Kupka and Vojtevch Preissig, clear influences on the work of Šíma.

If Šíma's painting eschews any overt social or political comment, such themes are nevertheless not entirely absent: Šíma, among this century's painters, is one of those most concerned with the fluidity of boundaries, the way in which – solid one moment, torn apart the next – boundaries have a tendency to dissolve without warning and this in itself has a certain political charge. These boundaries may be strictly metaphysical, existing in realms that are beyond those of ordinary perception, but they nevertheless cannot entirely be sundered from the latter. Šíma is clearly a painter who was profoundly affected by political events, to the extent that the rise of Nazism left him barely able to paint at all during the 1940s. Several paintings from 1937, all entitled 'Spanish Revolution', although one would be hard pressed to find any directly political matter in them, make clear the extent of Šíma's commitments, in which immediate events were not separated from cosmological reality, nor vice

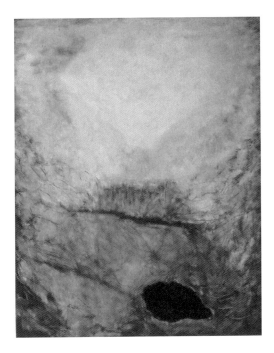

Figure 4.2. Josef Šíma, *Chaos*, 1959, oil on canvas, 100 × 81 cm. Collection of M and Mme Edwin Engelberts. Reproduced by kind permission of Aline Sima-Brumlik.

versa: recognition of the temporality of the here and now – even in the most terrible of circumstances – is crucial to his vision.

A friend of the surrealists, Šíma only very rarely participated in exhibitions of the group and surprisingly receives not a single mention in André Breton's *Surrealism and Painting*. Surprising because Šíma was concerned with a central surrealist theme: the nature of the other within the sensibility. And yet, perhaps not so surprising, for this surrealist theme was one that Breton failed to emphasize when it came to visual expression. Where painting was concerned, Breton was more interested in the configuration of the image, in what the work looked out upon, than in the plastic exploration of states of being, and it is perhaps this that explains Šíma's marginalization within orthodox surrealism.

Šíma's sensibility found a more responsive place to dwell within *Le Grand Jeu*, a splinter – or parallel – surrealist group, whose intense collective activity was centred in the possibility of going to the limits of human experience. The question of frontiers once more arises. The Great Game at stake here was that of Death, and might be contrasted with the game of life which tended to characterise surrealist activity. Not that this was an opposition, more a difference of emphasis. Surrealism – at least as a collective activity – sought the key to existence this side of the divide: 'I spoke of a certain "sublime point" in the mountain. It was never a question of my going to live in such a place.

Figure 4.3. Josef Šíma, *Le Point Un*, 1970, oil on canvas, 65 × 54 cm. Collection of M and Mme Edwin Engelberts. Reproduced by kind permission of Aline Sima-Brumlik.

Besides, it would, at that moment, have ceased to be sublime and I would also have ceased to be a man.'[1]

For the members of *Le Grand Jeu* it was precisely a matter of living at such a point and some of them paid a heavy price for the attempt: Roger Gilbert Lecomte and René Daumal, its two leading figures, were both dead at the age of 36, the former from drug addiction, the latter from the tuberculosis he had contracted as a result of experiments undertaken as part of *Le Grand Jeu*.

Šíma lived to a healthy age and he may not have been as inclined as his younger colleagues to indulge so intensely in the experiment that it affected his personal equilibrium, but he was still concerned to explore the essence of things. What is significant about this work is that it is not simply an expression of what is seen or even unseen, but that the process of creation itself, the mode of painting, offers what may be called an 'anthropological' exploration of the nature of reality.

In his philosophy, Emmanuel Levinas explored the nature of otherness in cosmic terms, showing how the Other is not merely other people or things but represents a primal frisson between being and infinity. Based on illumination, imagination and unity, the activities of *Le Grand Jeu* involved an intense questioning of the nature of existence that has parallels with the philosophical investigation of Levinas.

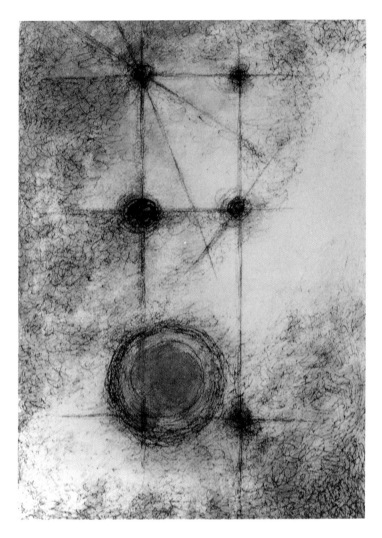

Figure 4.4. Josef Šíma, *Etude pour le Point Un*, 1970, China ink on paper, 55.5 × 38 cm, M.N.A.M. Centre Georges Pompidou. Reproduced by kind permission of Aline Sima-Brumlik.

For Šíma, the use of painting was a means by which to explore the essential nature of reality, in which the unity of the world was suddenly – but only momentarily – revealed. His work can perhaps be seen as centred in a single event when lightening struck close to him. The sudden sense of the fragility of life and yet of the unity of all things he experienced at that moment is at the heart of his enquiry. This involved the vision of an essential oneness of matter and energy, of a revelation of the relation between the whole and its parts, that led him to try to chart a restitution of man's original unity with nature. Šíma's mythical landscapes, in which the detritus of infinity – floating torsos, crystals, eggs – is cast adrift, perhaps to fade away, bring to mind the beginnings of things. Earth seems to collapse into sky; we are offered a vision of the world of unity in which earth and sky are not separated, in which the sky goddess Nut and the earth god Geb are still lovers. Here all is in transformation. Forms metamorphose, the world evaporates in sleep and hallucination is indistinguishable from perception. His work as a whole can be said to follow this theme: a meditation on lightning, or perhaps on the impact of a thunderstorm. The disruption of nature that a storm involves is one in which forms metamorphose in a glut of light and water. This is a moment in which the cosmos re-enacts a moment of creation and as such opens up our experience of life to an immemorial event. The most ancient memory of mankind is recalled in a sudden tremor. Light becomes matter and the visible is derealized.

In all of Šíma's work, illumination is connected with haunting. Nothing is forgotten, we are shadowed by all that has happened before we came to exist. The subject is not so much denied or dissolved as opened out to an encounter with the infinite. Memory here has nothing to do with individual recall; the trauma it reveals or plays out is, far beyond psychological explanation, a trauma of elemental forms enacted in terms of a cosmic drama of which human activity is but one emanation. Šíma follows this drama, exploring it, revealing it one moment, concealing it the next.

Water here represents a transitory order, or rather reveals the temporary nature of the human condition. It initiates us into recognition of the immaterial veils that constitute our personality. The human body, from this perspective, is but an evanescent cocoon that is as much absent as it is present and it evaporates each night in sleep. This can be seen most especially in the extraordinary series of portraits Šíma undertook in 1929 in which he presented his wife and friends like Gilbert Lecomte, Daumal, Leon Pierre-Quint and Berenice Abbott as shadows, only ethereally present in the world.

In taking us on a journey into a world that exists as a possibility rather than as a reality, as a perimeter of two lands, belonging to neither but imbued with the essence of both, Šíma reveals the contingency of life, the fact that we exist here and now only due to a chance configuration of happenings. Carried along by the current, we are only cast up on the shore for a short time in this limited, material world that ordinarily seems so solid around us. There is no seduction here: Šíma refuses the mystique of painting, which has no more permanence than anything else.

The artist perhaps closest to Šíma in these terms is Henri Michaux. Like Michaux, Šíma sought to penetrate into the heart of reality, to reveal what was beyond perception. Like Michaux, too, Šíma regarded painting as a material activity with the possibility of opening up the sensibility to what lay beyond it, of showing the unity of objective and subjective states, and of giving a glimpse of what the pressures of everyday living force us to suppress. In this respect, Šíma was less concerned with the production of a work of art than with the process of exploration that leads to it. He was not interested in realizing a process of inspiration, but in seeking the wellsprings of creativity by means of a collectivity of vision that opened up his world to anyone having

Figure 4.5. Josef Šíma, frontispiece to book by Pierre Jean Jouve *Le Paradis perdu*, Paris: GLM, 1938. Private collection, Paris. Reproduced by kind permission of Aline Sima-Brumlik.

the patience to follow his path. His approach has more in common with that of a scientist interested in exploring the nature of the world than that of an artist concerned with giving expression to what exists within himself.

I do not know if it is abusive to speak of Šíma in terms of anthropology, because there is nothing to link his work directly with any anthropological theme. At least, so far as we know, Šíma himself had no particular interest in anthropology and his work displays no overt concern with what are ordinarily considered to be anthropological themes. Yet if we are seeking to draw correspondences between anthropological knowledge and the process by which a painter seeks to gain an understanding of the sensible world around him, there seems to be something to be gained by subjecting a quest such as that implied in Šíma's work to anthropological scrutiny. For where the claims to scientific knowledge towards which anthropology once strove have become ever more tenuous, recognition of the complexities involved in sensual perception and in the processes of communicability between humans existing in an incomprehensible world have become more urgent.

If anthropological knowledge is to be seen as requiring the construction of an Other and as the study of what is external to us, a body of work like Šíma's can offer nothing (such an approach would doubtless deny any form of rapprochement between artistic and anthropological concerns). If, however, we are prepared to see it not as a thing but as a relation, in which otherness is located on a borderline of consciousness and in which it is important to seek out correspondences and continuities between perceptions as it contemplates the nature of reality and the phenomena of the world, rather than as being located in defined cultural configurations, then a visual exploration such as that of Šíma's can reveal parallels that – beyond the social masks they respectively wear – may bring together the concerns of the anthropologist and the artist. The philosopher Michel Serres has noted how 'literature gets through where expertise sees an obstacle', adding that 'philosophy can go deep enough to show that literature goes still deeper than philosophy.'[2] Might something similar not be said about the relationship between anthropology and art: the artist may be able go deeper into the nature of the reality of human relations, but still needs the anthropologist to reveal how deeply he is going?

Selected Bibliography on the work of Josef Šíma

Anonymous, *Šíma* Paris: Musée d'Art Moderne de la Ville de Paris, 1992.
Línhartová, V., *Josef Šíma, ses amis, ses contemporains*, Brussels: La Connaissance, 1974.
Šmejkal, F., *Josef Šíma*, Prague: Odeon, 1988.

Encounters with the Work of Susan Hiller

Denise Robinson

. . . of course its dramatic, he snarls self consciously theatrical, how could a spirit otherwise exist . . . it is because of their parlous reality that the spirits of the dead require deliberate artifice that allows them to be real.

Michael Taussig

[The] category of the 'other' includes the inhabitants of the realms of supernatural beings and monsters, the territories of real or imaginary allies and enemies, and the lands of the dead – places far from the centre of the world, where one's own land is, and one's own reality. The 'other' is always distant as well as different, and against this difference the characteristics of self and society are formed and clarified.

Susan Hiller

The work of Susan Hiller reminds us that altered states and phantasms are the ground on which we may move from one condition of knowledge to another. It also challenges the terrain on which so much has been built, and lost, in debates on difference that have passed through our 'interested' cultural agencies yet that appear to be always haunted by a need for a final translation of difference. In exploring these places 'far from the centre of the world' through their cultural representations, Hiller's work involves an ambivalent relation to the materials she works with – this is not indifference, for as Hiller says, 'I have never really had a formula for selecting what I work with. They usually turn out to be things which I deeply love and hate.'[1]

Hiller's work was developed in the context of an intense period of critical revaluation and questioning of the efficacy of art in the West, and a questioning of the autonomy of the art object. Yet importantly for artists, like Hiller, it was also a moment for a reconsideration of the margins to which so many practices in art had been relegated – what could not be ignored was the vividness of the margins from which Western culture had drawn much of its critique in the twentieth century: from the surrealists and the encounters that followed between modernism and postmodernism.

Having come from the US and having been based in Britain since 1970, Hiller's work is 'ghosted' by the development of the extraordinary phenomena of postwar popular culture and mass media in the US. It is not so much that the history of this phenomenon holds some founding moment that informs Hiller's work developmentally – for American culture is now felt politically and culturally everywhere, and returns to us in at times unrecognizable forms – but that her work's relation to this phenomenon holds something within it, some kernel that has always to be negotiated. Hiller's prolific body of work over the past thirty-five years is also ghosted by, and partly based upon, her refusal in the mid 1960s in the US to continue to engage with the anthropological project. She studied and practised anthropology prior to her decision to work as an artist, undertaking fieldwork in Mexico, Guatemala and Belize in the early 1960s, supported by a National Science Foundation grant. After 1965, however, Hiller's reasons for refusing to participate in the anthropology of the time, provide an insight into the basis on which it was then being conducted: a programme of complicity in the intellectual, economic and political colonization of what was deemed 'other' cultures. Her decision was based upon this deeply felt ethical dilemma, which she could see no means of challenging from within, and as a consequence she developed an insight that could be put to work: not to be in the position of being an observer of others but 'to be a full participant in the culture in which [she] lived'[2] and to refuse to be contained by anthropology's observer/participant model. American experimental film maker, theorist and anthropologist Maya Deren's relationship to the rituals of the Haitian Voudoun religion had a deep significance for Hiller, who early on recognized her as an ethnographer with a profound understanding of what is at stake in the model of observer and observed. A model refused by Deren's entering into a state of possession herself, a radical move that marginalized Deren's ethnographic work for many years. Hiller's work, *Fragments*, from 1978, described by Lucy Lippard as a 'complex, key work about the abyss between cultures and the colonisation of archaeological material'[3] is a work that also pivots on the refusal of this model.[4] The dilemma for Hiller is not so much some clearly demarcated shift from anthropology to art, from one discipline to another, but an indication of what is at stake and what it is possible to address when conditions arise that precipitate a radical shift in consciousness. Hiller has made a substantial contribution to mapping this terrain in her writings, especially in *The Myth of Primitivism*[5] where she commissioned a collection of essays to create one of the first places where art historians, artists, critics and anthropologists, 'spoke to and against each other about ways in which notions of the primitive inflect their work.'[6]

She also explored this theme in *Thinking About Art, Conversations with Susan Hiller*,[7] an anthology selected from Hiller's own prolific body of writing and interviews. On its cover is one of her photo booth self-portraits, *Midnight Euston* (1983) where the photograph's function of proof of identity is altered as it is recoloured and overwritten with automatic writing scripts. Suggestive perhaps of how the texts inside may be 'read', it also directs us to the points of eruption in language as one of the central foci of her work. As Jean Genet suggested, 'art should exalt only those truths which are not demonstrable, and which are even "false", those which we cannot carry to their ultimate conclusions without absurdity, without negating both them and yourself. They will never have the good or bad fortune to be applied',[8] and for Hiller, 'art with no overt political content can sensitise us politically'.[9]

Some of Hiller's earliest works, such as *Sisters of Menon* (1972-9), were developed from her automatic writing experiments – moving beyond the Surrealists' experimentation – and are still recognizable in much of her work. For example, she pursues this process as a critique of those claims for cultural neutrality so prevalent in the painting boom of the 1980s – pursuing automatic writing into a realm where she could see it as developing into a new language. Another early work, *Draw Together* (1972), a long distance postal event, was an experiment in non-verbal transmission of images and ideas and was shadowed by the significance of automatic writing. This connects with one of her more recent audio/visual works, *Witness* (2000), which however focuses on an elaborate construction of technologically manipulated verbal recordings. This is not a reflection of a parallel development of new technologies of communication (however much it is affected by this), for what binds the two

Figure 5.1. Susan Hiller, *Witness*, 2000. Audio-sculpture: 400 speakers, wiring, steel structure, 10 CD players, switching equipment, lights; suspended from ceiling and walls; approx. dimensions 700 × 900 cm. Commissioned by Artangel, London with the support of the British Council, the Tate Gallery and the Henry Moore Foundation. Courtesy of the artist and Timothy Taylor Gallery, London.

works together is a kind of tracking of a formless archive, 'out there' some-where. *Draw Together* acknowledges the unconscious and its challenge to the predetermined one-way address of language. In 'Witness' interpretation is made possible by resensitizing us to technology's relation to that speech which is relegated to the margins of discourse – in this instance, people who report having seen and experienced contact with extraterrestrials.

Witness finds its subject in what Hiller has described as, 'the unstable territory where the visible merges with the visionary. We are conditioned to think that the real visible world lies outside ourselves, and that what we see inside must be unreal'.[10] *Witness* is both a sound work and a 'site-specific' installation, yet its effect is shaped by voices. The first and most significant installation of *Witness* was located in 'The Chapel', a gospel church in west London in 2000. At the top of a small twisting iron staircase the beholder entered an interior transformed into a 'core', more like an internal mould in the shape of an oval. An oval formed from a drapery of electrical cables, each cable holding a small round speaker on the end, dropping down from the ceiling, from the darkness, in a controlled mass. Archaic within the economy of the speed of new technologies, they resemble car radios in a state of disrepair, speakers that appear to have been pulled out of somewhere else. But this is not where the 'shaping by voices' occurs, which is reserved for the encounter with the initially indecipherable voices transmitted through the speakers and the slow realisation of what the voices are saying. There are also other voices, heard and not understood, because they are in another language. All are stories told by people who have witnessed the presence of UFOs and extraterrestrials and approach a level of experience similar to Avital Ronell's desire for her own writing 'to alcoholise my texts, turn down the volume and let them murmur across endless boundaries and minuscule epiphanies'.[11] For Roland Barthes, in *The Rustle of Language* no voice is raised, and no voice is raised in 'Witness', and no emphasis given to particular sources, references or locations. For example, those sourced from government records have equivalence to those where people have recorded their stories directly on the World Wide Web – creating a tenuous balance between the specificity of the voice and the conditions of its emergence.

Held in the midst of a web of voices beholders are connected by what structures their distance from them – for the voices are citations: researched, selected and catalogued from the sites and archives that the artist has mined: MUFOX – Mutual UFO Network, UFO – Chronicles online, UFO, Master Index, UFO – hotline, UFO – Sighting Report Library. And the publications: The House of Lords UFO debate, 1979, 'Angels and Aliens': UFOs and 'The Mythic Imagination',1991. The palimpsest of languages includes: Portuguese, Spanish, French, Japanese, English, Hebrew, Hindi, Chinese, Zulu and Italian; and regional accents, which may hinder decipherability, also help to create the images we can't ignore.

Paradoxically, this polyphonic and polysemic assemblage is also speechless in the sense that 'the voice is never represented: it represents, it is the act of presence which represents itself'[12] 'for speech is not voice. It is voice that has run over and through language . . . (speech) differs, and it defers.[13]

Recounting my listening to *Witness*, I fall prey to what Hiller has built into the work: the inevitability of another migration of voices to the assumed silence of writing:

> in place of a face . . . there was an entirely black surface . . . the distance between us had been shortened . . . we looked for somewhere to hide, but no entry . . . across snow covered . . . it only lasted a minute but I have remembered all these details for years

> the size of a three story building, coral coloured . . . heads seem to give off a glow like a halo . . . our car radio felt dead and we felt a kind of coldness

These reports invoke the technologies of sound reproduction as they meet our senses, not so much to question the truth of the original telling by studying the many repetitions within these stories (hence their falsity, their 'non-uniqueness'), but what is at stake when our senses and language adapt to modernity's – now incorporated – 'shock' of technology. The last report is particularly loaded with this affect, the car radio didn't go dead it 'felt' dead, they felt not the heat of technology but its coldness. As Avital Ronell observes, 'technology as a neuro adventure'.[14] The reports also generate images like those which endlessly circulate within Western culture in pulp science fiction novels, the powerful place of movies such as the multi-million dollar friendly alien, *ET*, or the *X files*, as well as in non-Western cultures where these ubiquitous images may appear, radically appropriated – and in some instances where they may have originated. It is through the voice that, 'my words are alive because they seem not to leave me . . . not to fall outside me, not to cease to belong to me'.[15]

Clinic exhibited at the Baltic Arts Center in 2004[16] again installs us in the realm of the voice. For *Clinic*, Hiller chose a space with high ceilings and huge volume, one that evokes a place between transcendence and the echo of a chilling medicalized world. The space is apparently empty until we hear the voices: citations that retell the recorded stories of people who have had near-death experiences. With a speaker and electronic counters installed in each of the columns that stretch in two long rows along either side of the hall, the columns themselves appear to embody the voices. These voices have been 'collected', their context destroyed, torn from their given cultural order; they are now available for an experience in the present. They are encountered as a slow murmur, but erupt into something more when the beholder's attention wanders and momentarily locates a legible story. They may also become illegible when faced with the thresholds of life and death. Then there is the imbrecation of the voice with the illegibility of speech when encountering an 'other' language.

Hiller's work recognizes the opacity of what slips past and through the representation of such utterances and the subsequent faltering of a distinction between interior and exterior. For example, lucid experiences achieved through altered states – often assigned to an interiority – are reworked by Hiller, reinstating the experience by recognizing its connection to an outside 'I'm asserting that I am not identified with night, I am not nature . . . I want to show how one can claim a position of speaking from the side of darkness, the side of the unknown, while not reducing oneself to darkness and the unknowable'.[17] I have never thought of Hiller's work as anthropological. If it has something to say of the anthropological it is to the extent that the subjects of anthropology have too often been reduced to this kind of darkness, this kind of unknowable. Any sense of continuity through some perfect functioning of the apparatus of appropriation between art and anthropology is lost. Hiller's work may more productively be considered in relation to the work of the allegorist, due to her persistant practice of taking elements out of – and destroying – their context, in a sense draining them of life. For Walter Benjamin the object became allegorical under the gaze of melancholy – dead but eternally secure, any significance the object could have could only be acquired from the allegorist, hence 'alive' in the present.

Hiller also maintains a relation to her subject in part through her works' resistance to its incorporation within the trajectory of cultural history. Walter Benjamin offers the figure of the collector in place of cultural history. Writing of the collector, Edward Fuchs, Benjamin finds that 'he questions the hermetic self sufficiency of various disciplines . . . breaking with an historical view of the past (for Fuchs) truth lay in extremes, through his unique archive of the history of caricature, erotic art and the portrayal of manners'.[18] The work *Nama-ma/mother* (1991) is the first record in Hiller's book *After the Freud Museum*,[19] and is a reference to cave paintings at Uluru by Australian aborigines. The image of a container that holds Australian Native Earth found by the artist at Papunya, with the help of Papunya artists, is accompanied by a text which says, 'the title means mother in an aboriginal language I can't speak or under-stand'. This distance and untranslatability is an indication of the ambivalence that lies at the heart of this work. *After the Freud Museum* is an elaborate pseudo-scientific record, conjuring up ideas of the fetish in its presentation of artifacts. Records, objects, categories, histories, motifs, memories and modes of forgetting. The book is one collation of materials from an ongoing work that brings together Hiller's collections gathered over the previous 20 years and is a reworking of her installation of twenty-two boxes *At the Freud Museum*, exhibited at the Freud Museum, London, then extended to forty-four boxes and retitled *From the Freud Museum*. We are not only dealing there with the historical effects of psychoanalysis and the twentieth century's internalizing of Freud's theories, for it is a voracious museum – seemingly arbitrary – which registers the endless textuality of culture as it strains against the containment of cultural history. The fallibility of cultural history is recorded, deployed and catalogued through the artifacts assembled. Hiller has revisited ethnography, to cast a critical eye on its history.[20]

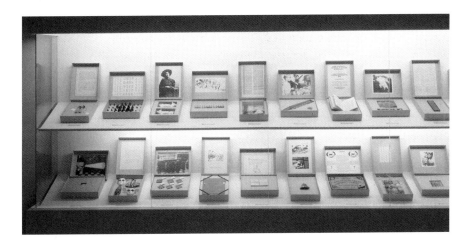

Figure 5.2. Susan Hiller, *From the Freud Museum*, 1991–97. Vitrine installation: artefacts, notes, in customized cardboard boxes, with video projection. Vitrine dimensions variable; 50 boxes, each 25.4 × 6.4 × 2.5 cm. Commissioned by BookWorks and the Sigmund Freud Museum, London. Courtesy of the artist and Timothy Taylor Gallery, London.

I am not suggesting that Hiller's work is exemplary of the figure of the collector, but that the collector shadows the figure of the artist. These collections meticulously categorize and retain the specificity of the cultural artifacts while juxtaposing them so that they move beyond discrete meanings. What Hiller deems suitable as an artifact is central to this. For example, it includes material from Freud's own archives, which he left uncatalogued: scientific specimens, miniature curiosities, traditional magic lantern slides and early Disney cartoon strips, replicated in 35 mm slides and now incorporated within the artist's own collection. Put to work by Hiller it becomes a revelation of the appropriative conceits of all museums.

An early work of Hiller's, *Dream Mapping* (1974) involved an event where the artist's friends became participants. They were asked to sleep within the fairy rings of a Hampshire farm, and in the morning to record their dreams. Hiller has spoken of this work, with its small range of participants, as limited in terms of its potential audience. Yet I encountered this work in her retrospective at Tate Liverpool in 1996, 25 years later. It involves framed remnants of the preparatory work leading up to the dreaming, now titled *Dream Diaries*. The diaries consist of visual notations for a dream record, as opposed to the temporal narrative of a dream, which we know is always constructed retrospectively. In the act of exhibition these diaries become more than a record of past occurrences. In the present it became a map, which in effect reterritorializes the efficacy of a record and the dream state. The maps were overlaid, not represented as escaping into isolated worlds of their own but marked with the shared internalizations of a given culture. As Hiller says, it is 'taking work past its point of completion'. Her work has a precipitous existence precisely because

Figure 5.3. Susan Hiller, *Dream Mapping*, 1974, three-night event, seven dream notebooks, three composite group dream maps. Additional documentation; exhibited in various configurations. Courtesy of the artist and Timothy Taylor Gallery, London.

it is vulnerable to being dismissed as an idealized portal to another world, rather than what it is: the recognition of the conditions of living in this one.

Hiller's work displays an engagement with what conceptual art recognized as the significance of the internalisation of languages – a process unrecognized by many art movements. Referring to the structuralist film makers and the New York branch of Art and Language, Hiller saw that 'conceptual art externalised and analysed those features of art activity that previously had been internalised . . .'[21] Yet this remained problematic for Hiller who offers a counter proposition, that artists may 'offer "para-conceptual" notions of culture by revealing the extent to which stated conceptual models are inadequate because they exclude or deny some part of reality.'[22] In effect then the conceptual model could not recognize those exclusions and more importantly could not then encounter the dilemma of their unrepresentability. The initial premise of conceptual art potentially evacuated a reference to the subject, and not some preformed subject which has been left out and can simply be reinstated to produce a better version of the real – which so much work succumbed to – 'not the subject as prime mover but the subject as desire, the impossible fantasy to account entirely for itself'.[23]

Hiller's encounter with conceptual art can be seen in her foregrounding the languages on which a work is structured, for example, when she archives 350 postcards in the work *Dedicated to the Unknown Artist* (1972-6). The work presents an apparently arbitrary number of postcards of a generic image – a rough sea – the familiar image of a wave crashing against a sea wall. In terms of content, it alludes to an atmosphere of collapse or sexuality or, in this form, popular sentiment about the boundaries of Britain as an island. Its initial conceptual framework could be narrativized or extended to metaphorical tropes. Yet for Hiller the original postcards become artifacts and are incorporated through the process of citation, then categorization to make categories of image within this one category of image. Arranged in a grid, not to establish a history but in a staging of languages, they form a kind of tableau. Through this process the work of conceptual art is retained but skewed. Hiller describes the work as, 'organised in the "ethnographic" present, that is, no historical data or suggestion about possible historic developments are introduced'.[24]

Amongst the many levels of selection, mapping and sourcing of the cards and the messages they carry, there is a meeting between object and event which each piece of material holds within it. The arrangement as a tableau also says something of Hiller's entire oeuvre: it spatializes time and refuses a neat fit between narrative and duration. Hiller's work might remind us of Foucault's proposed ethnography, one that finds history in 'sentiments, love, conscience and instincts, refusing memory as it is attached to metaphysics and anthropology'.[25] Her work continues to intervene in what has become for much of the photo/documentary art that currently commands the field of contemporary art, a confused relation to the methods of ethnography.

Michael Taussig's *The Magic of the State* brings us close to some of the propositions that arise in the work of Susan Hiller, not least of which is the place of the dead. Taussig's ficto/documentary, Dante-esque journey pulls the development of anthropological enquiry out of its rationalist, empiricist loop. Driven by his recognition of the response of the state to sorcery, taboo, and the fetish, within the fabric of the conception of the state itself, Taussig is concerned not with a state that hides its methods behind a mask, but with a state that is the mask. Like Dante's description of his journey, Taussig too begins in a kind of reverie reflected in his approach to his relation to anthropology. This is made possible through a writing that allows for its own sudden ellipsis and short circuiting: his 'pilgrimage' 'to travel tic-wise across this nervy wasteland of facial impulsions, awaiting the illumination that occurs with the interruption to the circuit'[26] to write and leave a document. Taussig's anthropological method – 'pilgrimage as method' – enables his 'descent/ascent' into the sites of various syncretic cults on a mountain outside of Caracas: to encounter spirit possessions at their interface with the figuring of 'the state'. As in Hiller's work, this too is an analysis of refusal and produces an image of the truly spectral nature of 'the state'. Taussig refuses this pilgrimage as a path to another world, acknowledging the excess of signification within the motifs and objects constructed to allow for the portals, namely the passage of the dead, through possession – at one point writing of the accumulated materials and cultural icons that construct the portals for entry as 'metaphor machines'. Taussig's writing opts for 'explanation as translation' and refuses the model of 'mindless and obsessional repetition that stays within the circle of exchange' – which Hiller identifies as the problem of much anthropology – and chooses to, not only permit the rupture but just that, testimony to unproductive expenditure, the need to squander.[27]

Multiscreened large-scale film projection characterizes much of Hiller's work from the past 20 years and her engagement with the technologies of mass media exploits its facility to fragment and interrupt. *An Entertainment* (1989), takes entertainment itself as an artifact. Punch and Judy puppet shows, which are staple fare for entertaining children around Britain, were filmed on Super 8 by the artist over many years. In *An Entertainment* these analogue images on Super 8 are digitized and reformatted – in fact, it is broken as a document – as if Hiller recognizes a ritualistic core in the event, and by 'breaking' it in this way and representing it in the museum she underscores a rupture in the representations of childhood experiences. It is also one more approach towards a culture in which one is never fully integrated. Installed in the museum, images double and repeat, coming out of corners, or from above and sinking into the floor – like unholy sunsets. There's no sense of continuity, just the symptomatic, uncanny return of the *mise-en-scène* of the terrifying family of Punch, Judy, Baby and Crocodile. Voices on the soundtrack strain to translate the words, reading as if they have no address, like reading in a language you do not understand, or the slow word-by-word sound made by a child learning to read.

Hiller's *Wild Talents* (1997), was inspired by the life of Stefan Ossoweicki the famous psychic known as the Polish wizard.[28] The work is a multiscreened projection that was initially devised for an installation in Warsaw in 1997, at a time when a model of capitalism had been reintroduced, bleeding back into a political and cultural landscape altered by the history of political incursions throughout and since World War Two. *Wild Talents* comes from a kind of psychic wound exposed through the cinematic representations of children who experience telekinesis, religious ecstasies, visions, hearing voices, communicating with animals, levitation, premonitory dreams, precognition, telepathy and psychic disturbances. These experiences are historically contained, if not through an idealization then as aberrations, perversely demonized and obsessively represented. Large screens with images sourced from the archives of Hollywood's trashy features, as well as its masterpieces, or the art of film makers like Tarkovsky sit alongside the downgraded aspirations of television movie production. Hiller selects from and destroys their context, all the time recognizing that these origins too are formed from an infinite surfeit. On two split screens bent by the corner of the room a fast moving collage of images is edited, digitized and reformatted, accompanied by fragments from the films' soundtracks: shrieking, screaming, toy trains crashing. In the foreground, a representation of a 1970s documentary film made in Yugoslavia of a pilgrimage to see children who experience the ecstasy of seeing holy visions, drags this spectacle to new heights. It too is reformatted, sound is erased and the illusion of real time is lost, the television bands rolling over the screen intercede

Figure 5.4. *Susan Hiller, Wild Talents*, 1997. Video installation: 3 synchronized programmes, chair, monitor, votive lights, 2 projected programmes, colour with stereo sound, programme duration 8 minutes, 36 seconds, 1 programme on video monitor, b/w, silent, programme duration 6 minutes, 30 seconds. Dimensions variable. Commissioned by Foksal Gallery, Warsaw. Arts Council of England Collection. Courtesy of the artist and Timothy Taylor Gallery, London.

between the documentary image of pilgrimage, the children and the technology that relays it; while rolling over it all, the derailed sound tracks of cinema fill the gallery.

Psi Girls (1999), like *Wild Talents* and *An Entertainment*, shows images projected on large-scale screens. Although more elaborate in its manipulation of the sensorium, *Psi Girls* is not an attempt at a total experience of the kind that moves us towards a virtual reality or the 'total work of art', because it reveals that there is no ground on which an experience can be fully replicated, nor can this work represent a subject, because each element and its elliptical trajectory leads us towards an endlessly ranging inscription machine. The sound and image are not so much working out of synch as against each other. *Psi Girls* sound track is like a visceral skin between the five screens and the beholder. The work recognizes that we are now separated from ritual, and confronts us with the psychic fallout in the work of art. Images of young girls with supernatural powers repeat, appear endlessly, and move swiftly from screen to screen, too quickly to rationalize. Flying between the five screens is a shimmering pattern of electrical interference accompanied by bursts of loud static, and a marked period of silence after which the clapping returns like an invocation. It shows that it is not the 'why' but the 'where' that reinterprets these dislocated motifs. The images are 'out of place', they point to the fact that something does not fit. The interferences are not interruptions but another sign of technology's translation of the gaps from which they have been selected. That the images are all of girls does not provide a narrative about 'girls'; it operates more like the 'sinthom', the repeated non-narrative motif, not connected to narrative structures but presymbolic, here refiguring by over-loading the correlation of the feminine with horror. Slavoj Žižek speaks of how the sinthome shows the gap that separates us from an explicit narrative to privilege one that is more diffuse, observing this effect in the films of Alfred Hitchcock.[29] Hiller's works are not films, but sit within the context of the endless returns of those motifs that form the core of all her work. With *Psi Girls* the uncanny intensity with which she navigates 'the real' also leads to a question of what is at stake in the figuring of gender. It is not so much that she uses the technologies of modernity but that she works through the effects of the technologies of modernity.

Like Hiller, Taussig does not idealise the formlessness of the spirit world. For example, he follows Benjamin's idea that the very structure of the police's efficacy is achieved through its 'strategic formlessness . . . nowhere tangible, an all-pervasive, ghostly presence in the life of civilised states.'[30] and goes on to say (in relation to the invocation of spectrality by the police in the context of Latin America) 'not only ghostly but rotten as well', and that this very 'spectrality opens the door to magical rituals of reversal'[31] Taussig's reference to the 'parlous reality' (cf. the opening quote to this essay) of those spirits that would take possession and the subsequent necessity of 'deliberate artifice' if they are to be made 'real', does not deny the reality of the experience, rather this is an experience of an encounter with the 'real' in the sense that Lacan would have it: 'the real is the void that makes reality incomplete, inconsistent, the function of every symbolic matrix is to conceal this inconsistency'.[32] This is what Hiller describes elsewhere as our culture's 'compensatory fantasies' or, as Taussig puts it, a 'hidden-ness performed'.

As Taussig says, it is only when 'the anthropology developed in Europe and North America through the study of colonised peoples [can be translated] back into and onto the societies in which it was instituted . . . that fetish, sorcery, taboo are redeemed and come alive with new intensity.'[33] Over the past thirty-five years, Hiller has always seen, felt and been highly attuned to the presence of this return in our culture. The very ambivalence of her work directs us to what is at stake in such a translation, and how and where that which is already present in our culture surfaces.

Reflections on Art and Agency: Knot-sculpture between Mathematics and Art

Susanne Küchler

> Just as mathematics provides us with a primary mode of cognition, and can therefore enable us to apprehend our physical surroundings, so too, some of its basic elements will furnish us with laws to appraise the interactions of separate objects, or groups of objects, one to another. Again since it is mathematics which lends significance to these relationships, it is only a natural step from having perceived them to desiring to portray them. This in brief is the genesis of a work of art.
>
> Max Bill 1949

The nexus of art and mathematics has produced some of the most vibrant sculptural, architectural and scientific works over the last several years.[1] In mathematics, new visual techniques have resulted from the availability of new tools aiding visualization, which has always played an important role in the discipline, just as the visual arts have made increasing use of these technologies. Interactions between artists and mathematicians became more and more frequent as each side began to realize the aesthetic and scientific potential of images generated with the new tools.

This chapter will discuss the potential impact of a particularly prominent example of contemporary 'mathematical' art upon an anthropological approach to artworks.[2] For reasons discussed below, I will focus on the aesthetics and mathematics of the continuous surface, embedded in the sculptural and mathematical exploration of knots, which now dominates research in architecture, design, mathematics and art. Two artists, the American sculptor Brent Collins and the English sculptor John Robinson, have been formative in the development of these complex geometric forms. Both artists share a concern with the sculpting of knot-spanning surfaces which illustrate basic methods of mathematics such as representation, classification, analogy, abstraction, and which illuminate the mathematics of the 'minimal surface'.[3]

Contemporary knot sculpture was 'discovered' by mathematicians who enthused about its intuitive application of mathematical principles whose abstract nature was recognized as hindering both research and teaching. John Robinson's bronze sculptures thus quickly became key tools for teaching mathematics through knots, displaying ways of thinking within a material medium that was both tactile and mundane.[4] From an anthropological perspective, the resulting collaboration between mathematicians and artists is of interest as it demonstrates the cognitive purchase of artworks whose formal properties appear to limit analysis to aesthetic or symbolic interpretation.

In the sense that the kind of sculpture discussed in this paper can be said to serve as a 'tractor' of thought, inciting thinking as much as embodying it in its patterned surface, it exemplifies Alfred Gell's reasoning on the theoretical basis for an anthropological engagement with art. It is to the credit of Alfred Gell's work that we can no longer bypass the cognitive purchase of artefactual form as a problem to be dealt with by the tools of symbolic anthropology, but must see it as an incremental part of a process of objectification.[5] His work suggests a Maussian reading of a theory of art 'which considers art objects as persons' and which considers, in line with the 'prototypical' anthropological theory, a 'series of problems to do with ostensibly peculiar relations between persons and "things" which somehow "appear as" or do duty as, persons'.[6] Patterned things, both product and inspiration of intuitive associative thinking, were presented by Gell as a locus of agency in the unfolding of person-object relations, a locus that has been overlooked in anthropological theorizing of objectification.

Knots, as Gell realized himself, are a prominent example of a physical/tactile pattern which simultaneously display what he calls 'cognitive adhesiveness'. For, 'once one submits to the allure of the pattern, one is liable to become hooked, or stuck, in it.'[7] The attachment between persons and things that we may find incited in Celtic knot-work or Melanesian sculpture is as we will see peculiar not just to 'most non-modernist, non-puritan civilisations [that] value decorativeness and allot it a specific role in the mediation of social life',[8] but to contemporary art and even architecture. Yet, we may ask, how relevant is the obvious investment of mathematical thought in such works and can such a concern also be found to underlie other, seemingly decorative works, from the play with continuous surfaces in contemporary Euro-American architecture and product design to the streetwise friendship-bracelet. What I have in mind is exemplified by the recent work of Ron Eglash on African decorative arts.[9] In the most systematic exploration of decorative design so far, Eglash traces pervasive fractal geometry across cultural and linguistic boundaries and a dazzling range of media. The question which resonates throughout this work, and which is pertinent to the artworks discussed in this paper, is directed to the notion of 'style' and its importance for an understanding of material culture. Is style, as Gell provocatively proposes, the product of the relation between artefacts, banishing culture from its role as 'head office?[10]

The current interchange between artists and mathematicians in the field of sculpture is thus of intrinsic interest to anthropology, as it may harbour key insights into possible future directions in anthropological research on art. Yet before returning to knot sculpture, a brief overview of the involvement of mathematics with art will serve to situate the appearance of the knot in artists' works.

ART AND MATHEMATICS: NEW PERSPECTIVES ON AN
OLD THEME

The interplay of mathematics and arts is well known from the history of Renaissance art which provides us with many examples of the centrality of mathematics in both the teaching of drawing and the interpretation of received artworks.[11] A famous example is found in Michael Baxandall's study of painting in fifteenth-century Italy which uncovered the socio-cultural conditions that provoked a sensitivity in visual culture to geometry and higher mathematics.[12] Paintings were openly searched for geometric riddles and valued for the complexity of problem-solving they showed. Morris Kline, a well known mathematician, describes Piero della Francesca as one of the greatest mathematicians of the fifteenth century.[13]

The nature of evidence was found not in images or words, but in the materiality of the artefact, and nowhere more explicitly than in northern Dutch Renaissance art. Here, seventeenth-century prints and paintings visually explicated observation and description in ways that united science with art.[14] Drawing retained its use for the classification and ordering of an increasingly expanding and chaotic perception of the world that was glimpsed through botanical and material collections of artefacts which filled seventeenth-century curiosity cabinets. This relation between science and art, however, began, barely a century later, to fall into oblivion.[15]

In many ways we are still under the influence of eighteenth-century thought, which harboured a growing separation of 'noumenal', the products of thought such as science, from the 'phenomenal', the world of experience, distinguishing scientific from artistic observation. The crucial role mathematics had played in visual culture was only taken up again, albeit in a new guise, with the advent of modernism, and only today are we beginning to see its full potential again.

The stage was set for a renewed concern with issues of representation by the re-'discovery' of axonometrics in the nineteenth century.[16] The possibility of representing a three-dimensional object from n-dimensional perspectives opened the doors for mathematics to branch into innumerable logical 'paper worlds' of its own construction, thus implicitly questioning Euclidean geometry with its assumption of the anthropomorphic, relative and egocentric conception of space. Euclidean geometry, which had remained unchallenged for centuries, was at last dramatically superseded in 1915, when Albert Einstein founded his new theory of gravitation upon the premise that our physical space possesses a non-Euclidean geometry that is created by the presence of mass and energy in the universe.

For art, this breakthrough in our understanding of the universe proved significant. Visual art could once again concern itself with the representation of the invisible, this time not under the guise of religion, but of science. Marcel Duchamp's representation of the shadow cast by the fourth dimension in his *Railway Track* may count as the first mainstream mathematically inspired work of art in the twentieth century.[17] But it was Impressionism and, still more,

Cubism that brought painting and sculpture much closer to what were the original elements of each: painting as surface design in colours; sculpture as the shaping of volumes to be informed by space. It was Vassíly Kandinsky, notably, whose work suggested a fresh conception of art that liberated painting from romantic and literary associations. He invoked a substitution of the artist's imagination by a mathematical approach to visualization, an idea carried further by Paul Klee, Constantin Brancusi and Piet Mondrian. Their works portray elemental forms and visualize, without representing, objects that have an existence in ordinary life.

The common interest of modernist art and mathematics lies in the visualizing of the fourth dimension. Belief in a fourth dimension encouraged artists to depart from visual reality and to reject the one-point perspective system that for centuries had portrayed the world as three dimensional. The full impact of the visualization of the fourth dimension was realized in mathematics only with the advent of computer modelling. Its rediscovery by mathematics was inspired by works such as those produced by the American artist, David Brisson, who developed the concept of hypersolids in the 1950s and produced perspective and orthogonal projection drawings as well as three-dimensional models of four-dimensional polytopes.[18] His *Hyperanaglyph*, a four-dimensional form projected on to three dimensions, established him as a leader in the visualization of higher solids. In 1975 he coined the term *hypergraphics*, which came to denote both concept and technical process that transcended traditional methods of making images by methods of visualisation that could blend contemporary thinking in art and science. Much of the hypergraphic art work is mathematically precise and enhanced by materials, colours, surfaces, textures, methods of construction and so on.[19]

Like most mathematically inspired work that came to represent the modernist spirit, the imagery of hypergraphics is generative and multiple. As 'mathematical recreations', it shaped the emerging 'generate-and-test model of creativity' that became celebrated as the new way of doing mathematics.[20] Fun-sounding explorations, such as 'how to tile a space with knots', became the hallmark of applied mathematics capable of constructing innumerable logical 'paper worlds', and leading to radically new ideas as to the nature of mathematics itself.

Mathematics, however, continued to regard the exploration of the fourth dimension merely as part of the description of non-Euclidean geometry. Observations derived from applied mathematics confirmed the predictions of Einstein's non-Euclidean theory of space – the real world was non-Euclidean after all and geometry was no longer just logical systems on pieces of paper, but multiple perspectives reflecting a 'decentred' spatial cognition that fully realized the possibility inherent in the pictorial equivalent of the fourth dimension. As foreshadowed by Cubism's multiple perspectives, the new mathematical visualization techniques began to realize a quasi-cinematic evocation of dynamic motion and change. The acceptance of alternative kinds of space, however, never achieved the widespread popularity of the fourth dimension among artists.

There is, as Max Bill suggested, a danger in mistaking the suggestion provoked by modernism that art is based on principles of mathematics, for an assumption that art is a plastic or pictorial interpretation of the latter.[21] In fact, mathematics and art are analogous processes of concrete thinking, 'the building up of significant patterns from the ever changing relations, rhythms and proportions of abstract forms, each one of which, having its own causality, is tantamount to a law onto itself'.[22]

The anthropological investigation of art and mathematics has been hindered, rather than helped, by the seemingly ubiquitous presence of mathematics in cultural activity: in the construction of houses and other buildings, in the making of textiles and baskets, in the turning of flat pieces of cloth or animal skins into clothing or shoes that fit, in the making of calendars to mark seasons, the planning of storage facilities or the layout of gardens and fields, in the depiction of kinship relations, or in ornamentation, as well as in spiritual or religious practices that are often aligned with patterns occurring in nature or ordered systems of abstract ideas. The greatest proliferation of studies has been in a branch of mathematics known as 'ethno-mathematics' which takes into consideration the culture in which mathematics arises.[23] Anthropology has developed approaches to mathematics as part of wider concerns with cognition, mapping and navigation.[24] Yet these studies tend either to exclude artefacts as data suitable for analysis or approach artefacts as evidence for the reconstruction of technique.[25]

The materiality of the artefact and its form has so far not been considered as a possible focus for mathematical thought, but merely as the visual antidote to textual or narrative forms. Gregory Bateson's classic recollection of Isadora Duncan's expression: 'If I could tell you what it means I would not have to dance it' did not provoke anthropologists to search for the thought processes resonating from certain forms of visualization.[26] Not, that is, until Gell rescued the debate on art in anthropology from sliding ever further into cultural determinism by alluding to the fact that artworks are objects that are scrutinised as vehicles of complicated ideas which are difficult, allusive and hard to bring off.[27] Such objects, he argued, thus embody intentionalities that are complex, demanding of attention and perhaps difficult to reconstruct fully.

The object that served to demonstrated Gell's thoughts on art as object of thought was the Zande hunting net, a tied bundle of knotted string, made famous on account of being selected as an artwork for a New York art exhibition in the late 1980s.[28] The debate stirred up by the inclusion of the net in an exhibition of African Art resonated far beyond the confines of the discipline of anthropology as the subject of the knot had already been well established across the humanities.[29] Cords had come to be seen as objects to be scrutinized, as vehicles of complicated ideas with the emergence of a climate in which learning and thinking about topological relationships became an accepted method for investigating ways of knowing.

Knotted things, in fact, had long been a focus of attention of mathematicians, partly because they allow the study of how geometric forms remain stable under deformation, a subject known as topology, but also because, as geometric forms, knots have a tendency to evoke a range of emotional and personal sorts of thoughts.[30] It was the evocative capacity of the knot that, in science, proved vital for an understanding of the nature of concrete thinking and its importance in the learning of mathematics. Mathematics found itself thinking of the knot as this kind of object, that is likely to touch people's lives in connecting with personal and 'affective' aspects of thought and thus as forming the springboard for associations that are both abstract and concrete in their mnemonic capacity.

Approaches to the knot reveal it as a 'tractor' of thought and thus as person-like in a way that enables one to see how thought can conduct itself in things. So it appears as the perfect object for examining the purchase of the interplay of art and mathematics in relation to anthropology.

THE KNOT: GENERATIVE AND NON-LINEAR FORMS IN ART AND MATHEMATICS

Consisting of variable, abstract components, such as surfaces, bridges and links that are connected through deformations, the study of knots was chiefly of interest to mathematicians following the discovery of a clear graphic system for describing the fourth dimension in the late nineteenth century.[31] Knot theory itself, however, only came into its own from the 1950s, when computing allowed the visualization of the capacity of the knot to be traced through n-dimensional space. Interestingly, it was artists, and not just mathematicians who now propelled new questions in the study of topology – questions, such as those surrounding agency and authorship, which are of unique importance for anthropology today.

It was the modernist artist Victor Vasareli who chose cordage for one of his prototypes, which, as he asserted, were capable of generating new artworks across differing media and dimensions.[32] At a time when mathematics had just begun to develop a theory about knots as a mathematical problem that was recognized chiefly to be one of classification, Vasareli had thus pointed to an affinity in the behaviour of material and organic forms which began to inspire new genetics and new biology in the following decades. His prototypes asserted that material forms, like organisms, are capable of self-organization – of generating new forms out of existing ones with the help of the intuitive intervention of the artist. Decades later, researchers into knots discovered not only some exciting new mathematics, but also relationships with physics, biology and insights into the structure of the DNA molecule, which supported Vasareli's findings.

Vasareli's work can be seen to suggest an approach to objects that draws on their constitution as 'manifolds', or internally connected images – an approach that today is visualized in the architecture of Neil Denari's 'Interrupted Projections'. Like much contemporary architecture, Denari's work aspires to the new aesthetic of continuous surface and wrapping imagery, such as the Guggenheim museum in Bilbao. Yet it is Denari's work, while more obscure perhaps than that of any of his contemporaries, that articulates most eloquently the implications of topology for architecture.[33]

Denari's technique rests upon a critique of the map, reflecting upon the resonance of the map with the sheet and the ribbon; the mapping impulse, itself synonymous with capitalism, being reformulated into a technical key called GALLERY-MA SPACE – visualized as an interrupted 'world-sheet or ribbon-like, 2-D surface'. 'In the contemporary world', Denari says:

> it seems as if architecture should not function as a vessel or container of knowledge or the social. Such a fixed/closed idea of function retards the pro-cesses, filtrations and overcodings that a supple architectural system could provide. Instead, it should operate more like an extrapolation machine, a device capable of re-spatialising the dramatic currents and flows of culture, not merely a mirror held up to reflect it. By BLENDING UP (OR DOWN) the world-sheet, architecture is a sudden spatialising and transforming third dimensional pheno-menon which actualises and sets into motion the intertextualised codes. My scheme for the Gallery-Ma space is an overcoded diagram of this concept.[34]

These aesthetic articulations of the continuous surface owe much to the new worldview which began to grip science and art – a worldview which aspired to organic, rather than mechanical models of space/time.[35]

Modernism and modern science thus arose out of the exploration of the implications of the reality of n-dimensional, unrepresentable and invisible worlds for representation. Anthropology, however, held fast to a belief in the universality of the conception of space as proceeding from the human body, constrained by the nature of the phenomenal world and by human physiology with its visual system and upright posture.[36] The failure of anthropology to recognize the implications of non-Euclidean geometry with its emphasis on the topological framing of space-time was only recently rectified with Jürg Wassmann's study of the Yupno of Papua New Guinea who, as he shows, use different reference systems at the same time in ways that are only compre-hensible when apprehending spatial conception as decentred from the body in everyday life.[37]

It seems fitting, given the affinity between organic and material forms alluded to in post-Newtonian science, that much of the mathematically inspiring artwork produced since Vasareli should have deployed neither painting as medium of expression nor cordage as material. Instead, the properties of bound form and continuous surface are explored in media suitable for sculpting, such as wood, metal and stone.[38] The figural, since the Renaissance regarded as the less refined and more 'primitive' art form, has emerged at the forefront of computer-generated art, using tools of visualization that are shared by mathematicians and artists alike.

For more than a decade now, Brent Collins has been creating wood sculp-tures that contain elaborate constellations of knot-spanning surfaces.[39]

Conceptually, the construction of such surfaces, also known as 'minimal' as they tend locally to minimize the surface area needed to span or close off a given opening, can be continued outward without limits. Until the mid-1950s, only a very limited number of such surfaces were known to exist. Among these are stacked criss-crossing saddles, to be envisioned in the simplest case as two planes at right angles with holes passing diagonally through their intersection line.

One of Collins' earliest sculptures, the *Hyperbolic Hexagon*, visualized an elaborate constellation of saddle surfaces, even though, originally, Collins was unfamiliar with this mathematical concept.[40] His 'discovery' by mathematicians created a lasting intellectual partnership whose impact can be detected in many of his later pieces, which display invariant symmetrical relations and uniform thickness from which one can abstract closed, knotted and linked ribbons curving through space (see Fig. 6.1).[41] The mathematical surface depicted by his artworks indeed constitutes what he calls a 'knot-spanning surface' or a 'framed link', with the knot literally being carved out of the wood and constituting the hollow, negative space of the sculpture.

Collins' sculptures remind one that artworks, both contemporary Western and indigenous ones, can be seen as interpretations in their own right of issues that preoccupy scientists, cultural historians and anthropologists alike and invite comparison with texts of various kinds.[42] The fact that Collins did not, at least in the beginning, perceive the mathematical nature of his objects, strengthens, rather than weakens this observation, as it draws attention to the intuitive level at which his sculptures visualise balance, proportion and rhythm crafted into objects that become a source of inspiration in often rather surprising ways.[43]

Another example of the creative use of the mathematics of knots in sculpture is the work of British artist John Robinson which has influenced the mathematican Rinald Brown.[44] Working from his studio in Somerset, Robinson came to Brown's attention in 1985 in a chance encounter with his work at the Freeland Gallery in London (see Fig. 6.2). At the time, Brown was working on an exhibition on 'Mathematics and Knots' to which John Robinson later contributed the artistic side.[45] The Leeds exhibit included thirteen sculptures and eleven tapestries. Today these sculptures are permanently at or near the universities at Bangor, Oxford, Cambridge, Barcelona, Harvard, Macquarie, Montana, Madison and Toronto.

In 1990 the sculpture *Immortality* was donated by Edition Limitée to the School of Mathematics at Bangor. In 1996, Brown and Robinson put some images of sculptures on the web; the project developed into a substantial web site on the sculptures and their relations to mathematics and science.[46]

Robinson's major work consisted of the Universe Series. It comprises more than 100 works, and ranges from representational work such as his 5 metre *Acrobats* and his *Pole Vaulter* outside the Canberra Sports Centre to his *Elation* and *Joy of Living*, which both express the idea of joy in achievement in an abstract geometric manner. Geometric form is used to express a theme of common humanity in 'dependent beings'. This sculpture is also one of a series

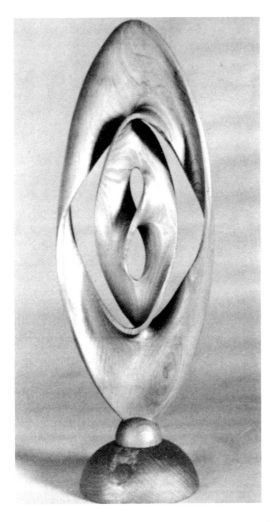

Figure 6.1. Brent Collins, *One Sided Surface with Opposed Cheiralities*, 1984, oiled cedar. Courtesy of the artist.

expressing what mathematicians call a 'Fibre Bundle'. Here, the 'fibre' is a square that twists as it traverses a circle, giving a boundary of two strips, in contrasting textures.

Others come to mind who have explored the geometry of the knot – such as Stewart Dickson whose 1990 stereolithograph was computer generated or Helaman Ferguson whose 1990 computer interactive sculpture in bronze and marble directs attention to the space defining capacity of the knot. Together they suggest a concept of the continuous surface with its play on the persistence of geometric form under deformation and its capacity for self-organization that has captivated contemporary architecture and science alike. Yet perhaps most interesting and suggestive is the serial nature of all these artworks, springing,

Figure 6.2. John Robinson, *Immortality*, 1989. Courtesy of the artist.

as it were, from a prototype that is both abstract – in the form of a program-assisted model – as well as utterly mundane, such as Collins's paper model consisting of cut and glued loops (curiously similar to a Polynesian 'soul-catcher').

The mathematician Carlo Séquin developed a 'sculpture generator' whose virtual forms were built by Collins, replacing the physical mock-ups from pipe sections and beeswax. In his collaboration with Collins, Séquin increasingly began to draw upon new computer controlled construction technologies that can turn a virtual shape into a physical model in a matter of hours. Neither the artwork nor the artist, appear to capture and dominate the interchange between Collins and Séquin, but rather what computer scientists have called 'the manifold', consisting of a series of interconnected images that appears to be imbued with an independent, self-originating template.

Science, backed by computer-generated forms, has merged with art in ways that are most explicit in these sculptural rendering of knot-spanning surfaces. The fusion of art and science as a topic extends beyond the scope of this chapter. Besides the many critical points that might spring to mind, the merger of the for-centuries distinct realms of science and art might have an unsuspected positive impact upon anthropology by freeing it to reconsider figurative, geometric and decorative artworks in other than aesthetic terms. Gell's call for tackling of agency inherent in art has yet to be answered.

Artists in the Field: Between Art and Anthropology
Fernando Calzadilla and George E. Marcus

INTRODUCTION (MARCUS)

By the mid-1990s, I had just about given up hope that the aesthetic issues that were implicated in the so-called Writing Culture critique of anthropology during the 1980s[1] would be developed by anthropologists themselves. Beyond the critique of the authority of ethnographic texts and of the conditions for the production of knowledge in the traditional *mise-en-scène* of fieldwork, these issues might have defined the ground for rethinking the long-standing forms and practices of anthropological research (the emblematic and defining fieldwork/ethnography paradigm of the discipline) that are so much challenged at present as anthropologists involve themselves with more complicated conditions and objects of inquiry.[2] For anthropologists to have explored the aesthetics of inquiry would have required styles of thinking, rhetoric, and practice – keyed to the notion of experimentation – that proved unacceptable to the boundary-keeping institutional and professional rules of order in the academy. While anthropology during the 1980s was influenced more than ever by theoretical developments in the academic humanities through interdisciplinary movements that were themselves caught up in self-images evoking historic avant-gardes (the 'theory' tendency in literary studies, for example, had this imago), it was still obliged to be social scientific, and definitely not art. Thus, any efforts at experimentation with the ethnographic form, beyond textual manoeuvres, were understandably limited, largely rhetorical, and when substantive, idiosyncratic and certainly marginal.

Perhaps this is as it should have been. While there have been some remarkable experimental texts exploring the relation between culture, the anthropological task, and aesthetics, produced through and from the trend of 1980s critique,[3] the urge to experiment in the sense of artists' practices within the restricted confines and norms of social scientific disciplinary practice was bound to generate many more works of unclear vision and uncertain address in terms of to whom and for whom they were directed. Still the most compelling aspects of the Writing Culture critique of the 1980s opened questions about breaking the authoritative frames, not only of traditional ethnographic writing, but by implication of the traditional practices and professional regulative ideals of fieldwork in the name of such notions as collaboration, polyphony, reflexive inquiry, and dialogue. These were indeed radical alternative suggestions or hints for practice, and they could hardly be served by mere modifications in the way ethnographies were written or even traditional projects of fieldwork were conducted. Attempts to do so – the body of "experiments" we have – were for the most part considered to be weak, rhetorical, and idiosyncratic. One might conclude then that more radical experiments, touching upon the aesthetics of fieldwork, were something that anthropologists, operating between the critiques of the 1980s and the changing conditions of research in the 1990s onward, could benefit from, but which, because of the weight of the professional apparatus of power, authority, tradition, and self-interest, they could not do for themselves in any coherent way. Only artists, who understood the task of ethnography more deeply than most other artists have in the heady era of disciplinary mixings that we have just gone through, might, in pursuing their own license, show anthropologists something important about their methods that they could not see as clearly for themselves. This is what the collective works of Abdel Hernández and his collaborators in Cuba and Venezuela offer anthropology.

Abdel Hernández is a Cuban artist, art critic, and cultural theorist. His work has evoked that of anthropologists, as in his performances, installations, and experiences in remote rural communities in Cuba, and in his exhibits/installations in the milieu of the everyday life of the urban poor.[4] He belongs to the 1980s avant-garde art movement in Havana, being one of its main actors and conceivers. The 1980s was a time of renewed possibilities for socially relevant and critical art within the socialist context (it was during this period that Hernández became acquainted with the Writing Culture critique in anthropology, among many other initiatives in the practice of critical cultural analysis that were then occurring in the US and Europe). The fall of the Soviet Union marked the end to this period of ferment and critical possibility in the arts. Many Cuban artists, including Hernández, went into self-imposed exile at the end of the 1980s, living in such countries as Venezuela, Germany, and the United States.

In Caracas, Hernández continued his anthropologically relevant work in conjunction with a diverse group of Venezuelan artists. During that time, he met Venezuelan-American artist-curator, Surpik Angelini, a resident of Houston. They formed a workshop, representing the work that Hernández and his collaborators were doing in Venezuela as well as works by members of Hernández's cohort of Cuban artists. They proposed to present the results of this workshop in a multimedia course and group of exhibitions and performances within the context of the Department of Anthropology at Rice University. With this presentation, our department, known for orienting its own teaching and research around the implications of the 1980s critique of anthropology, marked a serendipitous and unusual engagement between a practice of anthropology understanding the necessity of rethinking the paradigm of method at the heart of the discipline, and an initiative among artists strongly influenced by this same development in anthropology, but focused on disciplinary norms and constraints of art criticism (see the appendix to gain a sense of how this event was anticipated by the anthropologists at Rice). This event, known as *Artists In Trance* (subtitled, *New Methodologies in the Work with the Other in Latin American Art*), occurred at Rice in the spring of 1997, and was supported by the newly formed Transart Foundation.

The various performances and installations were meant to explore the concept of evocation[5] and its relation to ethical practice. In some cases artists developed ethnographies of themselves using installation as a spatialization of self-narratives and critique. In other cases, artists explored conceptually how cultural knowledge is constructed and how anthropologists represent cultures. Still other artists evoked the ethos of community mediating values in popular culture, questioning such traces of cultural domination as fetishism, colonialism, and textual authority in art history.

For me, the centrepiece of this workshop was *The Market From Here* (hereafter, TMFH) installation,[6] presented both in Caracas and Houston. This installation was produced through a fascinating collaboration between Hernández and Fernando Calzadilla, a well-known Venezuelan scenographer and artist of the theatre. They became engaged with the challenge of producing an ethnographically influenced installation of a marketplace – so diffuse and fluid in the human action it encompasses, so complexly polyphonous in the voices that define it as a place.

This is in part a task that involves ethnographic-like research and investigation, but where the outcome is not a work of analysis or a representation, but a particular sort of chronotope, to use Bakhtin's expression, for a drama. Hernández and Calzadilla designed and built an installation that could easily be interpreted as an attempt to represent the market, not by an ethnographic study, but by a *mise-en-scène*. Actually, the construction of the TMFH installation, with the involvement of numerous people of the literal marketplace they researched, is quite different from a mere representation as *mise-en-scène*. It was more the creation of a sort of imaginary of the people involved in the marketplace working with Hernández and Calzadilla, making intricate decisions about space, light, materials and so forth. This involved a much more complex and richer notion of collaboration than the ideal evoked in the 1980s critique, primarily by James Clifford, that limited itself to questions of authorship and writing texts. The heart of this paper is Calzadilla's account of the process that produced TMFH, which exemplifies for me the lost opportunity of the encounter between art and anthropology that did not quite occur in the opening created by the Writing Culture critique.

What I find personally most exciting particularly for the practice of anthropology in this evolution of Hernández's work to the production of the TMFH installation is precisely the kind of possibility in the ethics of collaboration that it develops. Ethnography is much richer in possibility if it collaborates with the practices of other intellectual crafts that have a kinship and resemblance to it – as in the case of scenography in the theater. The debates and discussions of collaboration in these cases promise outcomes more complex and interesting than just 'the monograph' or 'the essay' into which all experiments in anthropology seemingly must end, or merely the '*mise-en-scène*' of theatre or the installation of performance art, which otherwise lack the intensity and theoretical depth of ethnography. And of course such 'expert' collaborations in different genres are about a 'third' – people in certain settings in their everyday lives who become the subjects of interest to anthropologists and dramatists. What is fascinating about these expert collaborations is that they incorporate the 'others' of their mutual interest in a greater variety of ways and with different sorts of outcomes and products than would be possible if, say, anthropology refused to risk its authority by not entering into such partnerships with the scenographer, for instance. The result is messy, for certain, but I would easily trade the rather large anthropological literature on Latin American traditional marketplaces for Hernández's, Calzadilla's, and unnamed others' *The Market From Here*.

For some anthropologists, such collaborations might seem to go too far in that the disciplinary pride and authority of anthropology itself – its ability to ask and answer its own questions – became too compromised in its associations with ethnographic-like inquiry in other spheres of practice (like scenography). With all of its problems for anthropologists, an installation such as TMFH is valuable precisely because it has things to teach them by going beyond the limits of the rather narrow conventions in which experiments have been done by anthropologists themselves to areas of provocation that are too risky for anthropologists to develop, but that nonetheless work through strains of ideals and longing deep within their disciplinary tradition.

Here, I refer to the idea of ethnography as performance, which has been one of the 'key words' of possible alternative for anthropological practice in recent years. There has also been a more-or-less developed idea of ethnographic 'competence' being performative. That is, the true standard of judgment of ethnographic interpretation and translation is whether the anthropologist 'gets it right,' not as judged by his professional peers but by the people he studies. Competence always begins with language, and anthropological folklore often focuses on who among the specialists in an area or region speaks the language 'like a native'. To some extent, this very deep but underplayed and romantic ideal of very serious ethnography evokes the much disdained and naive 'going native' syndrome. Still, anthropologists have often sustained in their judgment of ethnography the related notion of competence or performativity. This perhaps had its most elaborate and scientist expression in the ethnoscience/ cognitive anthropology/new ethnography movement of the 1960s and 1970s.[7] Indeed, the ability to play back category systems in speech to natives, to 'elicit' action from them, was to become the highest scientific standard for anthropology. Of course, this movement eventually fell on hard times once it went beyond colour and kinship categories. But something of the same ideal has always been present in the interpretive/symbolic movement as well. In the field, one is constantly testing one's interpretations and understandings by finding ways to play them back to informants.

Figure 7.1. *The Market from Here*, 1997. At Rice University in the sculpture courtyard, between the Art and Anthropology departments. Photo: Fernando Calzadilla.

Finally, there was the brief surge into 'theatre anthropology' in the late 1970s and early 1980s, based on the interesting partnership of Richard Schechner and Victor Turner, and the writings of Eugenio Barba, among others. The main inspiration for this in anthropology was the later work of Victor Turner, who early on had a strong sense of the value of understanding ethnographic settings in dramatistical terms. However, what Hernández and Calzadilla are up to is quite different from this earlier effort at theatre anthropology. Turner was really bringing anthropology into the framework of theatre, and Hernández and Calzadilla have made the opposite sort of move (not so much theatre as performance/installation art) with more radical and interesting results for effacing the boundaries of both art and anthropology as institutions (see Fig. 7.1). Also, Turner was less interested in matters of epistemology and method than in universalist and transcendent questions about mind and emotion that could be explored by making theatrical the rituals that anthropologists studied in the field among peoples like the Ndembu and the Kwakiutl. There was never the more provocative bringing of the experiment and the performance to the field, as in Hernández's work.

Thus, TMFH as well as the other productions of *Artists In Trance* is a fresh initiative in the exploration of the practice of anthropology as performance. Why his work should be of interest to anthropologists is that it makes explicit and experimentally explores tendencies deeply a part of the ethos of the discipline having to do with a combination of scholarly distance and a more active participation in a culture but still within the frame of professional field work. The idea of collaboration, shared authorship, and 'the dialogic' stood for these tendencies in the 1980s critique, but they could (dared) not go beyond the conventional notions of fieldwork, even though they upset them from within their boundaries. The idea of performance had this possibility of going further, but it has remained mainly a theoretical artifact – another inspiration with which to frame the longstanding practices. Hernández and Calzadilla, I would argue, explore new space in this genealogy with their TMFH experiment.

THE MARKET FROM HERE: SCENOGRAPHY AS ETHNOGRAPHY (CALZADILLA)

Sometimes, waking up in the early hours, around 4.00 a.m., used to be a nightmare during my childhood in Caracas, Venezuela. There was this strange noise coming from the street that I could not identify. I asked Rosa, our old nanny, and she told me it was the devil going back to its quarters. Soon enough to my relief I discovered the noise's origin when I started to accompany my mother on early outings to the nearby Mercado Libre. Boys, not much older than myself, used to make carruchas, a kind of put-together wooden box with roller skate metal wheels to carry and deliver people's staples. Their large number and the metal wheels produced the noise I couldn't identify. That is one of the earliest marketplace memories I have, not to mention that my father had a wholesale food store near one of the city's food distribution main centres, Quinta Crespo, but I did not make contact with that world until I was a little older. I remember spice and grain sacs accumulated in the storefront filling the air with the strong aroma of cloves, cinnamon sticks in bundles, salted codfish, coffee, and cumin. The smell still fills my memories.

My fascination with the marketplace has been constant since early childhood. The relationship has been one of use and participation, observer and devotee. During my adult life, I have routinely visited the marketplace to satisfy my need, to recover portions of my past, and to enjoy the gathering, the accumulation of people and the diversity. That is why, when Abdel Hernández first approached me with a proposition to develop work around the relation of the marketplace with the art museum, I was more than enthusiastic, I was ecstatic.

The Museo de Artes Visuales Alejandro Otero (Mavao) and El Mercado de Coche (Coche) sat in close geographical relationship, but ignored each other as neighbours. The Mavao's curatorial department proposed an exhibition to Hernández that focused on the market, and Hernández's ideas went far beyond collecting works on the subject. Hernández invited young artists to create specific work that dealt with the relation between the Mavao and Coche. Mavao is a contemporary art museum housed in a Travertine marble building with a resemblance to Washington's National Gallery; Coche is the main food distribution centre for the city with trucks pouring in and out from all over the country. They are located in the outskirts, surrounded by low-income *barrios* in a densely populated area. The elitist museum is in the hippodrome grounds and its patrons are not exactly those of the community where it sits. With these premises, Hernández and I approached the artists and invited them to get in touch with Coche to develop works that would address issues of art market, community, the white cube neutral space of the gallery, and the rewriting of it, the desecration of the museum space, the separation between high and popular culture, how the market looked at the museum and vice versa, the ethnographic other, the ephemerality of the market against the permanence of the museum, and so forth. My job was to create the dramaturgy of the space, to place the artists' works in the museum and design the space to make a coherent statement of the whole exhibit, something for which my skills as theatre designer and market-lover were appropriate. As our meetings with the artists grew so did ideas and proposals. The museum authorities became concerned about the budgetary and political implications and the project was cancelled. But Hernández and I had been enthralled by the market idea.

After Hernández's visit to the Department of Anthropology at Rice University, where the course/event *Artists In Trance* was taking shape, the idea of presenting a major work on the popular market rose from its ashes. This time Hernández and I were co-authoring the investigation/realization. Bound by a set of given circumstances, such as a specific date and event with a pre-established theme, the project had a different process. We were not orchestrating the work of other artists; we were the artists realizing the work itself. The investigation was not centered on one specific locale but on the market's general relationship with the city, with the ephemeral, the transient, and the no-place that paradoxically constitutes 'market' because it only exists in the passing of hands.

Both Hernández and I, in different venues, had been involved in ethnographic research. Hernández during his Sierra Maestra projects in Cuba (see note 4), myself in the approach to scenic design and its later implementation as the ethnographic study of the people, their costumes, and places for the piece. Showing the structure that held together the scenic design served the purpose of emphasizing the ethnographic data that I collected in direct fieldwork or through others' accounts.[8] Although it was clear that this was an artistic endeavour, the fact that we were presenting it within the context of the *Artists In Trance* event at the Department of Anthropology of Rice University also made clear that it was a re-visiting of the debates about ethnographic method. We started with the ethnographic approach by roving the Venezuelan markets, talking to people, to vendors, establishing links and possible informants until we narrowed our interest to two of the most visited and populous markets in Caracas, El Mercado de Catia, and El Mercado Quinta Crespo.[9] This kind of market is under municipal control; they are administered by the city council and vendors are allotted a stand according to the type of merchandise they sell. Nemesio, a plantain vendor at Catia, had been in the same spot for forty-three years when we met him. The medicinal herb vendors prescribe and advise on matters of health, love, and happiness.

Mercados libres are class bound; they are not modern supermarkets. They evoke the street fair, the bazaar, the historical place of encounter marked by exchange. Both Catia and Quinta Crespo are situated in low-income areas of the city, quite central, and on busy nodal intersections. They are nested in their own early 1900s buildings, open naves with high ceilings; a mixture of church and industrial construction surrounded by a myriad of *buhoneros* (illegal street vendors) who use the circulation space to display their merchandise. The scene is one of sensual chaos: vendors hawking their wares, patrons, the aroma of cooked meals, peeled oranges, the colours of cloth, jewelry, the noise of children, the loud music, and so on. Except for Quinta Crespo and Coche, Mercados Libres are not open every day, which increases the number of people who might mingle during business hours, from dawn until noon. Catia's market days are Tuesday, Thursday, and Saturday. Others throughout the city vary, but most of them work on Saturday as opposed to the traditional Sunday street fair. Within this context, Hernández and I, both long-haired people, looked out of place without shopping, instead taking photos, recording, and making notes of everything. What is the role of the artist as ethnographer?

While describing the relationship between aesthetic quality and ideological tendency, Walter Benjamin in his 1934 essay, 'Author as Producer',[10] calls for artists of the left to side with the proletariat. However, this affiliation is problematic, because it suggests form versus content, political tendency versus aesthetic quality. This is an 'impossible place' in Benjamin's terms if it is not assumed from the inside, from the practicality of proletarian art; not *for* the proletariat, but *from* the proletariat – not beside, not next to it. In my case, one thing was going to the market to buy my food (as I had done most of my life) and another was going to the market as an observer, whether I was 'othering' or being 'othered'. The question of ideological patronage came to the fore with problems of misidentification and overidentification. Is there a critical distance? For artists working as ethnographers the relation informant/ethnographer was bound up in identity politics. It was either implicated in the problematic of class struggle and capitalist exploitation or it was implicated in the discourse of race and the colonial subject.

As we walked the markets, greeting people we were seeing repeatedly, talking to Nemesio, whom we had recently met, or Francisco, my orange *marchand* for some years now, we experienced the essentialization of identity, or the othering of the subject of study, thus preventing the kind of identification so necessary in terms of cultural pertinence or political alliances. Benjamin's 'impossible place' was turning into an impossible presence because the informant/ethnographer paradigm was not functioning for our project. There is no pure outside from where to observe nor did we want to be in that place (if it ever existed). Otherness is irremediably bound up in conditions of historical temporality where one prevailing other succeeds the old other only to be superseded by another. Joseph Kosuth asserts that '[b]ecause the anthropologist is outside of the culture which he studies he is not a part of the community . . . whereas, the artist, as anthropologist, is operating within the same socio-cultural context from which he evolved'.[11] Nevertheless, our role as observers of the market as phenomenon immediately placed us outside of its social matrix, despite my personal and biographical past involvement with markets. In our approach, the only difference with anthropology was that while the anthropologist is trying to acquire cultural fluency in another culture, we were acquiring cultural fluency in our own culture. Yet, the objectification created by the practice of observation negated the intention of the inquiry.

What we looked for in the relation informant/ethnographer was a subject that could relate to alterity without essentializing it. This subject is the subject of the threshold, the boundary, the liminal subject that can journey between subjects and objects, between sameness and difference; is the subject capable of inhabiting the betweenness of images and contexts? The subject that can explore the folds of the imaginary, explore the dialogue between the reflection on the wet asphalt and the shadows on the plastic covering the *buhonero* stand. A subject that can transit the betweenness of trance-gliding on aesthetic qualities, on beauty, without betraying ideology.[12]

The methodological response to the question was the othering of the self. The ethnographic fieldwork then, was not about the market, or its people, but about us in relation to the market. Self-othering is not without risks though. James Clifford's *The Predicament of Culture*[13] addresses the issue of ethnographic self-fashioning and ethnographic surrealism as we have seen it in Leiris and Bataille. The danger of self-absorption and narcissistic accounts was evident from the beginning. Vaccination against this danger, which could have resulted in ideological betrayal or the privileging of form over content, was in trance. However, let me rejoin the chronicle of our project before returning to our notion of trance.

After a day-long planning session at my studio, Hernández and I brainstormed scrutinizing the folds of the afternoon light on the windows. We began to draw on big pieces of paper cut from a roll of newspaper print. While the light faded outside, we drew and talked about the form of our investigation, the shape of what we were doing, looking for an analogy hidden in the creases of the imaginary. The charcoal sticks rolled up and down the paper covering the entire floor and a bird in flight began to emerge. We were looking at it from above, or we were on it; we were it. It had extended wings and a long tail. The bird in flight became the form we would work on, our analogy. We still didn't know what form the result of our inquiry was going to take. Being both trained in the visual arts, our first instinct was to draw.

Our outings to the market started to accumulate data about the materials used by the vendors and buyers. A closed system of ties, knots, bags, plastic sheet, wraps, sacs, and so forth, that dealt with issues of ephemerality, temporary display arrangements, mobility, precarious establishments that appeared and disappeared because the market closed, or because the police stormed the streets. Walking between art and anthropology had not given clear signals yet. Ethnographic accounts have traditionally been written, suffocated by the tyranny of language. Still worse were ethnographic displays, curiosity cabinet collections exhibiting 'native art' or 'cultural artifacts'. How to translate what we saw, what we had learned? How to evoke what we were experiencing without representing it? How to enact the shadows behind the plastic sheet when at night the street was illuminated by the *buhonero* stands, like paper lanterns illuminate a local fairground? All we were doing was gazing.

Sight has been the privileged sense in Western culture. A continuous 'preoccupation with visual and spatial root-metaphors of knowledge'[14] has been the backbone of Western metaphysics. According to Simon Goldhill,[15] classical Greek society was a sight related performance culture.

> The pervasive values of performance in Greek culture together with the special context of democracy and its institutions meant that to be in an audience was above all to play the role of democratic citizen. The political space of democracy was established by the participatory, collective audience of citizen spectators. *Theoria*, the word from which 'theory' comes, implies, as has often been noted in contemporary criticism, a form of visual regard; what is less often noted is that *Theoria* is the normal Greek for official participatory attendance as spectator in the political and religious rites of the state.

Goldhill succinctly synthesizes two of our major concerns to translate or enact what we were experiencing: visual regard and participatory attendance, *Theoria* in its full ascription. With this idea in mind, we then thought about a place, about the *topoi* of our work and how it was going to be presented. Participatory attendance could be performative in the sense that it could be an action carried through space, which would in turn give us 'the spatialization of time'. A space that could be walked, transited, read like a text without being literal took shape as the centre of our work. The space became the bird in flight and from there that structure became the work. It did not contain the exhibit, because there was no exhibit, the structure itself, inside and out, was the result of our interaction with the material and the experiences gathered in the markets. A movement between places, a spatialization of the imaginary.

In the garage of *Fuenteovejuna*[16] we built the structure out of scaffolding pipes, clamps, and use-mangled floorboards, a cross-like shape consisting of two naves, each one measuring 27' by 9', about 7' high walls, and 13' high on the apex (the roof was cross gabled). The floorboards were raised 18" above the ground. As soon as the structure was up, the relationship with the work changed. There was a physicality now that stopped all speculations about form. The space was readable and the fieldwork had accumulated plenty of know-ledge and experience to start filling it up. We began to bring materials and objects into it. The image of the lit *buhonero* stand with plastic sheet coverings became our metaphor for skin, for surface, for shelter. Diluted asphalt was applied to the plastic sheets before fixing them to the structure to gain opacity, to gain colour and a skin-like texture as it wrapped around the pipes following the structure's contours. The asphalt on the plastic became the medium where light refracted, tinted, and deformed the shadows that filtered through folds and stains. Asphalt was also a reference to the oil industry that had ruled the Venezuelan economy for the past 70 years. We covered the whole structure, giving walls to all of its sides and leaving only one open end to enter and exit. This solution, of course, was not reached without many hours, days of discussion and trials. Having the four ends open would have made it more accessible but we would also have had less control on how the work was going to be read, taken in, interpreted. Already the idea of text conditioned the way we wanted to spread on the structure. Hence, we decided to have a circuit, one way of entering and 'reading' the installation. We didn't want to leave anything open to the audience because of the many layers the work was piling up. Ordering the space and how the materials entered and were perceived followed the strict dramaturgy of the space; how proxemics worked in the placement of each object, its relation to each other, followed a strict relationship to the spectator, to *Theoria*.[17]

Cardboard boxes, onion sacs (red open weave), jute bags, rope, twine, thrift clothes, *guacales,* plastic bags, plus innumerable household and personal effects donated by friends and family became our medium. Even market vendors donated part of what made it into the installation. Again, each new phase of the work raised conceptual issues that had to be solved as we worked. By bringing the ready-made objects into the space, were we making a Duchampean allusion? What about the artwork's authorship, or the ethnographic authority?[18]

An answer to these questions was in the combination of a textualist model with aesthetic values, a 'readable' sequence yet an atmospheric environment that allowed the TMFH to develop a polyphonic language challenging both ethnographic authority and artistic authorship by placing the work in another betweenness, the betweenness of orchestrated voices speaking in the evocative mode of trance. I now want to discuss trance, the method that we followed during the creative process in order to 'give voice' by becoming rather than from a position of authority.[19]

According to the Oxford English Dictionary, trance stems from the Latin *transire*, which in spite of the later OF and ME *transir*, to depart, to pass away, it connoted to transit, to cross over, to pass, not necessarily away. The modern ascription speaks of *a sleeplike or half-conscious state without response to stimuli*. Let me put aside the dictionary's zombie inflected description and refer to a more specialized reference. Richard Schechner's *Magnitudes of Performance* discusses lying and the performer in the following terms:[20]

> . . . lying is a very complicated business in which a skilled liar – a person who can make a convincing face – *knows* he is lying but *feels* he is telling the truth . . . The half actor who 'does not forget' himself is the knower, the half who becomes the character itself is the feeler. Exactly how this works neurologically remains to be investigated. Possibly, there is a right-brain left-brain operation going on. This would suggest, even, that a skilled performer has 'three halves.' Both ergotropic and trophotropic systems are aroused, while the 'center' of the performer, the 'I,' stands outside observing and to some degree controlling. Clearly, a complex

operation engages both cognitive and affective systems simultaneously, without either washing out the other. A similar 'triple state' accompanies some kinds of trance, while in other kinds of trance the feelings may be so powerful as to blot out entirely the 'knowing half' of the performer.

Although one might conclude from Schechner's explanation on the different functions involved in the process that they are contradictory, if not opposite, another occurrence takes place, which Eugene D'Aquili calls 'rebound', during the trance experience[21]

In spite of the mutually exclusive relation between the ergotropic and trophotropic systems, however, there is a phenomenon called 'rebound to superactivity' or trophotropic rebound, which occurs in response to intense sympathetic excitation, that is, ecstasy, the peak of ergotropic arousal. A rebound into samadi at this point can be conceived of as a physiological protective mechanism . . . Meaning is 'meaningful' only at that level of arousal at which it is experienced, and every experience has its state-bound meaning. During the 'Self'-state of highest levels of hyper or hypoarousal, this meaning can no longer be expressed in dualistic terms, since the experience of unity is born from the integration of interpretive (cortical) and interpreted (subcortical) structures. Since this intense meaning is devoid of specificities, the only way to communicate its intensity is the metaphor; hence, only through the transformation of objective sign into subjective symbol in art, literature, and religion can the increasing integration of cortical and subcortical activity be communicated.

It is clear from the description how, once into the space, Hernández and I would go into the kind of trance described by Schechner in the liar segment, including the sympathetic excitement referred by D'Aquili. Take just this one example of the many in which this happened: while performing in the *Yerbatero* space, we would engage in the evocation of the market experience, the dialogues, the feelings imprinted in our memory and by 'becoming' the *Yerbatero* we would give voice, as in a mediumistic trance, without representation and never stopping being ourselves, to the experience and the collective memory we incarnate as members of the community where and for whom we were working. Seen from the outside, the creative experience might have seemed just a little off, maybe a feverish engagement in the process of creation, which is not strange for any artist who has experienced this kind of trance. From the inside, it was a schizophrenic dialogue of multiple voices, a vigorous activity that translated into building, tying, filling, displaying, all in accordance to a meaning 'devoid of specificity', being metaphor and synecdoche at the same time. Relating exterior and interior, public and private into a sequence of images, meta-texts and sensations whose syntax could only be that of the schizo. Every material had its own grammar within an overall structure that was out of joint with the really real. Saints' images and herbs were placed in the space next to objects that were 'grammatically' incorrect but that within the context spoke the same schizophrenic language we were experiencing. The *cachicamo* shells used by former peasants to carry seeds in the field looked like incantation charms when placed next to the carpenter's bench I recovered from a construction site, which after a 'treatment' became 'the table where I cut your image'. The hangings on the string-wall that separated the *yerbatero* space were scrap pieces of iron from a smith shop that resembled bells to keep the bad spirits away. Bullhorns from the municipal slaughterhouse in Clarines, a small town in the east, completed the grammar in order for the 'text' to be read correctly, as belonging to a *yerbatero* in a popular market. However, this transformation, the becoming of the objects was only possible because I was being spoken by the *yerbatero*, because the *yerbatero* in me spoke his knowledge through my identification with the material; because a memory that dwells in the collective imaginary was awakened in the space of the performance through the creative act. Embodied memory turned into trace, vestige, evocation.

At this point we felt that in spite of the trance experience, in spite of the reference we were making to the process as *mise-en-scène*, in spite of the schizophrenic language and the performance of embodied memories, our ethnographic experience was too close to the actuality of the installation. Something more theatrical had to be devised in order to alienate the spectator, to produce a distance from where to gaze, a parallax that would frame the observer as well as frame the framer. Out of this need was born the 'ethnographer'. A frame Hernández devised, the 'ethnographer' was a fictitious character whose 'office' was at the head of the installation. There, was an old desk with notes, anthropology books, photos enveloped in plastic bags like evidence in a crime hanging from a line like cloth drying in the sun. Three different-style scale models of the cross-shaped structure testified of his diggings into a fictional past of archeological discoveries and futuristic dreams. His notes, scattered through out the installation gave testimony to his incapacity to comprehend what he saw: 'I have been spoken,' claimed the vestibular notes. The separation between his office and the rest was an open structure of shelf units from where looking devices pointed toward different parts of the installation. Toy telescopes, reading glasses, magnifying lenses focused on a particular subject on a photograph, cardboard tubes tied to the structure at different angles signalled to an overlooked detail, a knot, a point in the structure. From there the spectator could see the others seeing, the framing device that frames the framer and separated our authorship from the work, making it one step removed, because now it was not our ethnography but 'his' though he was our creation. The invention of the 'ethnographer' opened the possibility for a critique of the ethnographic presence, the mapping of the other and his impossibility to grasp it. The ethnographer's office was also the place where the work reflected upon itself, an impossible inside/outside signaling a fiction. Which one? That is for the spectator to reflect on. This movement, the shifting point of view, created the necessary distance for the work to reflect upon itself and for the spectator to reflect on her participation: 'If this is not the representation of a market, if this is not an ethnography of the kind belonging to natural museums, then where am I?' For many of the Rice University workers who visited the exhibit, the immediate reaction was to say 'just like the market of my hometown' whether they were from Mexico, Ecuador, Peru, or Nicaragua. There was an instant connection with a memory, something familiar, recognizable. The paradox is that what people saw in the TMFH was the trace of a performed evocation for everything in the installation had been altered, manipulated through our subjectivity and distanced through the fictionalized layer of the 'ethnographer'. With space and time mapped onto a fictional character, 'the predominant mode of modern fieldwork authority . . . "you are there . . . because I was there"' was disrupted.

During the time of the exhibit, the class of anthropologist Quetzil Castañeda (Texas University at Houston) and Linda Seligman (George Mason University, Virginia) came to visit and we had a dialogue in the installation. One of the students, originally from Guatemala, said[22]

> When I walked in here it provoked memories from my childhood, memories which I had not transited in a long time: when I was eight years old and I went back to visit my grandmother she took me to the market. I had not remembered that until I came here, and heard the voices, and it was as if I was there in the market. Although I cannot remember the market in Guatemala, I felt as if I was there, I felt I was in a place that I can't remember. And that place over there . . . [*yerbatero*] I felt as if I had been there because there were many in my *barrio* but I never went there, hence, it's like walking into a secret place.

Neither Hernández nor I had been in Guatemala to research markets, and of course, there are similarities, both countries speak Spanish and are Catholic as a result of the Spanish colonization, but as I said before, TMFH is not a representation of a market, it is an evocation, the trace of a performance in the space. Evocation enacts the past while representation re-presents the past. Evocation does not resort to mimesis while representation does. While in trance during the creative process of the *yerbatero* space I was not re-presenting any of the vendors with whom I had interaction; I was evoking a situation, enacting a memory through my own subjectivity, therefore the outcome is different from the representation of a market, that which would be more akin to the curiosity cabinet, the natural science museum, the ethnographic exhibit, the object as historical evidence of ethnographic authority.

What happened in the other spaces, for example in the *buhonero* space, the first one after the 'ethnographer's' vestibule, was similar to that of the *yerbatero*. We bought the *catre* from a vendor at the San Juan market in Barquisimeto and later placed it in the installation along with the altar, the razor blade, the knife, but not in the manner the vendor we bought it from would have had it in 'real' life, but in relation to the space we were proposing, a spatial consciousness where fiction and reality mingled in the surface, in the skin of the plastic covering that wrapped around. The bags full of cloth spoke of the violence in the streets, the bags hanging from the chicken wire that served as ceiling and deposit spoke of the transitory placement of their lives. Similarly, in the woman vendor's space, the empty dry-cleaner's bags spoke of the violence against women, women violated, missing testimonies, like ghosts among the party dresses sold in the market with the illusion of a Cinderella night. Old vinyl records 'framed' the space as they went around, like music in a jukebox.

The last space, the space through which one exited the installation, was dedicated to the *Fiesta*, the celebration of the event and the gift, the vendors' presents to their foreign audiences: carved figures, rice bags with saints inside them, women's decorated false nails, and a parrot that spoke English. Since the parrot could not travel (it is prohibited to take them out) we substituted the parrot with a cock when we got to the US.

The Market From Here explored the language of the *mise-en-scène* as ethnography and as installation art.[23] In doing so, it proposed a discourse that intersects with its parental disciplines: anthropology, art, scenography, and ethnography. The hybrid that resulted, although some art critics preferred to categorize it as artifact, as ready made, spoke of the new crossroads opened for those artists and ethnographers who transit between art and anthropology. In our case, we chose to use some of anthropology's methodology and content and make them complementary to the creative process, to the subjectivity of the artist, in this way liberating them from the burden of 'othering' and ethnocentrism, allowing difference to coexist. What the discourse of the TMFH proposed was the dismantling of anthropological authority, leaving the trace of the performance, the scenography of a play that created its own script as it played itself out in space. Most interesting is the fact that this trace, the act of installing, the performance of an evocation corresponds to ethnographic knowledge exercised in field work. It is not about the objects themselves transcending essentialist categorizations but about a method of inquiry that opens conditions of possibility for the existence of experimental spaces within ossified disciplines.

Although anthropology made an in-depth critique of the discipline in the early 1980s, the shock treatment has not produced the results that would expand the field of the discipline. Retrenchment quickly took place after acknowledgement of the crisis and old forms of ethnographic narrative readapted to the new paradigms. Art on the other hand has been moving steadily toward the commodification of the art object, regardless of its political involvement. In this regard, TMFH as discourse proposed an installation that experimentally approached social issues concerning violence, indigence, and marginality at the same time that it subverted the art market on its own turf. Having no object, no product, anything to sell or save, there was no commodification. What remains is its discourse (see Fig. 7.2).

Figure 7.2. *The Market from Here*, 1997. Herbs and Saints – In Quinta Crespo, an herbs and saints vendor stand. Detail. Photo: Fernando Calzadilla.

APPENDIX: NOTES BY GEORGE E. MARCUS PRESENTED TO THE DEPARTMENT OF ANTHROPOLOGY IN ANTICIPATION OF THE ARRIVAL OF *ARTISTS IN TRANCE*, 4 JANUARY 1997

I suspect that there is a set of as yet unarticulated reciprocal desires between our department and the visiting group of artists that gives a particular edge of anticipation to the *Artists In Trance* project, on both sides. In senses yet unknown, they desire anthropology in and as represented by us, and we desire, I think, an unfulfilled aestheticism at the level of our practices as anthropologists. Of course, as actual communities and sites of enduring relationships we don't know each other at all. This is the fascination that the imminent encounter holds. In a powerful sense, the classic frame of 'culture contact' with all its ambivalence, hopes, and needs for translation fits very well our project. In the meantime, imaginings, hopes, and suspicions fill our minds in anticipation as we prepare to take up our role as 'hosts' to unknown 'guests', whom we think of (I'm sure far too simplistically and stereotypically) as artists from 'the Third World' who seek an academic anthropological context in which to introduce themselves to North America. Given the inevitable misrecognitions of any situation of first contact, Abdel Hernández's idea of actually writing in anticipation of the encounter is a hermeneutically wise and ingenious strategy for making presuppositions, biases, suspicions, and pre-imaginings explicit so that at least they might not dog our responses as unchallenged and unrecognized already existing 'attitudes' with which we experience the project as it unfolds.

For me, the critiques of the 1980s of anthropological rhetoric and representation (and more broadly of rhetoric and representation themselves) with which we are associated distinctively as a department are unfulfilled in their possibilities for changes in the doing of anthropology. Certain versions and degrees of the sense of the limits of representation were broadly received by anthropology and associated academic fields without a thorough exploration of changes in practices. This potentiality lay in the unfulfilled aesthetic dimension and ideal of the critique. Without nostalgia for that moment in the 1980s, and without any expectation of recapturing unexplored possibility raised by *that* moment, one hope and desire for us in the *Artists In Trance* project is the opportunity to see some of the issues that were alive in the 1980s critique return in wholly unexpected and novel forms in the work of the artists performed and presented in this project. Being tired of and a little disappointed by what has been made of the critique in anthropology, I personally want to see what has been made of the same issues from a completely different point of origin (and not one that we can necessarily easily share or even fully understand), but while trying very hard not to submit the work of these artists to the enclosed 'anthropological court of judgment'.

For me personally, and my own previous interest in the ethnography/sociology of art worlds, my hope is that we will be participating in a fascinating case study of art world politics, appropriation, and value creation. What is to be made and understood by the choice to present this work as a 'course' within the academy and within anthropology (but at one of the centres known for the strong self-questioning of these contexts)? Artists once well supported in the academy of socialist Cuba, now living by whatever means in exile, and wanting to present themselves within the confines of a relatively secure, privileged, and mundanely critical US 'ivory-tower' outpost, but inevitably attracting more or less attention from art world institutions, configure juxtaposed sites of activities that are bound to stir ambivalence on the sides of both guests and hosts that will bear watching and understanding.

At least part of my own anticipation is in terms of this ethnographic 'eye' and context for understanding of what we are doing. As of now, we, the Rice anthropologists, are already as hosts in the posture of spectators, reactors, responders, rather than performers along with the artists. Will this initial posture be changed for any of us? If yes, then there is real unforeseen possibility for us in these events. If no, then we will have to struggle mightily not to be just an audience, or to fall in the comfortable role of anthropologists of trying to figure out this piece of 'otherness' which initially is very much presented to us as such.

I think there is in our department much openness and unarticulated positive feeling about what we might see and experience, but given the wary point-counterpoint, critical edge of academic environments, I also think the initial reception 'in anticipation' of this project is articulated primarily in terms of doubts, suspicions, and concerns. I think it is precisely the nature of these defensive responses that it is so important to make explicit here in this 'writing in anticipation' exercise, so that they cannot innocently dominate later discussions as embedded and extremely resistant attitudes that are unacknowledged at the outset and merely there to be confirmed. It is thus important to present them for what they are before the event, so to speak, as opening desires, anxieties, and suspicions, that may or may not have any relevance for the project as it actually unfolds. 'Writing in anticipation' thus is like an inoculation that gives at least immunity from the complexly motivated critical faculty with which academics consume everything including themselves.

So, here, in brief list form, are the sorts of 'concerns' or scepticism both that I have thought of myself and that I have heard when I mentioned this project to various colleagues both here at Rice and elsewhere (for example, at New York University and Columbia on a visit in November):

1. Again, our tendency to submit this entire event to the anthropological or ethnographic 'court of judgment'. The artists in trance themselves become immediately an ethnographic object for us – objectivized and distanced. Our tendency will be to make them – the artists – the primary 'other'. While there is value in this, and it is probably inevitable since in the first instance, we are to be more spectators than participants, still, the danger is that by participating as 'anthropologists' we might miss the point, or at least crucial dimensions of the experience. So against the reinforced tendency to define this event in terms of the anthropological *mise-en-scène*, we should also take this opportunity and space to play once again with the identity 'anthropologist'. To do this, we will have to think carefully what other us-them identities are available to us, besides that of anthropologist and artist (as anthropological subject).

2. Relatedly, there is a proprietary mood in contemporary US anthropology, heightened by the recent appropriations by humanities movements like cultural studies of things like culture and ethnography with little credit to or involvement from anthropology. Thus the possible sensitivity that this project might be yet another appropriation, with implied incompetence, lack of conviction, and so forth, of 'our' anthropology without consultation. The point for those of us in this project is that this proprietary reaction formation is very much alive and easily stimulated. Particularly in our 'culture contact' setting it can take up a lot of time.

3. In New York, the immediate response of someone who quickly read over the brochure for the project – why are there no women artists in this group, indicating that by this lack of inclusiveness, that the project is of less interest, less progressive than it might otherwise have been (see Fig. 7.3). The general point is that identity politics predominates in US academia, and it is bound to have a strong impact on the reception of this work.

Figure 7.3. *The Market from Here*, 1997. Etnógrafo – reading the Ethnographer's notes and 'evidence'. Photo: Fernando Calzadilla.

4. After the failures of so-many historic avant-garde, there is a general scepticism about the (false) hopes of contemporary avant-garde or the capacity of groups such as *Artists in Trance* to escape being avant-garde in any of the diverse modernist senses. Can *Artists In Trance* escape, even in the moment of its operation in our department, from the authority of art world institutions, which if they do not secretly desire, then at least with which they must negotiate? Is there any possible avoidance of the seduction of this appeal and the art world's inevitable ability to define artists in trance completely within its field?

5. Relatedly, without more prior knowledge of the group, there is probably some suspicion of the *Artists in Trance* conforming to the sociological model of a charismatic cult, enclosed and with strong internal principles of authority operating. While our department itself has often been described, accusingly, as this sort of formation, and while there is nothing illegitimate about such groups – in fact, the most creative things historically have emerged this way through circles, teams, partnerships, intense associations – they are not currently politically correct. It is as much their doctrinaire or authoritarian side that is likely to be pointed out, even by their friends, as their creative side (such groups were received much differently, and perhaps more naively in the 1960s, but alas, the mode of reception is very different now).

6. Finally, and again relatedly, there might be the sense from this side that the
   artists are too theoretical, too 'academic', and not transparent enough in
   their social commitments and concerns. This feeling might relate to the
   present moment here of exhaustion with theory, or at least theory, as a mode
   of discourse. Abstract theoretical discourse was a challenge of the 1980s that
   some regret and others are relieved is now in 'bad odour,' so to speak. Much
   more desired are performances, through art, anthropology, or whatever
   named field, of the implications of theoretical debate that were aired in the
   1980s. If the genre of ethnography has truly blurred with others, anthropologists seek some sort of kinship in the practices and performances of
   artists in trance that cannot be resolved by theoretical exposition. Of course,
   as we all know from the classes we teach, we are still mired in theoretical
   expositions of the world in a didactic context. And so, we approach with a
   certain amount of trepidation the *Artists in Trance* who have chosen to
   communicate with us and others in the very context - a course - which
   has traditionally been constrained by a proclivity for the lecture, for
   theoretical exposition.

And now that we have made these complex attitudes in anticipation explicit,
on with the show!

EPILOGUE (MARCUS)

Of course, I cannot present here an extended account of how the actual events
turned out in relations to the hopes, fears, and cautions expressed in the above
document. In retrospect, I can only say that it was a mixture of successes and
failures in terms of expectations (at least, the anthropologists' expectations),
but that the experience of the failures was at least as valuable for us as of the
successes (see Fig. 7.4). Along with the performances and installations were a
set of public lectures and departmental seminars with Abdel Hernández at their
centre. He characterized these as a course.

These turned out to be a disappointment for the anthropologists, because
we had expected them to be more like performances (entertainments, even),
and they felt more didactic and scholastic to us - just more of the same.
However, these events, which dealt with a review of contemporary art in Latin
America, were a great success among the diverse community of Latin Americans
in Houston, who attended the lectures in great numbers.

The performances and installations were another matter. They created a
much more interactive atmosphere between ourselves and the visiting artists,who made themselves available to discuss their creations. *The Market from
Here*, the most sustained installation, became the most observed, participated
in, and discussed of the works presented. Classes of undergraduates were
brought to it and discussions of it were incorporated into course curricula.
Additionally, there were one or two memorable seminars between the anthro-

Figure 7.4. *The Market from Here*, 1997. Audience among the Buhonero's bags and testimonials. Photo: Fernando Calzadilla.

pologists and the visitors about the process of creating TMFH and other works. Most of all, though, we were reminded of how complicated and how mysterious sustained cross-cultural encounters remain, even among people who believe they share an intellectual agenda and a common set of issues.

Photographic Essay
Dave Lewis

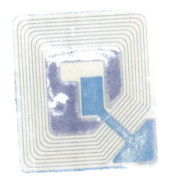

Dialogues

With Dave Lewis, Rainer Wittenborn, Claus Biegert, Nikolaus Lang and Rimer Cardillo

Arnd Schneider and Christopher Wright

DAVE LEWIS

Dave Lewis's photographs frequently challenge the viewer to ask certain questions; questions that can be difficult and uncomfortable but which reveal otherwise obscured histories.[1] His work appears often in major surveys of black British photography.[2] A recent series of photographs based on the Stephen Lawrence case – a notorious murder case that instigated a large-scale examination of institutional racism in the British police – focused on the sites at which the story unfolded. Lewis was aware that any images he made would be seen in relation the media reporting of the case and chose what at first seems an oblique approach. But these powerful images, which take the form of extreme closeups of textures and details, such as rain on the steps of the Crown Prosecution Service, effectively conduct an anthropological exploration of place. In creating such a strong sense of experience, Lewis also makes you question the relations between individuals and institutions; the effects of racism are in one sense given palpable form. Lewis is also concerned with his native south-east London and the ways in which different communities use and adapt their environments. He has worked with local schools and community groups on photographic projects and continues to see this work as an important and ongoing part of his practice.

The relation, or lack of it, between individuals and institutions of many kinds has been an enduring focus of Lewis's work. For his series of images for an exhibition, exploring the relations between anthropology and photography, he staged a series of confrontations in British archives and collections of nineteenth-century anthropological photographs.[3] For one of these he posed a naked black model on the Director's desk at the Royal Anthropological Institute underneath a painting of the famous anthropologist A. C. Haddon wearing his academic black gown and holding a human skull.[4] Lewis's own sense of unease about being in such collections is apparent and the photographs are a direct response to this. But, rather than a solely negative critique, Lewis is concerned with the possibility of reclaiming histories and the photographs form points of departure for questioning anthropological representations of others and for critically examining the role of the archive. Such direct affirmations of individual presence challenge the premises of anthropological investigation in a subtle but fundamental way.

For this book, Lewis was invited to produce some new work that related to his concerns about anthropology. He chose to focus on the teaching of anthropology; on the ways in which it institutionally recreates itself as a discipline. Basing himself at the University of East London, Lewis attended anthropology classes run by Jayne Ifekwunigwe[5] and talked to students. As well as drawing attention to the physical base of anthropology in the sense of a series of teaching methods, Lewis wanted to evoke a sense of anthropology's relation to what is outside it; to the local community as much as any imagined 'world' available for investigation.

INTERVIEW WITH DAVE LEWIS, LONDON, 20 DECEMBER 2001

Christopher Wright (CW):   What was the motivation behind your work at the University of East London (UEL)?

Dave Lewis (DL):   What I started thinking about was how you teach other people to become anthropologists, what do you tell them to look for? It wasn't so much the specifics, because I'm not an anthropologist and I probably wouldn't be able to hold onto the stuff anyway, it was about how you pass on that knowledge to a group of people. How people are trained.

CW: About becoming qualified or becoming a professional?

DL: Yes, how do you achieve the status that allows you to say 'I'm an anthropologist'? I've always been interested in how knowledge is arrived at, how epistemologies are formed. What has struck me in the past are the parallels between anthropology and photography, and there are some parallels but also differences, particularly in terms of institutions. You would only get so much credibility with a doctorate in photography.

CW: You're talking about relations between theory and practice. How do the two influence each other in your own work?

DL: When I was in Jayne's class at UEL, although I was there to take photos, I found myself becoming more interested in what she was saying and what the students were saying. They talked about how you approach a 'site', and the differences between participating and observing. How much do you tell the people you're observing? We talked about proxemics. She was asking us to think about who it was asking the questions, that's of key importance, rather than any illusion of being objective. And I started to think that's like being a photographer in some ways. In some shows I've had I've been standing on the outside with a 5 × 4 camera trying to take the 'whole scene', and trying to make these huge statements about a site. I took a series of photos looking right over Hampstead and then over Peckham, and if you're not thinking about the theory then you just have these different landscapes. But when you think of the theory you start to see how things are organized differently, the way people react and interact within these landscapes is different. This is a different thing from being closer within a site, and talking to people and becoming part of the social events and having to interpret in another way what you see through the camera. So I can see these parallels with anthropology in the way you approach and interact with sites.

CW: You've encountered anthropology before, and it seems as though there is something that resonates on a practical level as well as a theoretical one?

DL: In terms of what I've read – although a lot of this stuff stays dormant for a long time – I've looked at how anthropologists worked in the nineteenth century, and this was brought home when I visited institutions like Oxford, Cambridge and the Royal Anthropological Institute (RAI). So to see this woman, this black woman, teach this group of kids with earrings and 'tams' on their heads, seems a long way from the beginnings of anthropology.

CW   Did you come out with a positive view of anthropology?

DL: Yes, at least from that class. That was the only class I went to so I don't know about the others. I always get a bit worried about some aspects of anthropology, the basis of some of it really disturbs me.

CW: There's still aspects of anthropology that are relatively untouched by some of the theoretical arguments you've been reading.

DL: I don't know how they make some aspects of it relevant to today.

CW: There's an institutional basis for things that doesn't necessarily change, how do you get taught to look as an anthropologist? And what are you taught to look at? It seems to me that anthropology could be usefully taught on photography courses.

DL: The basics of photography are involved with fundamentally anthropological concerns, unless you're doing something which is totally technical. A lot of photography is about people, and 85% of photography is about communication. I was told by my photography teacher that when he was at college the first thing they were asked to do was photograph the first twenty people they met, and everyone had to do that. Photography is about participation, you have to deal with people. In anthropology there seems to be more scope to make up stuff, to stand back and for that to be a credible stance, in photography I think its harder to do that. Today, we expect the photographer to have had a relationship with the subjects and the communities, I'm not sure I feel like that when I read anthropology. I don't know what kind of relationship the anthropologist or ethnographer has had with those people apart from asking questions and observing. There's something that appears to be distant about anthropologists and their subjects, there's this thing about living with the natives and I find this a real sticking point, I'm not sure you can go off and do that. I haven't really come to terms with what it is I find difficult with this, and I don't know if its because I'm not white, I'm not English, and I'm not middle-class, or because I've always historically been the subject or the victim. Very rarely do I see black anthropologists, I know there are some, but if you look on the boards of university departments you know . . . then its hard for me to then accept what those people are saying, it's just another bloody exercise.

CW: Some of the changes in anthropology have been student led in the sense that students are going out into today's marketplace and saying 'I've got a degree in anthropology how's that relevant? How's that going to get me a job?'

DL: I think anthropology is relevant, but I'm a bit wary of saying it's this and it's that, because my experience of it is that it's changed and is changing. It feels like it's changed even since I began looking at it, in Jayne's class you had this whole group looking at the movie *Carwash* and thinking about the people in it. And I found myself thinking this is close to film criticism, and this is not a criticism, I think its good that these things cross-over. But then I keep thinking what's anthropology then?

CW: People talk about the ethnographic turn in contemporary art, work which is trying in some way to be ethnographic and often claims some kind of authenticity or truth as a result of this. But perhaps there's a lack of perception about the differences between anthropology and ethnography? Between anthropology as a kind of distanced more general theorizing, and ethnography as a more specific encounter with people; the two get conflated. A lot of times, you read a book and think someone has just spent two years in an African forest, and yet I have no idea of what that was like from the writing, it becomes something removed from experience.

DL: I can see how that would happen, and I think the perception of what it is you're doing is weighing so heavily on the actual practice, the theory weighs down your doing of the thing, and then it becomes really problematic. You end up trying to squeeze things into different shapes. As long as you have the kind of systems and institutions we have now, that's going to be hard to change.

CW: That's what I find interesting in your focus on the institutional aspect of anthropology; there are things about the way its taught that make you think it doesn't want to change. For a long time, visual anthropology was to do with acquiring purely technical skills once you were already a trained anthropologist. But if you compare this to teaching in art schools, if you're going to do photography you don't just learn to use bits of equipment. The whole thing is geared around developing ways of looking, and ways of interacting in producing work, which seems to be something that would be very relevant to anthropology. You're trained as an anthropologist but in any given situation how do you look differently from a photographer? Is there a difference in what you look at, or how you look? It seems to me that you'd want to look at a lot of the same things and share similar problems. Does that mean it's a matter of intentions, or of sites of exhibition and audiences?

DL: The project that I'm thinking about doing now involves working out how I approach people. What questions is it that I want to ask, how far do I take my engagement? Some of these things are influenced by the kind of questions raised in Jayne's class. I want to get the views of different groups like lawyers and working-class youth, within the same area about how they think the environment should be shaped. Totally different responses from people who live in the same place, although perhaps 70% of the rest of their lives are the same and they have to deal with the same things. How do you go about identifying that and recording that as a photographer in twenty-first century London? That's when you start to look at some theory. That's where I think there is a similarity between anthropology and photography.

CW: What do you think motivates anthropologists?

DL: I'd like to think there is a genuine curiosity, but when they start taking apart things which they don't really know anything about, even if they've spent two years there, I'm not trying to be flippant . . .

CW: There's a slightly arbitrary decision about the amount of time you need to spend somewhere, a year, or a year-and-a-half, but why not insist on longer?

DL: It's about what you're prepared to say to the reader; this is where I was, this is where I went, I jumped from here to there, this is what I thought it was about, and this is how I think we should go forward – that's fine. But what finally gets produced seems to forget that and be such a closed book.

CW: There are issues of authority. If you did a photographic project and displayed it in a gallery that's one kind of product, whereas an anthropologist would write an academic book. Because they're seen in different spaces, they have different authorities. But you go and see an exhibition and sometimes that's more 'realistic', anthropologists tend to make things that are less open ended. Rather than openly engaging in a process of making things visible, they often act as if they're accurately reproducing the world.

DL: People don't expect anthropological writing to be open ended, people expect it to be solid so that the product is finished. And I have big problems with that because things change and things move on. I'd like to know what people's aims were when they set out, that would make it more interesting and be more reality driven. Because that's what usually happens, you don't end up where you thought you'd be. In anthropology books you usually end up exactly where you thought you'd be.

CW: When you speak to anthropologists they admit that of course you end up with something different than what you started out with, but you don't write about that process. What you write leaves that out, it's a product for a particular market.

DL: But where does that leave you? We're talking about disciplines which have ongoing exploration at their core.

CW: The model for an anthropologist is still the lone anthropologist. You get some couples who collaborate, but not much collaboration makes it into the final work, in the sense of actual dialogue, unless it's with a named 'informant'.

DL: Isn't that adventure story stuff?

CW: It is, and that's perhaps why some artists like anthropology. There's the trendy theory and then there's the authenticity and the authority of that; there's still a romance about anthropology.

DL: That's how strongly it's fixed in our minds; it takes a long time to try to take that apart.

CW: There needs to be a willingness to engage with other audiences. Anthropology that has tried to be popular is often not seen as being as serious as its more academic counterpart; it's somehow unprofessional. But presumably that's what anthropologists have a duty to do – to engage other audiences, to move beyond academic confines. They need to look at various ways of addressing new audiences. It's also about a willingness to deal with other spaces of exhibition.

DL: But don't anthropologists really want to be just left alone? (Laughter.) Maybe that's why we don't see more relevant anthropology. You know where are the ethnographies of mixed-race youths in London, with their mixed-race families and their BMWs ? It would be good to see stuff that more people can relate to. I'm not sure if it's laziness on the part of anthropologists or fear, fear of dealing with subjects that might look too much like sociology or cultural studies.

CW: There have been relatively few collaborations between anthropologists and artists . . .

DL: Because anthropologists would hate it. If I took a series of photos and started to call it anthropology, it would threaten their gravitas. In terms of work I think it would be interesting to trace over stuff that's already been done by anthropologists, going back to places and working with a different medium. Anthropology is a written thing, but you never give other people the pen. I think that would be too scary for anthropologists to do. They're very sensitive. Why? It's about authorization.

CW: Anthropology should be about dialogue . . .

DL: But the anthropology I've read seems to engage in very little dialogue and have very little to say about my context. There's a lot of allusion to anthropology in contemporary work but I'm not sure how much people actually know about it, it's just popular right now. I originally put these photographs of UEL together as pairs to create a kind of movement. What I was trying to achieve was a kind of dialogue between the images. I was trying to show how 'un-standard' anthropology is, and what is outside it.

RAINER WITTENBORN

Rainer Wittenborn and Claus Biegert's *James Bay Project* (1981) was a multi-layered work that focused on the impact of a large-scale Canadian government hydro-electric scheme on the environment and the local Cree people. Wittenborn and Biegert undertook several months of fieldwork with communities in northern Quebec (both Cree and those of construction workers on the scheme), during which they produced drawings, made botanical collections and collected other artifacts, took photographs, recorded interviews and oral histories, made videos, and mounted exhibitions. Plant samples were gathered and allocated names, uses, and histories by Cree and also by Canadian scientists; revealing the disparities between the two systems. The range of objects and events involved in the project, which also included a substantial book, meant that no single form of representation was privileged above any other, and this allowed an equally diverse range of audiences to be addressed.[6] It was important

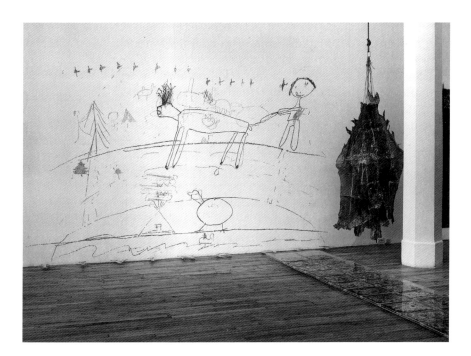

Figure 9.1. Rainer Wittenborn, *Living Off – Skin and Body*, 1995. Wall drawing, caribou raw hides, felt letters, granite sheet, 26 square of caribou lichen (+ detail) installation at Center for the Arts, Wesleyan University, Connecticut. Courtesy of the artist.

that the exhibition was shown in Cree communities to counter the way that researchers of different kinds 'come up here and milk us dry and then they never show up again', as Cree spokeswoman Susan Pashagumscum pointed out,[7] and the exhibition opened in the Cree village of Chisasibi before going on to Montreal and San Francisco. Wittenborn commented on the reaction of Cree people: 'It was the best audience I ever had. The people didn't look at it from the purely aesthetic point of view, they were following my journey as an artist. They read every line, they checked every detail . . . They could identify with my work, there was no barrier of artificial respect between the audience and the art.'[8]

The project used art as a tool to *do* things – 'they have assumed a participatory stance to call attention to vital issues and stimulate dialogue that might affect change'[9] – and the work effectively blurs distinctions between art and science; 'aesthetics never becomes an end in itself in Wittenborn's work, rather, it enters into the service of an endeavour to document and enlighten.'[10] Aesthetics remains only one factor in a 'comprehensive totality' which combines the abstraction of anthropological (and other) research with the authenticity of experience. The work engages the senses but does not neglect rational argument, or rather, it refuses to acknowledge any division between the two. They 'combined exact ethnographical and geographical documentation with artistic and journalistic means of expression. Their approach thus provides a new dimension for traditional anthropological fieldwork methods.'[11] Wittenborn and Biegert undertake what Latour has suggested as a remedy for current divisions between science and social and political theory;[12] they abandon territories in favour of tracing the complexities of networks.

In 1989 Wittenborn and Biegert where invited by the Cree Grand Council to return and document the changes that had occurred in the intervening decade. The resulting exhibition *Amazon of the North – James Bay Revisited*[13] used a similar combination of media to the former exhibition and explored the continuing impact of the hydro-electric scheme and other environmental pressures on the Cree way of life.

RAINER WITTENBORN AND CLAUS BIEGERT: ANSWERS TO QUESTIONS BY ARND SCHNEIDER AND CHRISTOPHER WRIGHT

What are the influences of anthropology on the contemporary art world? It is not so much the influence of (cultural) anthropology. In the past it was mostly the influence of native art with its exotic elements; today it is the indigenous worldview and the message of tribal people to the industrial world. Stuck at the end of a dead-end road, the industrial world is looking for solutions. While the majority of the dominant society is searching within its own boundaries, a small group is looking beyond. It goes almost without saying that visual artists, probably artists of all kinds, belong to this small sensitive group. Artists have always been seismographs of a society's social and political development. As Minneconju-Lakota Medicine Man Tahca Ushte in his conversations with writer Richard Erdoes put it: 'You artists are the Indians of the white world. You should understand our problems.'

What have been the anthropological influences on your work, in either a generalized way or in the sense of specific works or theories? How does this influence manifest itself in your work and how do you encounter anthropology, through museums and exhibitions and/or through written work? We were very careful not to repeat the mistakes of early anthropologists, who mostly showed little concern about the wellbeing of the group they were studying. Their commitment was directed towards the university they were employed by. We associated ourselves with those representatives of anthropology who were very critical of their own academic discipline and committed towards the people they were working with.

During our time (1979/80) on Cree territory we worked very closely together with anthropologist Rick Cuciurean who had gained the trust of elders and the younger generation in Band Councils in almost all Cree settlements. Rick functioned as a mediator between the indigenous communities affected by the

James Bay hydro project and the government body responsible for destroying the traditional hunting grounds with this project. We benefited enormously from this contact by a common sharing of experiences. Rick practised what was emerging in the United States at the time as action anthropology. In this radical branch the field study is undertaken only with the full consent of the indigenous group, the study's subject often being defined by members of the indigenous group. Another unorthodox academic we worked with was Professor Michael Asch from the University of Edmonton, Alberta, who was the president of the Canadian Society of Ethnology at the time. Michael Asch did a survey of hunting and trapping routes of Dene people in the subarctic of the North West Territories – in collaboration with Dene hunters and university cartographers. The Dene Mapping Project became a milestone in scientific work serving hunting people. We worked on our project with a similar approach. We knew: only with the Cree would we be able to create an exhibit about the conflict at James Bay. Very early during our research we came to the conclusion that the Cree have to be first in reviewing our work before we would present it to the public in Canada (starting at the Musée des Beaux Arts in Montreal), the US, Brazil, Europe and Thailand, eleven venues in total. This decision was triggered by a remark of Susan Pashagumskum in Wemindji: 'Anthropologists, film makers, photographers – they all come up here and milk us dry and then they never show up again.' Our exhibition had its premiere in the Cree village of Chisasibi. The indigenous people appreciated our collection of sub-arctic plants from their territory, which offered the white scientific view next to the herbal knowledge of Cree elders, including nutrition, medical use – even mythology.

Do you see your work either directly or indirectly addressing any anthropological questions or concerns? What are they and how does your work achieve this? We were only interested in the concerns of the indigenous people we visited and the questions they had. Like in action anthropology we were open to their wishes. Since there was no reserved attitude towards artists (unlike in the white society) we had no problems in communicating our vision and combining it with theirs. And there is a side effect: leaving home and diving into another cultural cosmos will transform you and enable you to see yourself and the society you come from, with different eyes.

What kind of anthropological methods do you, or could you, see as relevant for your own practice and for contemporary art in general? It goes without saying that the collections of natural history and anthropology from the eighteenth and nineteenth century always have great impact on a visual artist. Before we headed up north we spent time at the Royal Ontario Museum in Toronto to become acquainted with relics of the past in order to be equipped to judge the modern situation. Because there was a lack of historical photographs in the museums, we requested old photographs from people wherever we went. And we were most successful.

It is of utmost importance to open yourself to the unknown and become a sincere listener and sensitive observer and – if necessary – a participant. The basic requirement is time: you have to adjust yourself to a different time flow in order to experience a different worldview. You should keep in mind that you are also a source of information for the ones you visit. The encounter can have a creative impact on both sides. We were glad to have a series of postcards with us that gave them a picture of Bavarian mountains, animals and flowers. We were also aware of our own background: on a larger scale, we did belong to the civilization that was killing their culture. And we came also from a situation of struggle; we also had stories of destruction and defeat, like the resistance against nuclear power or the initiatives to save the forests.

Our decision to make the impact of the James Bay Hydro Project on Cree culture the subject of an international mixed-media travelling exhibition made plain our commitment. The Cree considered themselves as a sovereign indigenous nation of Canada and not as citizens of Quebec. We had to express this in our work knowing we would not please Quebec officials. While Quebec is considered bilingual we experienced a trilingual situation as we zigzagged through the north. As a result, in our exhibition the writings on the wall were French, English and Cree.

What chances do you currently see for new productive dialogues between art and anthropology? What would be the shared ground for any such dialogues?   Both sides have to review their attitude towards tribal cultures in the past and they have to explore their potentials in the future. Both disciplines can gain from each other if they are willing to make a stand: tribal cultures are the lifeblood of the world's cultural diversity, and they are under attack. Artists as well as anthropologists who enter the field of conflict cannot remain neutral.

The collaboration between Rainer Wittenborn and Claus Biegert was a joint venture of a visual artist and an author – resulting in an exhibition and a catalogue, entitled The James Bay Project – A River Drowned By Water, *followed by a book in German,* Der große Fluß ertrinkt im Wasser. *What can be gained from such cooperation?*   We equipped ourselves with the skills of the partner crossing the borders of his own professional field. We gained a freedom of transmitting an exotic issue into our own society. Our concept developed during our research and continued during the two years in the studio. In the process of combining artefacts, drawings, paintings, photographs, words, video and sound, we were able to deal with the complex situation much better than if either of us had been alone. It is not only the combination of different media that describes an issue more precise than one medium alone; it is also the space between the collected and created pieces, as well as between the collaborating persons. 'The space between' for us has been the space where the unexpected could happen and where the spiritual moments would have their place.

In 1989 and 1990 you went back to James Bay for further research. What triggered this decision? The Grand Council of the Cree – who in 1981 had ordered 10 000 copies of our catalogue – invited us back to look at the changes. We considered this a great sign of trust and appreciation of our work. They paid for our expenses and we experienced a great welcome in all the communities. Our travels coincided with the protest against the Great Whale Project, the flooding of their most northern rivers where their territory overlaps with the Inuit. This conflict was included in our second exhibition *Amazon of the North – James Bay Revisited.*

How does Amazon of the North *differ from* A River Drowned By Water? During our first research in 1979/80 we realized that the Canadian public was unaware of the different culture up north. This lack of knowledge caused us to choose a more pedagogic concept in laying out and explaining the basics of a sub-arctic hunting culture. A decade later, the James Bay issue was known all over Canada and the US, and the Cree had begun to send delegates to the United Nations in Geneva, Switzerland. The isolation was broken. This gave us more artistic freedom. Now we were able to create a space in which images, thoughts, faces, tracks, horizons, sounds, fears and visions could relate to each other. For example: the impact of mercury poisoning through fish caught in the reservoirs was captured by huge portraits of pregnant Cree women looking at you. This gallery of faces corresponded with installations dedicated to two animals, the Beluga whale and the freshwater seal; both species would become extinct if the project would ever go ahead.

If you are involved in any form of teaching practice or giving lectures, does anthropology form a component of this in some way, perhaps through the use of ethnographic examples or by referring to anthropological theories? We both are in teaching positions: Rainer is a professor for interdisciplinary arts at the Technical University of Munich, and Claus is a freelance lecturer at the German School of Journalism. We have become sensitized by our experiences with people who have been exploited culturally and this forces us to look at our own society with different eyes. Respect is no longer an abstract word.

NIKOLAUS LANG

Nikolaus Lang has worked in Japan, Italy, Sweden, Bavaria, and Australia collecting and ordering objects. In an early piece *For the Götte Brothers and Sisters* (1973/4) about his native Bavaria, he collected and displayed the objects of the Götte family's rural life, providing biographical information through material traces and effectively invoking a way of life.[14] He first visited Australia in 1979, inspired by reading about a long journey Aboriginal people made to collect a particular red ochre, and his *Australian Diary* (1979) presents diary entries of Lang's own journey, next to ochre samples and his finds of prehistoric

Figure 9.2. Nikolaus Lang. *Wearing Somebody's Jacket* (detail of *Culture Heap*). Courtesy of the artist.

tools (collected with the permission of Aboriginal people). Back in Bavaria, he collated and combined these to make a kind of 'store cupboard'. Later works, assembled under the title *Nunga and Goonya*[15] – from Aboriginal terminology for 'blackfella[ow]' and 'white person' in present day South Australia – included *Peter's Story* (1986/9), a reconstruction through photographs of a tragic incident from 1856, recorded by a settler and preserved in his unpublished manuscripts at the South Australian Archives in Adelaide. Through 'reliving and re-creating',[16] Lang wants to bring to light that which has been lost. The story concerned a case of mistaken identity in which an Aboriginal man from the Flinders Ranges was imprisoned and eventually died for a crime he did not commit, and Lang himself re-enacted elements related to the story. The process of 'trading places' is also referred to in Lang's work *Your Eyes, My Eyes – Tindale's Legacy* (1988/91), which is based on plaster casts of a Pitjandjara man taken by the anthropologist N. B.Tindale in 1933 at Ernabella mission station. The taking of such a cast violates Pitjandjara beliefs that identity is extinguished at death. In reusing it, Lang consulted tribal representatives and the work is dedicated to the seven tribes of the Flinders Ranges. From the original bust Lang made seven negative moulds in which the eyes were 'opened', and from these negatives he made a further seven positives in which he inserted casts of his own eyes, questioning notions of looking through others' eyes.

Through these works Lang is seeking

to re-open the historical imagination to the very possibilities that his predecessors work had closed down: the possibility of constructing a new expressive interpretation of social activities, through pursuing interconnections of meaningful, reciprocal interchange across the spaces of difference, through investigating, re-contacting, re-awakening, reliving and reshaping the imaginative meanings of two starkly different cultures' interaction with each other.[17]

An anthropologically motivated interest in the functioning of human societies forms the core of his work and in his concern to trace the effects of one culture on another and bridge gaps in mutual understanding, 'he undertakes an interdescriptive engagement of both cultures'.[18] Lang focuses on pluralities and the historical inscription of one culture upon another; he fashions sculptures out of abandoned pieces of machinery, as well as natural forms and reconstructions of Aboriginal tools. *Culture Heap* (1986–91) is a hybrid grouping of artifacts from both cultures; objects that Lang found, made himself, or altered in some way. The cast of an Aboriginal skull is filled with shredded pages from a book by Pastor Johann Georg Reuther, a Lutheran missionary who arrived in the Flinders Ranges in 1888 to work with the Dieri people. The Dieri people have not survived but their language does in the form of Bible translations undertaken by Pastor Reuther. The 'heap' also includes recent Aboriginal woodcarvings, fossils, farm implements like sickles and shears, a spanner inscribed with 'Fucking Mother Earth, Fucking anthropologists, Fucking missionaries, Fucking artists', a Catholic prayer book tied up with string made of human hair, mineral pigments in bark containers, spears, a jacket on which Lang has sewn mother-of-pearl buttons to form 'wearing somebody's jacket', wooden implements, the remains of dead animals found on the road, an emu egg with the inscription 'coconut: inside white, outside brown', a metal 'billy', bark bowls (coolamons), prehistoric stone implements and stone implements made by Lang, and *Terra Nulius* a 'caption' made out of arranged stone implements. This inventory of artefacts 'turns the space of difference into a transactional space, across which a variety of meanings and interactive effects may be articulated, and new possibilities raised'.[19]

NIKOLAUS LANG: ANSWERS TO QUESTIONS BY ARND SCHNEIDER AND CHRISTOPHER WRIGHT

The first time I came across anthropology was as a child, when after 10 o'clock mass one Sunday morning, I went to my father's mayoral office in Oberammergau and saw an illustrated anthropological encyclopaedia in his library. From then on I used to go there week after week for years to consume the contents. I was hooked on foreign worlds.

From the age of eight or nine, I started to collect things: minerals, fossils, artefacts from Papua New Guinea and eighteenth-century Oberammergau woodcarvings, insects and plants. By the time I was ten, I had the third largest alpine garden in the village.

My approach was empirical then and it is basically still so now. As an adult, I was able to pursue my childhood dreams. The main reason for my visual work in Australia over many years was and is my intense interest in Aboriginal culture, past and present.

What are the influences of anthropology on the contemporary art world?   The influence of anthropology on the contemporary art world is enormous and growing, due to globalization and the dominance of industrialized nations.

What have been the anthropological influences on your work, in either a generalized way or in the sense of specific works or theories? How does this influence manifest itself in your work and how do you encounter anthropology, through museums and exhibitions and/or through written work? Anthropological influence is an important part of my work. The techniques I often use are very close to anthropological ones. Before visualization of a project, I involve myself first with theoretical concerns, then confront myself with a particular situation on site or in the field, I collect and put objects into a pseudo-scientific order.

Do you see your work as either directly or indirectly addressing any anthropological questions or concerns ? What are they and how does your work achieve this?   Yes. See, for example, 'Your Eyes, My Eyes – Tindale's legacy' (*Nunga and Goonya*), a piece based on the anthropologist's Norman Tindale's research and field work, in this case the collecting of casts/busts of living Australian Aborigines in the 1930s. In my re-casts of one of Tindale's busts of a fifteen-year old boy, I exchanged the boy's opened eyes with my closed eyes, and in so doing , I am questioning the view of both the white and the black man.

What kind of anthropological methods do you, or could you, see as relevant for your own practice and for contemporary art in general?   As an example of the relevance of anthropological methods in my work and practice, in Australia I collected Aboriginal stone tools (with permission!) and on the basis of this collection, I knapped stone tools myself and put them to practical use on wood, stone, and bone. ('Culture Heap', *Nunga and Goonya*).

How has anthropology influenced your approach to the preparatory stages or 'research' that leads to particular works?   I was invited to participate in an excavation at Arkaroo Rock painting site in the Flinders Ranges, South Australia, in the 1980s. The study of the painting led me to an interest in earth colours. I looked for identical pigments in the surroundings, I was able to identify the materials that had been used for the painting – and started my collection, which led to my piece 'Colour Field – Ochre and Sand' in 1987 (see *Nunga and Goonya*). Thereafter, collecting earth pigments has been an ongoing process.

What chances do you currently see for new productive dialogues between art and anthropology? What would be the shared ground for any such dialogues? I can only see a chance for productive dialogue between art and anthropology if the white man questions his dominant view. Above all, anthropologists should question and examine contents rather than what often tends to happen, to aestheticize an object by putting it on pedestal, whereby the spiritual content of an object is frequently not taken into consideration.

What could be gained from dialogues between artists and anthropologists? The collaboration art/science could lead to a better understanding for both parties.

Would you consider, or have you, collaborated directly with anthropologists? What are the possibilities for this? I have no difficulties in collaborating directly with anthropologists, whether in a museum, or in the field, or privately. At the moment I am dedicating my next show to the anthropologists, Katharina and Andreas Lommel, and am including some of their work, paintings after Aboriginal rock art, produced in 1955 in the Kimberley, N.W. Australia. However, in the past I have experienced unbelievable misunderstandings, due to what I believe to be misplaced political correctness, when working in the field. When well-intended politics overshadow and replace science and clear thinking, the results can be disastrous.

If you are involved in any form of teaching practice or giving lectures, does anthropology form a component of this in some way, perhaps through the use of ethnographic examples or by referring to anthropological theories? As a professor at the Academy of Art in Munich, I offer lectures and workshops that are directly or indirectly concerned with anthropology to my students – for example, I recently gave a lecture on Aboriginal rock art – Wandjinas and Bradshaw style paintings, to be found in the Kimberley, north-west Australia, or I am preparing a workshop at the Academy on natural earth colours, which have a direct reference to rock art in Australia.

RIMER CARDILLO

Rimer Cardillo has been preoccupied with the plight of indigenous people in Latin America, and particular in his native Uruguay,[20] and beginning with his 1991 show *Charrúa y Montes Criollos* he has developed a consistent body of work engaging with their troubled history. Obliteration from the historical

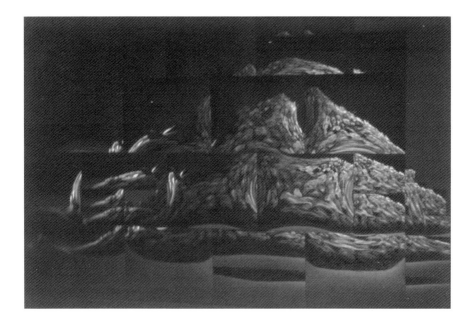

Figure 9.3. Rimer Cardillo. *Reflections*, 2001. Walls covered with mirrors photo silkscreen, dimensions variable, Venice Biennial, 2001. Courtesy of the artist.

record, as in the case of Uruguay's original people, the Charrúa, marginalization in present day Andean countries, and the resonances from the archaeological past have all been explored in his works.

Cardillo's approach is led by a great curiosity about the practical craftsmanship of past and present artists and artisans – the producers of those works we later encounter as 'archaeological remains' or 'ethnic arts'.

Cardillo shows a kind of 'material empathy' to the products of the other, yet he does not try to recreate it, but to achieve an understanding of the original working processes, and the spiritual motivations behind them, through his own work.

This is the reason why he has on many occasions collaborated with archaeologists and anthropologists, and also participated in excavations. Cardillo actively seeks dialogues with practitioners from those fields and also had his work shown at anthropological museums.

His installation *Charrúa y Montes Criollos* (Charrúa and Creole mountains), mounted in Montevideo in 1991, was intended as an explicit critique of Uruguay's official history, and lack of recognition of its indigenous past. It was shown as a large-scale, multi-media project at the Municipal Exhibition Centre and then at the Museo Fernando García (a disused railway station) where it has since remained on permanent display. The show involved the co-operation of other artists, anthropologists, artisans, lighting designers, musicians, and museum personnel. The artworks themselves evoke at the same time large ant hills called *cupi* in Guaraní, and ancient burial sites from the Charrúa, called 'little hills' (*cerritos*), both of which are typical of the rural Uruguayan landscape known as 'creole mountains' (*montes criollos*) – the former habitat of the Charrúa and other indigenous peoples. Yet the terms *cerritos* and *montes criollos* wiped out any explicit indigenous references. Cardillo studied the available literature on the Charrúa and also visited several excavation sites. He takes knowledge out of the specialized confines of academic archaeology (a rather small field in Uruguay) and makes it available, aesthetically and materially reworked, in the public domain in order to provoke a discussion of history, 'origins', and identity.

Cardillo uses techniques that display an intuitive empathy with the archaeological artefacts. What he terms the 'logic of indigenous construction'[21] implies the use of primarily those (non-industrial) techniques that, potentially, could also have been available to the Charrúa, using soil, charcoal, sand, ash, and ceramic casts of fossilised animals in the construction of an artificial installation-mound entitled *Ancestor with Fossils*, another variation is the *Cupi IV*. Cardillo transcends the immediate material vocabulary of indigenous people (by using wooden artifacts, plywood scored with electrical routers, photo silkscreens). At the same time, he retains references to ancient techniques and materials, which are evident in many of the pieces shown in a retrospective at the Bronx Museum of the Arts in New York and at his large installation for the Venice Biennial in 2001.[22] This kind of retrospective empathy with indigenous materials and techniques suggests that the now extinct Charrúa could have been, and in fact *are*, co-authors of Cardillo's artworks along with the artist and his collaborators who create them in the present.

Cardillo's appropriations question accustomed anthropological methodologies of representing other cultures.

RIMER CARDILLO: ANSWERS TO QUESTIONS BY ARND SCHNEIDER AND CHRISTOPHER WRIGHT

What are the influences of anthropology on the contemporary art world?
Traditional artistic techniques within disciplines are at this time no longer enough to express the ideas and feelings connected to the era we are living in. The current international art scene is involved in crossing boundaries between disciplines and thereby creating a richer vocabulary for artistic expression. There is a need, at this moment, for research and the creation of new venues to express concepts related to our historical present.

In a very remote *estancia* (ranch) in the northern part of Uruguay, I recently met with a gifted craftsman, a *guasquero*, that is an artisan who creates with rawhide all the artifacts needed to ride horses. He showed me a commissioned piece, a *rebenque* (whip) with a handle made of a shiny chrome car antenna. This given object was preciously incorporated into the woven strings or strips of hide. I tend to compare this behaviour with those seventeenth-century

German metalsmiths who marvelled at the new artifacts brought from the New World and incorporated them into very elaborated metal pieces – the series of objects with *ñandú* eggs (South American ostrich) and coconuts shells found in the Albertinum Museum, in Dresden. Most notable. The Coconut Goblet (the so-called Holzschuher Goblet), model by Peter Flotner, a goldsmiths' work attributed to Melchor Baier, Germanisches Nationalmuseum, Nuremberg.

Contemporary artists do not have all the answers in the political, historical, or artistic compartments, so they naturally embrace anthropological methods in their work.

What have been the anthropological influences on your work, in either a generalized way or in the sense of specific works or theories? How does this influence manifest itself in your work and how do you encounter anthropology, through museums and exhibitions and/or through written work? As a child I experienced an enormous attraction to objects made by early cultures like a set of humble ceramics attributed to the Charrúas, decorated with fingerprints, displayed at the Santa Teresa fortress, Rocha, Uruguay. Later, my attraction continued with my confrontation with the ethnographic museums of Hamburg, Berlin, and Leipzig, with all the marvellous collections of objects from the old German possessions in the Pacific islands.

My late childhood and adolescent years were spent at the general store owned by my father and uncle. The store was located in the frontier zone between the city and the countryside in Montevideo's outskirts. A place of confluence of unique human characters: gauchos, Indian descendants, factory workers, industrials, guitar players and singers, ventriloquists, billiard players, thieves, soccer players, bicyclists, *murgueros* (carnival actors), medicine men, and other unforgettable people, the store was a scenario for cultural anthropology.

Later in my trips in the Amazon forest in different parts of Latin America, I encountered again the 'frontier town', the limit between 'civilization' and the unknown: the jungle. In this shared space there is a confrontation between the most diverse cultures and the most diverse interests: economics, science, artistic, religious, and so forth. And everybody has a cautious and enormous curiosity to know about the other.

Do you see your work as either directly or indirectly addressing any anthropological questions or concerns? What are they and how does your work achieve this? Perhaps the need to create an iconography of the past, a past taken away by the ruling classes. American history is written by winners of wars against native peoples. How was the New World created? The structural model argues that language itself produces reality. What was the 'reality' of the other? How do we know the countless cultures that were exterminated and that continue to seep away, without leaving a written or oral history?

In 1991, I spent 5 months in Uruguay, I created an installation entitled *Charrúas y Montes Criollos*. The project opened at the Salón Municipal de Exposiciones and is on view at the Fernando García Museum in Uruguay. The region had been occupied for millennia by several native tribes. In 1516, the Spaniards arrived at the River Plate and started the conquest and the Charrúas defended their land in a war that lasted 300 years. In 1831, they were exterminated as was the indigenous flora (Montes Criollos), which at the beginning of the conquest covered 25 per cent of the land. Today, it has been dramatically reduced to a little over 3 per cent of the landscape.

What kind of anthropological methods do you, or could you, see as relevant for your own practice and for contemporary art in general? Cultural anthropology, field research, a personal and natural way of investigation reinforced by anthropological analysis, towards the investigation of indigenous cultures, their environment and the life of people is what I practice. Horacio Quiroga, a writer and early ecologically inspired artist from Uruguay, moved at the beginning of the twentieth century to San Ignacio a 'frontier town' in Misiones, Argentina. There, in contact with nature and its various people, he created a series of powerful short stories named. *The Stories of the Jungle*, published in weekly instalments in magazines and newspapers of Buenos Aires. I believe Quiroga is a model of an artist (albeit not visual) who integrates anthropological methods in his work to great effect.

Time and space, different layers of time, overlapping each other. In my travels I participated in many different experiences that involved people, animals and objects. I distilled from my life pieces of reality, almost short theatre plays. In my installations I want to obtain many layers of visual information by almost a reconstruction of images from a remote reality.

How has anthropology influenced your approach to the preparatory stages or 'research' that leads to particular works? My research and creation is guided by my being a product of two cultures, and by my lifestyle that moves from the Hudson Valley in New York to the Orinoco river in the Amazon. I inherited the attraction for the oral tradition. Many members of my family were notable story tellers, who told tales of immigrants and their life in the countryside. Some other narratives originated in Europe at the turn of the century. I recorded and keep recording stories from family and other people. These methods of approximation and knowing a system has fuelled my projects.

A good example was my contact with the Piaroa in the Ventuari River, Venezuela. I lived within these people: recorded conversations and interviews, kept a small journal fundamentally with drawings, took photographs, and witnessed the conflict and confrontation of interests in the area. Later, the rich information I collected was used to create an installation, *Pachamazon-Hunters-Jorobados- Missionaries* at Cavin-Morris Gallery in New York City in 1996.

What chances do you currently see for new productive dialogues between art and anthropology? What would be the shared ground for any such dialogues?   I think artists and anthropologists can benefit in their respective areas of work by overlapping their experiences. There is an area of creation and investigation in both categories; artists and anthropologists should learn from the other. There is intensive creative investigation on both areas.

I have been enjoying and investigating the 'will for form' by peoples around the world in different times and spaces. My first interest was visual, for instance, how people in contact with animals need to translate their respect and emotions through visual objects, 'art objects'. I collected clay horses made by farmers in Peru, Yugoslavia, and Paraguay during the 1960s, and they share the same formal characteristics. Different groups in contact with one rough material, in this case clay (and I suspect under similar environmental circumstances), react in the same formal manner (will for form). I also found this in old Greek, Mayan, Egyptian, and Japanese terracottas. I would benefit from working with an anthropologist to further develop a more cohesive investigation in this area.

I can't forget the reaction of anthropologists when they first saw my show *Charrúas and Montes Criollos*, a massive installation where the enigmatic, forgotten and extinct Charrúa tribe was metaphorically recreated. They confessed to me that they were inspired by this visual and physical experience, and that the experience would help them find new ways to approach their investigation. Based on this contact, a young anthropologist gave me photo material of recent excavations done in 1993 on the Atlantic coast of Uruguay. An important finding, a perfect bone bag from 2000 years ago, evidence of a second burial, was later manipulated by me and incorporated in a series of silk-screened canvases. This not only influenced my will to formal expression but also informed the conceptual background of my project.

What could be gained from dialogues between artists and anthropologists?   Common themes of interest bring together artists and anthropologists. In 1991, I worked with an anthropologist who was investigating the indigenous mixed-descent among the inhabitants of Uruguay. I made some contacts with these 'mixed blood' people and gave some other information to the anthropologist about possible areas where they could find people interested in knowing their native descendents.

Would you consider, or have you, collaborated directly with anthropologists? What are the possibilities for this?   In 1991, during my installation Charrúas y Montes Criollos, I worked closely with anthropologists. Later, in 1996, I had another intense collaboration in Venezuela and Paraguay when I was advised by anthropologists with experience in the Ventuari, Orinoco and Paraguay rivers and also in the Gran Savana and the Pantanal region.

If you are involved in any form of teaching practice or giving lectures, does anthropology form a component of this in some way, perhaps through the use of ethnographic examples or by referring to anthropological theories? I teach at the Art Department in the State University of New York, New Paltz. Rather than teaching from only an aesthetic point of view, my teaching methods depart from the individual and their own environment, past and present. I have students from all around the world; my class is a 'frontier town'. I teach according to the dynamic that you encounter in those zones. Rather than being technically oriented, my classes are focused on merging different media to express a concept. In my lectures, I talk about the origin of my works, the anthropological methods I have used, and I also bring in and show ethnographic objects.

Travels in a New World – Work around a Diasporic Theme by Mohini Chandra
Elizabeth Edwards[1]

Displacement, the silences of histories, the complexities of double identity, the longing for 'elsewhere', and the attempts at coherence in experience have become focusing themes of the late twentieth and early twenty-first centuries. Mohini Chandra's series of installation and video works, *Travels in a New World 1* and *2, Untitled* and *Album Pacifica* engage with the complex manifestations of these issues through an ongoing and developing conceptualization of histories represented within overlapping narratives of displacement and identity. The work emerges from an exploration of personal photographic practices and usages articulated in everyday experience within the Fiji-Indian community and its diaspora in Australia, New Zealand and North America. It explores not the 'facts' of history but the way diaspora histories are made, transmitted and actively maintained in personal engagements with the present. It is work that has developed from a personal exploration to a contemplation of multifaceted histories. As such, it addresses a community's colonial and postcolonial experience as represented in the overlapping discourses of a specific colonial situation and its aftermath. While at one level the work operates as a critique of colonial anthropological constructs of an essentialized 'Fiji', what concerns me here is the way in which it is heavily inflected through a methodology, which might be recognized as 'anthropological', in the sense of the reflexive and auto-critical methods that have emerged over the last two or three decades. In this context, I shall argue that Chandra's work constitutes a significant interface of anthropology and cross-cultural history with contemporary arts practice as differently figured sites for the translation of the quotidian, the subjective and the specific into broader representation, explication and theoretical analysis.

Chandra's starting point is her own family's history of double displacement. The first displacement was as indentured labourers brought from India to Fiji, under British colonial rule, to work the sugar plantations in the late nineteenth and early twentieth centuries. The secondary diaspora is that of the well established, successful fourth generation Indian community, who left Fiji in the face of the racial and economic pressures that followed a military coup in 1987. Continued racial tension between the Fijian and Indian communities was equally the cause of the rebellion, parliamentary hostage taking and the ousting of the democratically elected Fiji-Indian Prime Minister Chaudray by the Nationalist rebels under George Speight in 2000, and the continuing political and economic instability in Fiji. However the history of the sizable Indian community, established in Fiji to further colonial economic progress, is largely invisible in the powerful fantasies of both the nineteenth-century imagination and the twentieth and twenty-first century tourist paradise of an Edenic Pacific, despite the manifest success of the Indian community in business and professional life in the postindenture and postcolonial period. The conventional discourse was dominated by ethnographic notions of 'pure', 'traditional' Fijian culture, which in popular usage revolved around contrasting primitivist tropes of the 'noble savage' and 'barbarous primitive'. The Indian presence both disrupted such notions of the exotic and was marginal to colonial hierarchies that stereotype. Further, the colonial administration valorized the political and cultural institutions of traditional Fiji, isolating the modern, dehumanising and potentially disordered world of the Indian labour lines. Such a racialized discourse of nation – 'in' it but not 'of' it – was the source of tension and enforced an invisibility.[2]

This situation shapes the traditional photographic representation of Fiji. The indentured Indian labourers are absent from its frames, allowed to exist photographically only in terms of the celebration of colonial progress. Brigitte D'Ozouville has described this position in terms of a dualism of the visual field which reflects the dualism of the society.[3] While this released the Fiji-Indian population from the dominating colonial stereotypes, at the same time it orchestrated a silence and invisibility.[4] The divide between personal and private visibility and collective and public invisibility, which emerges in Chandra's works like *Album Pacifica*, is integral to the dualist discourse which reinforces the dualist vision of a racially divided society. It is these silent and marginal histories and the conceptual issues they raise that interest Chandra.

The focus of the work is on family – Chandra's own family as it happens – but it could be any of the parallel personal histories that constitute the Indian diaspora experience in Fiji and beyond. This intersection of the personal and collective, a key methodological node in anthropological translation and interpretation, was her starting point. Chandra is both insider and outsider, belonging to space both here and there, spaces defined as being 'elsewhere'. In comparison with many non-Western artists, for whom anthropological appropriations are linked to a critique grounded in identity construction, Chandra occupies a more liminal space. As in contemporary anthropology, there is a blurring of the boundaries of the spatial separation between 'home' and 'field' as the sites of different anthropological activities.[5] She moves through all the worlds with which her work connects and thus moves the visual into different spaces of articulation. In focusing on how individuals positioned their experience in relation to wider global dynamic she uses the significant features of contemporary Fiji-Indian culture and inserts specific human experiences into more generalized discourses of displacement and diaspora in which individual voices have become submerged. Yet simultaneously, her personal position offers coherence to her account and interpretation, demonstrating the world in which subject individuals live. For instance, an early work, *Fear of the Dark (Rivers of Blood)* (1996), is concerned with mixed marriages in the political climate in Britain in the 1960s. In it an historical family photograph, a wedding photograph, is printed on a mattress shot through with nails.[6] It was from such a subjective position that Chandra's thinking developed.

If the family and subjective experience are the starting point for *Travels in a New World* and other works, Chandra's methodology as an artist and the shape of her questions draws heavily on recent thinking in anthropology, postcolonial and subaltern studies.[7] Her work is constituted through the reflexive and expressive moment that has characterized these academic movements. The value of metaphor, figuration and narrative within style, and of novels, autobiography and diaries within genre, have become recognized as capable of contributing to cultural exploration, interrogation and description as well as to both anthropological and historical understanding.[8] This argument has been extended beyond textual forms to arts practice and photography as potential contributions to the representation of non-Western cultures.[9] Likewise anthropology itself, in Western tradition the privileged and authoritative voice in the description and definition of culture, has expanded into precisely the form of self-criticism and cultural criticism (including criticism of its own photographic forms) which, in recent years, has attracted those artists interested in questions of cultural construction, memory, cultural transmission and identity. As Marcus and Myers have argued,[10] both anthropology and contemporary art have culture as their object and are concerned with the construction and processes of cultural knowledge. Anthropology and art can no longer be wholly conceptualized in terms of an 'objective'/'subjective' opposition, but rather as complementary stances in cultural and historical interrogation. They are overlapping sites of tracking, representing and performing the effects of cultural difference and the values these imply within contemporary life, offering alternative strategies to a 'scientific' understanding of culture. The artist might be seen as operating in the space that Walter Benjamin saw as the true role of the translator. In grasping the genuine relationship between the original and a translation so as to articulate the intended effect and the essential nature of the original, it recognizes the space between them and its representation.[11]

Chandra's work not only draws on anthropological notions of cultural explication concerning identity, memory, social and cultural reproduction and continuity. It is situated on the more experimental edges of both anthropology and history through reinserting the subjective into a consideration and exploration of human cultural experience to expressive effect. She has used many of the techniques of contemporary anthropology in establishing the strong research base that informs all her art work: detailed archival research in institutions such as the National Library of Australia, Fiji Museum and National Archives, and the Mitchell Library in Sydney, extended fieldwork, interviewing and photo-elicitation, and collecting (in this case hundreds of family photographs that were rephotographed and documented to create a research archive). This constitutes an ethnographic process from which emerges a descriptive and analytical ethnography – for instance the oral history of Prasad studios, one of the major photographic firms serving the Fiji-Indian community.[12] At the same time, the methods embrace the serious fictions and signifying metaphors of more contemporary anthropological expressions.[13]

These form coherent tools for the exploration of the specifics within the multiple, overlapping, sometimes contradictory experience of Indians in Fiji. At the same time, in the tradition of postcolonial analysis and contemporary anthropological theory, such a methodology allows not only a destabilized authority but has experimented with ways in which to reinsert individual subjective experience, originating in fieldwork, in a refigured cultural discourse. Similarly one can argue that Chandra's artwork constitutes history 'writing' but in a different way. All the pieces in *Album Pacifica* and *Travels in a New World* are integral and insistent in their historical references. In the past, Western histories have been characterized by a construction that is dependent on linear narrative, causal links between facts, and on textual expression. Further, the idea of 'history' as collective and distant, and 'memory' as individual and immediate, is itself a product of Western conceptualization of 'history' and 'individual' that cannot be assumed to be universal. On the other hand, Pacific islander histories themselves have always been characterized by a blurring of those categories such as history, memory and myth that have defined the inclusions and exclusions of Western histories through which Pacific histories have been articulated. It is thus significant that many historians from the Pacific itself, as well as maintaining the traditional forms of oral history, have chosen to write in expressive forms such as poetry and short stories as expressions of historical consciousness. Similarly, Fiji-Indian articulations of memory and autobiography, inflected through performative fictions, play an important role in historical expression. Indeed '[c]ontemporary Fiji Indian fiction could be seen as the most closely related cultural practice to the photographic, in its autobiographical nature and in it the way that vernacular experience is expressed through a process of inscription.'[14]

Photography as a medium for a poetic historical strategy and photographs as the material focus for Chandra's conceptualization are at the core of her concerns. In using photography as the form of her 'text', Chandra is in effect writing in the 'vernacular', excavating the mainspring of both past and present, personal experience. Photography is the medium used extensively by the Fijian Indian community itself to articulate history, memory and identity. Within this, photographs link 'history-as-lived' and 'history-as-recorded', connecting personal histories to collective histories, and thus to regional histories and to global histories. Using the material practices of photography and video, as used by Fiji-Indian community, to explore its cross-cultural forms, the work becomes a continuation as well as a translation.

In her detailed concern with the relationship between history and lived, subjective experience Chandra avoids reproducing the 'bounded other', where

Figure 10.1. Mohini Chandra, *Travels in a New World 2*, (1997). Installation, video, film, sound, detail from six screen projection. Dimensions variable. Courtesy of the artist.

individuals are merely representative of specific societies. This again represents a conceptual link with contemporary anthropological thinking that departs from the kind of traditional conceptualization which understands individuals in terms of bounded cultural groups. Indeed the diaspora loci of much of Chandra's work mitigates against this construction of culture from the start. It is especially explicit in *Travels in a New World 2*. In five large video screens separate voices are filmed telling of their personal experiences against the background of the Pacific Ocean in Fiji, Australia, New Zealand, US and Canada (Figure 10.1). The subjects speak of a remembered family photograph common to all of them, made in the 1960s before they left Fiji. While the photograph is not seen by the speakers, in the installation they face it, a flickering ghostly presence uniting them, a still photograph extended in time on the video screen. Although absent for the speakers, its existence dominates, the photograph is somewhere, the linking indexical trace of times that unite and cohere different narratives.

The ocean itself is common to all the component videos in *Travels in a New World 2*. It forms the space that both unites and divides, the vastness and relentlessness of ocean becomes a potent metaphor for the distance over which diaspora links must be maintained. Like the cohering photograph, the edge of the ocean, the beach, is invisible but ever present. Here Chandra is taking up Greg Dening's model of the beach as the space of cultural negotiation, boundary and frontier, beginning and ending, and the liminal space of identities in flux.[15]

Diasporas are made up of many journeys, the intertwining of multiple travels, of arrival, leaving, settling and staying put. It is 'a text of many distinctive and perhaps even disparate narratives' which conclude and intersect in many different places and many specific historical experiences.[16] As the mosaic of separate voices in *Travels in a New World 2* move into the public sphere, through the video performance in a gallery space, they become less clearly distinguishable from one another, they merge into a more collective voice of memory of displacement. In this public performative and collaborative work, we are reminded that the photograph is the link that enables this particular family diaspora to 'catch up' or to 'construct' a missing life history. In speaking about the photograph the participants also raise issues of migration and identity through their own stories. In so doing Fiji is located as 'the imagined but denied "past homeland" and therefore as a contingent space in the continuing history of Fiji-Indian diaspora.'[17]

Yet Chandra's work is ambiguous. Individual experience is not only singular; it is socially informed in its overlapping themes and forms. In translating 'memory' into 'history' through analytical engagement, she brings to the fore an historical reality constituted in a series of unfinished encounters, linking different parts of the globe through a succession of unresolved political and economic dynamics. Ironically, within this, Western tropes of the Pacific paradise, of palm trees and beaches, become refigured and internalized as part of Fiji-Indian identity and its photographic expression. Memory cannot after all be wholly distinguished from imagination,[18] even as it connects to the outside world, recalling simultaneously real and imagined geographies, such as those that have dominated imagery of the Pacific. Thus the whole work is redolent with appropriations and Fiji-Indian expressions and refigurings of modernity. Pacific paradise is inflected through popular visual forms from religious iconography to Bollywood film.[19] If, as I have suggested, performative fictions constitute a legitimate cultural and historical voice, Chandra's source materials themselves include complex theatres of self that employ complex studio backdrops and montage in the creation of non-ordinary spaces through which to project identities.

The theme of photography and photographs as an expression of self and as a linking device is thus strongly interwoven throughout the whole series. In small communities individual and collective identities are so tightly bound and culturally specific that ideas of history position both self and community within a set of interrelated relations between past and present, self and other. The diaspora experience destabilizes this cohesion, but the photographs are used within the community to maintain and encourage the networks of community and thus encourage self-conscious formulations of identity and history. Related to this is the metaphor of *travel*, which is central to *Album Pacifica* and the *Travels in a New world* project. It is given its expression through a strong spatial and temporal sense, both in formal nature of the installation and as a metaphor working through the pieces. They suggest an interplay amongst peoples in different spaces which must characterize the encounters of displacement. Further, it erodes the rigidity of boundaries and perhaps points to social and cultural identity in terms of an intricate amalgam rather than an absolute or essentialist notion of 'identity'.

Photographs travel like people, they are material objects which circulate. They forge links across the spaces as in *Travels in a New World 2*. Despite the almost ritual production and exchange of images that constitute the making and use of family photographs, familial bonds are precisely expressed and experienced over the distance of displacement through the photographs. In their inclusion and exclusion in specific formations of memory, they denote absence as well as presence The significance of this is strongly articulated in *Untitled*, a video piece in which the pages of a family album are slowly turned, but one never reaches the end of the album – the story is unresolved (Figure 10.2). There is no sound, not even the sound of pages turning, only an eery silence of absence in the presence. The piece moves in and out of different spaces as the viewer sees different pictures but returns to the point of departure in a continuous cycle of repeated rememberings. Turning the pages through a narrative of images which always returns to the 'home', wherever that might be.

The interconnectedness of metaphor and materiality also resonates through *Travels in a New World 1* where the tea chests, a metaphor of both travel and

Figure 10.2. Mohini Chandra, *Untitled video*, 1997, installation, still from continuous Video loop, Dimensions variable. Courtesy of the artist.

Figure 10.3. Mohini Chandra, *Travels in a New World 1*, 1994. Photography, sound and mixed media. Installation, dimensions variable. Courtesy of the artist.

Indian labour, are imprinted with the specific – family photographs (Figure 10.3). The piece links identity and heritage. The tea chests constitute an apt metaphor for the transformed labour of indentured workers, referring back to the tea-plantation workers of the Indian subcontinent. Tea chests suggest storage and transport over space and time, just as the photographs printed on them here are vessels for the storage and transport of memory/history. The electrical wires that link and light the installation are transformed into ambiguous physical attachments to an unnamed centre, are they controlling leashes or umbilical cords? Which way are they travelling? This piece is the earliest of the series that now constitutes *Travels in a New World* and was the fertile ground from which *Album Pacifica* emerged. It sets up the ambiguities and complexities of histories' material traces which undergo a conceptual shift in *Album Pacifica*.

Movement over space and time is central to *Album Pacifica*.[20] This installation brings together photographs that had been scattered, as linking objects, through the diaspora. These photographs were collected during fieldwork and copied for the research archive. However, in the art installation Chandra concentrates not on the content of images but on the photographs themselves as *objects* as the focus of exchange and contemplation.[21] We see only the backs of the photographs: they do not show us 'people' but the marks of 'their-having-been-there' – names, dates and happenings barely legible – 'Died in New Zealand', 'Before departing for USA'. The 'invisibility' of the photograph's content works as a poetic in that it brings imagination into play. Through the textual accretions the atemporality of the photograph is punctured with the precise placement in time, a specific point of reference.

Such photographs – kept in wallets, pockets, carried in suitcases or positioned on walls and mantelpieces, are fragile relics linking past to future. Their inscriptions point to the social uses of the photographic object in a fragmented existence.[22] Yet in their 'blindness' the photo/objects have a resonance that requires feeling and thought. They require a willingness to engage with another world, and from a precise ethnographic point, to imagine their possible significances. The viewer is confronted with their own role in the construction

Figure 10.4. Mohini Chandra, *Album Pacifica*, 1997. Installation (100 pieces). Detail view, photography, black and white prints at 10 × 8 inches approx. Installation dimensions variable. Bluecoat Gallery, Liverpool.

of historical and cultural knowledge. Further, as an installation, *Album Pacifica* refers to ethnographically observed display practices of the way in which photographs operate in Fiji-Indian social space. The formal arrangement is that of framed photographs hung densely across a wall and high over doorways in the style of Fiji-Indian domestic space (Figure 10.4). Yet the way in which it inverts display practices in translating forms of visibility into invisibility, a with-holding of the image, also points to conventional institutional ways of displaying photographs. In another formation the latter idea is taken further; Chandra has produced the backs of some of the photographs as massively enlarged colour C-types prints. At first glance they appear as minimalist conceptual art performing in a gallery space. But multiple traces of the social object emerge as a dense layering – the invisible image that we *know* is there, the thumb prints and the pencilled comments – 'Nice Nice Ugly' of past and absent viewers. On what terms, after all, do we see photographs? Or know culture?

Such work, as I have discussed here, is not simply an idiosyncratic articula-tion of fragments of method and concept but a carefully formulated response and translation of research data. In this register, *Travels in a New World*, *Album Pacifica* and related works together function like a contemporary ethnographic monograph, translating and extrapolating general understanding from explicit individual observation and experience through a conscious subject positioning of the author. One is reminded of the anthropology of Rosaldo or Rabinow or the history of Dening. Conversely, throughout Chandra's work, larger social forces become represented and articulated as personal experience. This brings us back to the fundamental tension of history and of anthropology, the relationship between the specific and the general. Within this, displacement is not treated by Chandra merely as a discursive trope. She positions historical actors, however insignificant their lives, as active producers of that critical discourse, of *being* the diaspora, rather than being passive objects within it. This element, simultaneously reflective and active, is central to Chandra's work, as it must be ultimately to all histories. Again Benjamin's characterization of the translator as reinvigorating and marking a stage in a continued life seems relevant here. In the context of the political and colonial history of Fiji, the historical placing of specific diaspora experiences sharpens our ability to sort through the deadening multiplicities that can mask our understanding of the elements active in the constructs of difference.

No Borders: The Ancient American Roots of Abstraction

César Paternosto

> . . . the history of America, from the Incas to the present, must be taught in its smallest details, even if that means that the history of the Greeks archons is not taught. Our own Greece is preferable to the Greece that is not ours . . . we need to graft more of the world onto ourselves, but our Republics must be the trunk . . .
>
> José Martí, *Nuestra América*

> the only original creations of America are those of the pre-Columbian times[1]
>
> Octavio Paz, *The Labyrinth of Solitude*

After several years of absence from the art milieu of my native Argentina – I have been living in New York since 1967 – I had a show of recent paintings in the southern winter of 1977 at the Artemúltiple Gallery in Buenos Aires. The exhibit was well received, but the most significant outcome of this trip came after the show closed: I accepted an invitation to travel to the Andean region.

The trip – a sort of conquistador sweep – started in northern Argentina, where I visited the remains of Tastil, an ancient site discovered only in the late 1960s. For some inexplicable reason what called my attention was the agricultural area, where the grooves of the ancient furrows spoke of the toiling of humans long ago. After this first, indelible exposure to the remnants of the past, the trip progressed by land, crossing into Bolivia. After stopovers in the colonial cities of Potosí and Oruro, constantly climbing through the highlands I reached the capital city of La Paz at a dizzying altitude of more than 4000 m above sea level.

From La Paz, I visited the ruins of Tiwanaku, where I photographed, among other monuments, sections of the stone walls just because they reminded me of a Joaquín Torres-García constructivist painting. My first, spontaneous connection between past and present art was thus established. I then continued on to Lake Titicaca, which spans the border between Peru and Bolivia; it is the highest mass of water in the world: in the thin air and under the impious sunlight the deep blue waters make for a truly unforgettable experience. I later entered Peru, and riding the memorable local train, I reached Cuzco, the ancient capital of the Inca state, the 'navel of the world'. Sadly, of the former grandeur, only isolated stone walls remained, coexisting with (or rather submerged by) the colonial buildings as well as the modern edifices. From there, I visited the ruins of Ollantaytambo where the massive six-monolith monument that crowns the ceremonial area, known as the 'Temple of the Sun', struck me as a most compelling piece of 'minimal' sculpture (Figure 11.1). But there was more to come: while the experience of the 'lost city' of Machu Picchu and the magical ambiance of its setting was in itself worth the trip, it was the *Intiwatana* ('the place where the sun is tethered') – a stunning piece of abstract, constructivist sculpture that became, for me, almost the main focus of attention there (Figure 11.2).

In a sense, this trip to the Andean region was long overdue: pre-Hispanic art was not, on the whole, a foreign experience to me. I was born in La Plata, 60 km south of Buenos Aires, a quiet city of streets shaded by linden, *jacarandá*, maple and sycamore trees, which is the seat of the provincial government as well as of the formerly prestigious National University (Albert Einstein lectured at the Physics Institute in the 1920s) and its Museum of Natural History. The museum is well known in scientific circles around the world, mostly because of its paleontological holdings; it also houses a remarkable collection of ancient artifacts from the Andean region. When I revisited it towards the end of 1961, I was so strongly impressed by this collection, particularly by the Santa María and La Aguada white-on-black ceramics of northwest Argentina, that this vision inspired a series of paintings on which I worked through 1962. These paintings consisted of thickly built impastoes of dark earth tones into which I scratched

Figure 11.1. 'Temple of the Sun', ceremonial area, Ollantaytambo, Peru. Photo: César Paternosto.

Figure 11.2. *Intiwatana*, Machu Picchu, Peru. Photo: César Paternosto.

archaizing symbols of a rustic geometry.[2] But soon I felt that that approach was too 'provincial' and, by 1963, I drifted back to mainstream modernism, working within the parameters of geometric abstraction. By the end of the decade, and already living in New York, my painting evolved towards an even more radical abstraction: the frontal surface was left blank – just painted a stark white – and, instead, the enlarged sides of the stretchers were used to depict spare geometric notations, such as small squares, or contrasting bands of colours, which could not be seen from the usual frontal stance, so the viewer had to move sideways to find them (Figure 11.3).

It was at this point of my evolution when I travelled to the Andean region. Nothing in my previous exposure to pre-Hispanic art could have prepared me for the sudden 'discovery' of the abstract sculpture of the Incas – something that amounted to a true, undiluted revelation. It is interesting to note, on the other hand, that I had somehow 'readied' myself for that encounter: in the works I exhibited in the two previous shows before that trip (at the Galerie Denise René in New York in 1976 and the one already mentioned in Buenos Aires) I had already abandoned the 'modernist' white, turning to a gamut of pale earth tones, similar to those I found in the Andean landscape. More importantly, however, I had the overwhelming feeling that I had met with a vocabulary of forms, which, if distant and hermetic at first, was so very much like my own.

So, as fascinated as I was, I was still left with unanswered questions. 'Abstract', 'minimalist' sculpture in the heart of the ancient Andes? What did it mean? Why did I not know about them beforehand?

Figure 11.3. César Paternosto, *Who Was Who in Last Night's Dream?* 1970. Acrylic emulsion on canvas, 60 × 60 inches (152 × 152 cm). Courtesy of the Galeria Durban, Caracas-Miami.

Back in New York, my painting started to reflect this experience; whereas the *Intiwatana* in Machu Picchu was a genuine three-dimensional, 'in the round' sculpture, the six-monoliths of the 'Temple of the Sun' at Ollantaytambo with its carved reliefs lent itself for a frontal reading akin to painting, even in spite of its massiveness. It came to have, in fact, a lasting influence on my work: the frontal plane of my paintings remained monochrome, working now more deliberately within a limited range of earth and sandy grey pigments. But I also started parting the surface in two halves and mixing the paint with marble powder, thus obtaining a subtle textural diference in one of the halves (Figure 11.4). In spite of its intrinsic pictorial nature, this textural nuance evoked, for me, the subtlety with which the Inca mason-sculptors joined the giant mono-liths at Ollantaytambo. In sum, from the structural or compositional point of view, my paintings did not change as much as I felt 'reconfirmed' by the aniconic ancient monument.[3] Yet, it was my deliberate restriction to shades of earth pigments which was to carry, now with total awareness, the symbolical weight: colour became the signifier, a metaphorical reference to cultures closer to nature, to the earth – or, in Barnett Newman's words, 'the majestic force of our earthly ties and natures'.[4] In order to emphasize this connection, I titled these new works with the Quechua name of the month in which they were painted adding the ordinal numbers; for example, *Pawqar*, 2, 1978 (March, #2, 1978). At other times, I would use symbolic Andean words, such as *Inti* ('sun' in Quechua, the central god of their pantheon) or *Inti Raymi* (the name of the festival of the winter solstice which also designated our month of June), as well as names of archaeological sites, such as *Saywite*, and so forth.

Figure 11.4. César Paternosto, *Saywite*, 1977. Acrylic emulsion and marble powder on canvas, 64 × 64 inches (162.6 × 162.6 cm). Courtesy of the Galeria Durban, Caracas-Miami.

All this, I felt, meant a big step away from the dominant formalism of the 1960s. And, all along, I was telling the friends who witnessed these changes that if from Paris Picasso absorbed the lessons of the tribal sculpture in Africa, would it not be even more natural for a South American artist to evoke the experience of the monuments of the ancient American past?

Itching to know more, I began reading about pre-Columbian art; little did I know at the beginning that I was facing a many-sided, complex epistemological question. First off, I was directed to the 'social sciences' section of the New York Public Library, not to the art or architecture sections. Yes, of course, I soon discovered the fundamental treatise by George Kubler, who arguably more than anybody else did the most to establish the discipline of the art history of ancient America, wrenching it (as far as he could) from the clutches of anthropology and archaeology – as he himself states in his long and illuminating introduction. It was, indeed, crucial for my research: I found in Kubler a scant reference to the Incas' distinct inclination for carving rock formations, which, in his words, 'mark the presence of man without representing him in images or statues.'[5] Yet it was his reference to Heinrich Ubbelohde-Doering's *On the Royal Highways of the Inca* (published in German in 1941) that led me to the rest: the German archaeologist had surveyed, as well as photographed with a most sensitive eye, a comprehensive number of these sculptural manifestations so peculiar to the Incas. I was elated – there was actually much more to it than the 'Temple' at Ollantaytambo or the *Intiwatana*. I knew, by then, that I wanted to write extensively – a book, actually – on this subject, to, in the very first place, start defining these tectonic carvings as what they truly are: *sculpture*. For, twenty years ago, the sparse references in the literature referred to them, if at all, as 'architectural stonework', or just 'stone carvings', never as 'sculpture'.[6]

Soon it became evident that anthropologists, as well as art historians, were bound to evaluate the ancient American forms based on the projection of the (classical) Western canon, that is to say, the representation of natural forms; J. Alden Mason's assertion that 'The ancient Peruvians built no Parthenons or Colosseums, sculpted no Venus di Milo, painted no masterpieces' (*The Ancient Civilizations of Peru*, 1957) typifies the ethnocentric, even reactionary, canonical view; other art historians, like Kubler or Geoffrey Bushnell, exalted the figural sculpture of the Maya or Aztecs, calling the authors, without hesitation, sculptors. I have no difficulties with this; only that they were writing in the second half of the twentieth century and they were manifestly oblivious of the already established forms of geometric abstraction whereas I, as a life-long abstractionist, was able to read immediately those geometric reliefs or cubical carvings of the rocks *in situ* as meaningful sculpture.

There was more to this projection of the Western canon, though: while the prevailing figural representations in Mesoamerica greatly facilitated their perception of it as 'art' – as foreign to the Western canon as they might have been[7] – the central, most influential art in the Andean region was weaving. This medium, whose orthogonal matrix – the crossing of warp and weft – to a great extent influenced the totality of the sub-angular, planar Andean icon-ography (when not originating plainly geometric configurations) is, for the West, only a craft to be relegated to a second-class citizenship in a world dominated by the 'fine' or 'high' art; and so are the other artistic manifestations of ancient America, such as ceramics and metal works. Therefore, as the centrality of these practices is lost for the Western observer they remain, almost without exception, enmeshed within the nets of anthropology, archaeology, or ethnohistory. In other words, a fresh, new approach to these practices as the *central arts* of the ancient culture would bring about unforeseen conse-quences for the research in art and anthropology – a little of which I am trying to put forth here.

By the time I finished *Piedra abstracta*, in 1989,[8] I had found answers (mine, at least) to the 'abstract' nature of the Inca sculptural works. Based on Andean mythical narratives it could be surmised that stone was infused with a numinous sense: the first humans had been fashioned in stone; or turned into stone because of misbehaviour; or else they became combatants who came to the rescue of the Incas at a crucial point of their history. In short, the minimal modifications inflicted to the stone were their way of exalting, or releasing the intrinsic symbolism of the material; or, as in the rock formations of Kenko and Suchuna in the vicinity of Cuzco, their modality to emphasize the sacred-ness of a space.

Furthermore, I found out an even more fundamental aspect of the ancient American art practices: that, unlike in the post-Renaissance West, they were inextricable from their symbolical or practical functions. In other word: if, just as in our culture, the ancient practices involved deliberate modifications of matter (carving of stone or wood; painting on walls or ceramics; modelling, as well firing clay; metal working, and so forth), unlike ours, and from the start, those manipulations were intended for a *use*, a use that could be graded from the ceremonial/symbolical to the practical. In other words, ancient America never developed the media for a 'pure' artistic activity; consequently, the purely aesthetic activity was foreign to its inhabitants. It was just as well that the (Western) distinction between 'art' and 'craft' or, for that matter, 'decoration', as distinct from 'high' or 'fine' art, made no sense to them.

The English translation, *The Stone and the Thread*, was also to carry new insights: taking stock of the totality of the arts in ancient America, it appeared clear that if during the colonial times they were displaced by, or otherwise blended with, the European practices, then after the Latin American countries declared independence from Spain, the scientific paradigms arrived. Later, the creation of the Societé des Américanistes in Paris in 1876 formalized the nineteenth century's positivist criterion, enforcing the perception of the aboriginal symbolic production as 'artifacts'; that is to say, the material culture that provided the auxiliary documents for anthropology, archaeology or ethnography. Thus the official pattern that still prevails was established, and, not least, a *border* was created.

This reception of the scientific paradigms was a substantial part of what I call the neocolonial statute – the body of laws or educational systems inspired by the Enlightenment and established by the ruling elites of European descent to create norms of behaviour and cultural representations intended to perfect the replica of the Old World in the Americas. Acting as internal colonial powers the creole elites continued with the destruction of the aboriginal cultures by institutionalizing a most effective and enduring denial. (That is why in Argentina, for instance, we never learned at school that the north-western part of the territory had been part of the Inca empire: somehow 'history' began with the arrival of the Spaniards. Or, worse, ponder this fact: in 1894 the Bolivian army used some of the sculptures at Tiwanaku for rifle practice[9] – the Latin American armies being, of course, the epitome of the neocolonial powers).

What has ensued is a conundrum of ambiguous, still unresolved cultural and epistemological situations of which one thing remains unabatedly clear: even if we have now institutionalized the discipline of 'pre-Columbian *art*', it still remains isolated, removed from mainstream (Western) art history and, consequently, their masterpieces are largely consigned to anthropological or natural history museums, languishing, one might say, in the unresolved status of half breeds, scientific specimens yet of an inescapable, tantalizing beauty. Neither the specialized collections, nor the departments of basically Europhile encyclopedic museums, entirely dispel the notion that we face an isolated, self-referential phenomenon.

The ambiguity is palpable: if there is a measure of recognition, all along the prefix *pre*-Columbian, *pre*-Hispanic is implying that which was *before*, alien, a perennial reminder of an *otherness*, and therefore something that we better put in the hands of specialists, scientists or *pre*-Columbian art historians. In fact, it is this intellectual alienation (a ghettoization, actually) rather than the physical separation in specialized museums which is most deletereous for a desegregated conception of an art of the Americas that would seamlessly encompass the ancient arts and architecture with the arrival of the European models.[10] All the more so since the more idiosyncratic ancient works, the aniconic *horizontal* sculpting of rock formations performed by the Inca (as opposed to the figural verticality of the Western sculptural tradition) (Figure 11.5), or the enigmatic mega-drawings scratched on the Nazca arid pampas (Figure 11.6) seem to resonate stronger than ever in the art of the second half of the twentieth century – not to mention the planarity of the textile-grid-generated forms,which, though being an entirely independent sequence, we cannot avoid noting its long precedence over the modern evolution.[11]

This fracture is exacerbated by a sorry symmetry of deeply entrenched misperceptions that epitomize the neocolonial culture: on the one hand, you have the nationalistic/ethnic appropriation of the ancient American traditions by the modern political entities that evolved in the areas in which the ancient cultures peaked, namely, Mexico, Peru or Bolivia. On the other, you have the willful alienation from those traditions by the self-perceived 'whiter' peoples of the southern cone of the continent: 'We don't have Indian blood' you hear them say often enough. So, following the logic of both views, we could ask, then, whether the Italians or the Greeks are the only ones entitled to the Renaissance or Classical traditions.

None of these questions matter when the artists of the Americas 'discover' the ancient arts. They find no borders to be crossed. As I described it at the beginning, there is an *instant recognition of the art* in the *art*ifact, not, by any means, an appropriation. This would occur, in my view, *only* when there is an outright lifting of the ancient motif on the part of the artist. Though, lately, foggy postmodernist theory does not disparage 'quotation', as the euphemism goes, the exposure to the ancient arts should function as a motivation, a source of inspiration, a springboard that should be translated into a visual metaphor. This would be the result of a transformation, an equivalent image that the artist finds by distancing him/herself from the source, yet keeping a connective tension with it.[12]

On the other hand, and in the particular instance that concerns me here, what for anthropology, or even current art history, is an almost incidental, mute, 'geometric decoration' in a textile or a ceramic vase, for the artist becomes a learning experience, a 'lesson in abstraction', which, reverberating with the ancient symbolism embraced by the social group, in the receiving process bestows a generic sense of *cultural validity* to a modern abstraction practised in the Americas.[13]

Although I cannot deal extensively with the subject here, let me point out that some geometric designs, known as *t'oqapu* – so often overlooked as 'decorations' – that appear on Inca tapestry tunics (Figure 11.7), or engraved

Figure 11.5. Sculpted rock. Inca period. Suchuna area. Cusco, Perú. Photo: César Paternosto.

Figure 11.6. Trapezoidal figure. Nazca desert, Peru. Photo: César Paternosto.

Figure 11.7. Inca tunic with t'oqapu designs; interlocked tapestry, cotton and wool. South Coast of Peru. 35³/₄ × 30¹/₈ inches (91 × 76.5 cm). The Dumbarton Oaks Research Library and Collections, Washington DC.

as well as painted on *keros* (ceremonial cups) have been deemed to be semantic units, akin to the Chinese logograms. The entire Andean cultural context, pre- and post-Hispanic, appears to support the ancient viability of the system as an efficient, though partial, substitute for writing, even in spite of the fact that their decipherment did not progress beyond a limited number of signs. Recently, though, this research is gaining qualified reception among Andean scholars. In short: we face here the strong possibility of overturning once and for all the traditional sterilization of geometric designs as 'decoration', as well as accepting that, on the contrary, they may have been 'full of language'.[14]

Artists, like myself, may travel to the archaeological sites or may visit the anthropological collections, but it is not in pursuit of a scientific taxonomy. They are there in search of an art tradition, absorbing the lessons of art history that the mainstream discourse has denied them. Again, it is this wilful search, this voluntary connection with the art of the past in a basic attitude of learning that confers cultural significance, a meaning, to a true abstraction of the Americas and which differentiates it from analogous or isomorphic approximations.

In 1946, Barnett Newman organized an exhibition of aboriginal art from the Pacific Northwest Coast for the inauguration of the Betty Parsons gallery in New York, gathering objects from private collections as well as from the American Museum of Natural History. Edmund Carpenter acutely observed that as the organizers of the show transported the pieces across town 'they declassified them as scientific specimens and reclassified them as art'.[15] This is precisely what happens in the artist's mind.

The encounter with the aboriginal arts of the Americas historically echoed the European *avant garde*'s embrace of the tribal arts arriving from the colonial dominions. Yet that encounter meant, for the American artists, a recognition of a different sort: the Mexican muralists incorporated the Mesoamerican iconography as a substantial ideological component of an art of heightened social awareness aimed to a large public; Torres-García extolled, and was decidedly influenced by, the 'geometric thought' he found in the Andean arts, advancing the utopian vision of a (his) telluric constructivism as *the* art of the Americas; early in his career, Barnett Newman saw in the aboriginal traditions – thus summing it all up – a 'common cultural heritage'.[16] In other words, if they could not deny the Western tradition they inherited, by fusing it with the perception of the native arts – the *only* arts originated in America – they sought a distancing from the European traditions.[17]

Now, if for the Mexican muralists there was a rather smooth transition from one figural tradition to another, the search for the structural principles of an abstraction of the Americas involves a process that is implicitly as profoundly political as the muralists' message – though less vociferous. Those structural principles are to be found in the textile grid, in the designs on ceramics, or in the cubical shaping of the stones, all of which have been characterized in the dominant anthropological or artistic discourse as 'decorative' or 'ornamental'. Yet, as they are assimilated by the artist, they re-emerge in the artistic conscious-ness as *art sources*, re-gaining the centrality they had in the ancient past, or, as the case may be, in the surviving so-called 'ethnographic' cultures.

That re-emergence in the artistic consciousness means – at the very least within the reduced environment of the arts – a cultural retrieval, a modicum of recomposition of a fractured culture, the overcoming of the old segregation of the aboriginal arts.

All along, my immersion in the original art of the Americas had stimulated an eagerness to know more about other art traditions in which geometric forms are pregnant with symbolic meanings. Back in the early 1980s, I learned from the Tantric *yantras* and the mandalas the possibility of a different, meditation-inducive geometric structures. In the 1990s, the series of 'Porticoes' and 'Facades',[18] a group of structured canvases with actual rectangular apertures on the pictorial screen, reflected the influence of the 'sun doors' in Amerindian, Egyptian or ancient Greek architecture. Lately, my renewed interest in the grid, within which I inscribe lines (the '*hilos de agua*') spaced at rhythmic intervals and traced with water colour pencils, issued from the textile structure rather than from the modernist grid.

Finally, after all those years writing on the sculpture of the Incas, I finally embarked on projects involving ideas for three-dimensional works I had put off many times. In 1991, during a month-long residence at the Study Center in

Figure 11.8. César Paternosto, *Northeast Window*, 1995. Pigmented cement sculpture, 13½ × 24 × 24 inches (34.2 × 61 × 61 cm).

Bellagio, on Lake Como in Italy, happily unhindered by daily chores, I began working on a series of wood models, which, after further reworkings, I later cast in cement (in order to colour them I added earth pigments while the mix was still dry) (Figure 11.8).

Though realized in a modest physical scale, with these works I was coming full circle, for it had been my perception of the Inca stone sculptures which started this long process of self re-education. In all, it has been more than twenty years of a transformative and spiritually nurturing experience that not only has broadened my view of art as a touchstone of human culture, but also has served me as an efficient antidote *vis-à-vis* the rampant commercialism or the maddening pursuit of celebrity, to name but two of the most pervasive ills that sap the true creative energies of today's art.

ACKNOWLEDGEMENTS

I thank my wife, Cecilia Vicuña, always my first reader, for her suggestions regarding the focus of the text. Dr. Arnd Schneider and Gabriel Pérez-Barreiro also made pointed observations. My gratitude also goes to Rosa Alcalá who, as usual, generously came to the rescue in making my non-native English thoroughly readable.

Carlos Capelán: Our Modernity not Theirs

Jonathan Friedman

THE ANTHROPOLOGICAL NATURE OF ART?

Carlos Capelán is a very down-to-earth person who has specialized in part in the collection of earth from far corners of the world. He is very well travelled and has lived in Europe, and the Americas. He now lives with his family in Santiago de la Compostela, renowned historical pilgrimage site, a site of healing and gathering in moist green hills. Life is not art, but lives can make sense in ways that art can reveal. Capelán has dealt with the concrete, with the collection and ordering of the things of the world. His art is about the gaze itself, about assemblage and the making of sense. It is in a very important sense about modern life, the modern world and about the modern subject and its others. His work has varied with his career and I cannot do justice to it all. I am primarily concerned with a series of art works that have taken the form of exhibitions. While some anthropologists busy themselves trying to grasp the art of the other and playing museum by collecting other people's representations and products, Capelán does something that is on the surface a parallel activity to this museology but is simultaneously a structural inversion of the latter. The anthropologist has and still is somewhat blind to this activity itself – to collection. In fact much recent anthropology has become increasingly ensconced in precisely the genealogical mode, one that seeks to identify objects by tracing their origins: 'who are you really?' 'where do you really come from?' This is a field that has been virtually exploded by intuitions of mobility. There are prerequisites for this current situation. Quite a few years ago, for those who remember, there was a self-conscious theorizing in the field, a concerted effort to account for and explain the realities that we confront as anthropologists. This was a modernist predisposition that was at home in modernism with its thrust toward bigger and better understandings of the world. This was a spirit of adventure of movement toward new and unknown horizons. This was an anthropology that saw the museum as a mere appendage, a spin-off of a larger project – the filing cabinet of research. After all we had to have our ethnographic artifacts stored somewhere! There was a period in the 1960s a final surge or high point of modernism in which museums were seen as the enemy, as inhabited by old fashioned collectors who had no interest in tearing down old-understandings to make way for the new. Cultural objects were simply another arena, a low status arena at that with respect to the soaring adventures of theory.

This was a fragile world, but exhilarating for some. At its purest and most powerful it had room only for 'good ideas', good argument and the modernist mechanisms of theoretical breakdowns and theoretical transcendence. But this world was dependent on a population or generation of intellectuals who had no interest, or only peripheral interest, in formal status, were not worried about jobs, which they all seemed to obtain, or believed that they could obtain, and could occupy themselves with a purely intellectual and social engagement for society as a whole. Now this world never existed, especially in the social and humanistic fields, but it was an ever-present ideal type, a tendency that formed the ultimate last resort of seminar disagreements. Its egalitarian openness, to the degree that it existed, depended upon a certain social and especially economic security, which made revolting intellectuals a viable social phenomenon. The paradigm began to crack in the mid-1970s with the economic downturn throughout the West. The future began to fade rapidly, a future that was the anchor of a modernist present. Without a future to stabilize the movement of the present a surging desire for security began to emerge, one that became increasingly fixed in fixity itself, at least for the great majority of those who began to find themselves without jobs. But there was also modernist spin into the postmodern, the deconstruction of all fixity, of all forms of classification, understood as imprisonment. Category-bashing became a new pastime. One of the hallmarks of modernism was the self-evident nature of the project, the idea of moving forward, even into the unknown, the trajectory of the self, of society, of mankind, all forming a cosmic success story in which the contradictions of the present could be overcome through the struggle for a new world. As this project disintegrated there ensued a new kind of critique, one that aimed at deconstruction for its own sake (exemplified by Derrida)[1] at the same time as most people were on a quest for new identities. Deconstruction is no stranger to modernism of course, but it was formerly part of a larger project of critique and construction rather than an end in itself.

THE INVERSION OF MODERNISM AND THE RETURN OF THE COLLECTION AS MODE OF SIGNIFICATION

The primitivism of the modernists was a project of assimilation, a discovery of form in itself that could be transferred to the project of modern art. It was neither a return, nor a longing for the primitive as such, not a sign of the failure of modernity, but an expression of its success. The decline of modernism has ignited a new search for the primitive, one that is more focused on what it has to offer us in the more general sense, its holism, wisdom, closeness to nature. This is another kind of project, one that turns away from the modern and attempts to root the subject or re-root the subject. This is only one moment in the change, however, because there are those who are still located at the locus of the modernist position even if the latter is devoid of content. These are the new postmodern elites who instead of *roots* would have *routes*, who cherish displacement and deterritorialization as a mode of being. This latter development emerged after the previous plunge into indigeneity and has led to a new oppositional configuration between cosmopolitanization and localization, in social reality, between new elites and downwardly mobile majorities. But both cosmopolitans and locals are embedded in the sea change that is the decline of modernism, both are ensconced in the discourse of rootedness. The difference is one of position alone, whether the roots are entangled in elite identities or homogenized in territorialities.

It is in such circumstances, beginning, we recall, with the decline of modernist theorizing, that the genealogical mode becomes dominant. When modernist anthropologists deconstructed locality, which they did at least as early as Max Gluckman, they did so in order to reconstruct it as a produced reality. When postmodernists deconstruct locality they do it in order to attack it as a bad idea, smacking of cultural essentialism, ethnic absolutism and ultimately and by some sort of quite mystical if popular association, fascism. This is no longer an attempt to understand and explain but a moral critique. It seeks not to understand how placeness exists but seeks to advocate nomadism as an idea-type, modelled on the nomadic existence of the travelling academic. Otherwise the apotheosis of diasporas, known empirically for their endogenous, endogamous and of necessity strongly bounded existences, could never have occurred. It is in such circumstances, as well, that collection and museological thought has again come to the fore.

The first official cultural anthropologists were absolutely clear about the difference between genealogy, the filiation of objects, and the structured nature of ways of life that make use of so many imported objects in their own making of specific worlds of meaning. But this period was the first move away from a previous era of genealogical modes of thought in which the identity of objects, people, peoples were the crux of thinking about the human world, a kind of thinking that produced diffusionism.[2]

ART ENCOMPASSING THE ANTHROPOLOGIST

Capelán's work is very much about collection but, unlike that of the anthropologists, it is distanced from itself, it is an imaging of collection itself, completely self-conscious. His exhibits are cosy collections of the world, enveloped in warm brownish hues, but they open up a series of questions of utmost seriousness. The light is soft, like in a living room (see Figure 12.1). There are artifacts and substances gathered from the ends of the earth, roots are gathered in the living room, but there are comments by various and sundry intellectuals that do not refer directly to the objects but are themselves objects. The walls are also covered by maps of the world in outline, maps that concentrate the

Figure 12.1. *The Living Room* installation, Graz, Austria, 1996. Courtesy of the artist.

experience of collection, of the world in the room. The world is the representation of the collected things, the localization of the global in the hall of the museum or gallery, but it is also the representation of the commentators, the representations of the representations written on the same walls on which there are reading lamps and Capelán's well-known images of powerful primordial humans striving for the unattainable. The colours are fashioned of real earth. This is concrete art. The books are piled and held down with rocks. This is the earth, the whole earth at home. It is controlled, yet there is a tension and an ambivalence. There is a museum case, the kind well known from early museological exhibits where stone tools were aligned by size and shape in a mechanical pattern accompanied by minute descriptive labels. Capelán's museum case contains finger nails arranged in the same fashion. The irony is striking. Is this a parody of the museum? Yes and no! It is more! It is a collection of human parts, fingernails arranged carefully by size. Fingernails are the dead clippings of human beings which represent or express the hands from which they come, hands that did important social things. Here the nails are abstracted from their living context and aligned according to a schema that is irrelevant to their concrete use yet expressive of something else, the order of collection itself. On the walls of this collection are painted figures. They are stereotyped figures like the collections themselves, but they represent whole human beings stripped bare and clearly primordial . . . they are in struggling and striving movement and perhaps in anguish as well. These are figures that have also appeared independently in other parts of Capelán's work. They are constructed as muscular human forms seemingly constituted by weblike non-Euclidian geometrical maps or perhaps wires. Something is wrong. The collection is disturbed and perturbed by this odd combination. This is not the mere collection of the world. It is literally the *drawing* of the world into a locality in which the tensions and contradictions emerge in concrete forms. Nails and human figures, often in movement, on the run, not the cosmopolitan run but the run toward another realm, toward the primordial perhaps, toward that which seems perennially lost in the collection itself with its fragments ordered according to other rules.

These exhibits are about the world as a collection, about the relation between collectors and collected, about centres and peripheries, however much positions may be changing. They are about the creation of identity by means of collection as well. We are what we place in our spaces. These are living spaces, living rooms, rooms as consumption, worlds populated by the objects of the world. But this is emphatically our world, our modern world, a world of the book of the text of things-in-interpretation where the interpretation is never inscribed in the things. It is a world broken and fragmented, held together only by the closed space within which we practise our collections. The anthropologist is usually unreflexive, even in his newfound hyper-reflexivity, of the degree to which he is implicated in the project that he takes for given. Let me illustrate.

James Clifford, not an anthropologist, but closer than most to the anthropological project, studies exhibitions and museums in his latest and perhaps most brilliant book *Routes*.[3] In an otherwise fascinating discussion of the exhibition *Paradise*, which deals with Papua New Guinea today, he clearly has a problem with distinguishing his own perspective from those that he analyses via the exhibition, if that is even a possibility that ought to be entertained. The issue is a war shield, traditional in all respects except for the fact that it has an advertisement for a local beer painted on its surface. The exhibitor asked the artist for an explanation and was told that beer is associated with life force and with warfare and that just this beer is consumed before battle. In other words for the locals the beer advertisement is in no sense 'matter out of place'. But for the erstwhile anthropological observer the object seems odd combining the modern and traditions. It is categorized as hybrid for this reason. But whose reason is it, the reason of the producer of the user or of the western consumer of the image itself. There are clearly differences and tensions here, but they are eliminated in favour of hybridity. Kwakiutl Indians who performed potlaches with sewing machines a hundred or more years ago were also engaging in hybridity. But without knowing it. What is missing in this analysis, otherwise so astutely focused on the anthropologist, is precisely the classification of the classifier. What is the act of classifying something as hybrid?

Capelán's exhibits are structured so as to avoid this problem because their very organization concerns the classifier as well as the classified. The visitor to the exhibit is an observer of the act of collection as well as the content of the collection. As art, of course, it is not explicit and abstract but implicit and concrete. But this interpretation is clearly a strong possibility. In a recent interview, Clifford addresses this problem in the sense indicated here.[4] He stresses that life is about construction, about articulation in the here and now, not about the meaning of the genealogy of elements but about the way that they constitute lived realities. This does not mean that there is no history, but that the latter is a negotiation of continuities in the formation of the present. The negotiation is contradictory as well. The articulation is fragile and historically unstable.

These exhibits could well be the objects of ethnographic investigation. Here I have suggested that they are structured to say something about the state of the world. This is not a statement of the mere conglomeration of difference. It is collection, of course, from the point of view of the assumed subject of Capelán's exhibits, but it is a collection in tension, a tension between Western classification and the forces that appear on the wall in the figures of those who are not so easily captured. Of course, this difficulty is not the difficulty of real conquest and colonization, it is the difficulty of Western modernist identity itself, which is predicated upon the attempted transcendence of the primitive defined by the repressive-expansive act of civilization itself, repression in the body, expansion overseas. But Capelán is doing something special in his art: he is parallelling and parodying the anthropological project, the project of collection of the other. Here is the humour but also one of the powers of this artistic production.

ART AND MODERNITY

Art is an act of construction. In structuralist interpretations it lies between the bricolage of *la pensée sauvage* and science. The former is the recombination of elements expressive of the same underlying structure in which the goal of the expression is precisely the exploration of that structure, a structure of meaning, the latter is the creation of new structures that refer to the same natural or otherwise objective phenomenon. Whereas the former are concrete rearrangements of reality, the latter are abstract statements about reality. Scientific theories do not express variable forms of fixed underlying realities of the social, but are themselves statements of such realities. Different theories of the same reality emerge via the elimination of former theories and they are not, by definition, reducible to variations on the same themes. Art in this scheme of things is the creation of representations of the world that contain an interpretation of the world in their very organization. Art is both concrete and abstract, it is a form of reality that embodies an insight into that reality. This is the aesthetic core of art, its ability to arouse insight and interpretation via its configuration of concrete form. Even abstract art is concrete in this respect. Art is as free as science in its ability to fix its gaze on any aspect of the world. In this approach art is a product of modernity or of modernities. It requires distance with respect to the world. The distance engendered by modern sociality is one based on alterity where the individual endures a certain separation from his own practices, from his social identity and his forms of experience. It is perhaps an illusion to assume that this state of affairs is particular to modernity, but there is some indication in the anthropological literature that this is indeed the case.[5] If it is not the case then existence is basically universal in form, differing only in what specific content it has. I shall not argue about this absolutely essential issue here but shall simply assume that the differences in worlds are truly existentially significant and not mere matters of the rules, objects and symbols that enter into them. In such terms artistic forms in the mode of *la pensée sauvage* are necessarily extensions of that mode, as a mode of existence.[6] They are, thus, aesthetic without conforming to the notion of art as a modern endeavour. And insofar as art can be said to exist in non-modern situations, I would argue that such situations are in fact equivalent to those of the modern as forms of social experience in that they permit the kind of distanced insight that is typical for art as an activity. This would imply that there are always spaces of distanced reflection in all societies even if they are more or less restricted. It also implies that, as implied in the work of Lévi-Strauss, the real world is not divided into modern thought and traditional bricolage. But the combinations of different kinds of thinking vary in important ways. In this sense, the freedom of the modern artist is not of his own making but a product of a situation of separation, even of alienation from any particular life form. This mode of existential alterity is not a historical universal and where this is not the case the freedom of the artist is similarly curtailed, focussed on a more limited set of objects.

SAME PROJECT, DIFFERENT MEANS

Capelán's constructions are concrete spatial forms within which we move. They are anthropological spaces as well, spaces of the collection of the world, the localization of the global. The writing on the wall is also the concretization of the reflexivity of this imploded world. It is not meant to exist outside of the exhibition of objects but it is part of the concretization of the total work. Reflexivity is just as much part of the world as that which is reflected upon. This is not a bowl of fruit. It is not the world in a grain of sand, the penetration of a pair of hands by Rembrandt. It is another project indeed. It is an attempt to encompass a political reality. If it is hybrid in any sense, it is our hybridity, hybridity for us, the effect of collection itself. Collection always has a subject and the identification of the world always occurs from a position. Capelán's art is an exploration of this position, our position. It is not a study of other people's realities, but of our own. Isn't that how it can resonate with our experience? Isn't that what art is all about? The artist claims to be a modernist. This is, perhaps, because he is aware of his own position in the world. There is no conflation of Indian consciousness with his own. True art must be produced from within a given world of experience. We can not produce art out of other people's experience. Some anthropologists of a globalizing persuasion might tend today to deny that there are different experiential worlds but this is not the aim of Capelán. To deny the real differences in experiential worlds is the ultimate imperialist act, as Sahlins has suggested in another context, since in the name of globalization it denies to others their specificities even if they do it with Coke.[7] No real artist could ever confuse the issues, only anthropologists and other academics.

The Case of Tattooing
Nicholas Thomas

In a 1995 essay, 'The Artist as Ethnographer', Hal Foster identifies an 'ethnographic turn' in contemporary art, which he finds problematic on a number of grounds. This development owes something to the long-standing mutual engagement between art and anthropology, but reflects a new sense of a shared paradigm. If anthropology is seen as a self-critical and contextual science of otherness in the field of culture, it matches what Foster calls the 'rote' demands and values of contemporary art and theory. 'It is along these lines that the critical edge is felt to cut most incisively', he suggests; hence 'the ethnographic mapping of a given institution or a related community is a primary form that site-specific art now assumes.' Foster acknowledges that there is a productive side to this trend – in, for instance, the recovery of suppressed histories, and in innovative forms of collaboration between artists and communities – but is in the end sceptical. He cites the well-known works by Lothar Baumgarten, which feature the names of indigenous peoples of north and south America, often mistranscribed or imposed by explorers and ethnographers. He suggests that

> these names return, almost as distorted signs of the repressed, to challenge the mappings of the West: in the neoclassical dome [of the Museum Fredericianum in Kassel] as if to declare that the other face of Old World Enlightenment is New World Conquest, and in the Frank Lloyd Wright spiral [of the Guggenheim] as if to demand a new globe without narratives of modern and primitive or hierarchies of North and South, a different map in which the framer is also framed, plunged in a parallax in a way that complicates the old anthropological oppositions of an us-here-and-now versus a them-there-and-then.

This sounds like approbation, but Foster points to the 'complication' that such interventions in museums are often commissioned; they are imported critiques, which may do more to validate than subvert the institution. Outside the art gallery he finds that things are no better, that quasi-anthropological collaborative art projects involving communities typically do more to recapitulate 'a remaking of the other in neo-primitivist guise' than produce some form of genuine participation, or question the authority of the ethnographer.[2]

Much of what Foster says is acute, but a curious equivocation that runs through the essay comes to the fore in his concluding paragraph. 'The other', he writes

> is admired as one who plays with representation, subverts gender, and so on . . . the artist, critic or historian projects his or her own practice onto the field of the other, where it is read not only as authentically indigenous but as innovatively political! Of course, [he continues] this is an exaggeration, and the application of these methods has illuminated much. But it has also obliterated much in the field of the other, and in its very name.[3]

It seems that artistic engagement with an 'other' is pernicious, except when it is not.

We seem to face a familiar theoretical impasse, and a chronic source of anthropological anxiety. I do not, however, want to rehearse the pitfalls of cross-cultural representation. Instead, I suggest that anthropology need not be conceived as Foster conceives it, and that accordingly the interplay between art and anthropology can be approached in other ways altogether. His essay presumes that the discipline is constituted around the object of the other, and that it works on what he calls the horizontal axis, in engaging with institutions and communities at particular times, rather than vertically or historically. These presumptions are both justifiable and indeed commonplace, but fail to reflect the orientations of a good deal of recent anthropology, and consequently diminish our sense of the possibilities of the present.

It is true, of course, that the discipline has largely been about 'other cultures'. Even anthropology 'at home' has frequently reproduced the intellectual operations of exotic ethnography, by treating marginal groups as the equivalents of discrete non-Western cultures. But the historical anthropology that has developed in tandem with anthropologically minded history over the last twenty to thirty years has done something other than move from the study of the other to that of the self, leaving the premises of exoticism and cultural relativism intact. Historical anthropology, which has come to be particularly concerned with colonialism, and with the shaping of both European and non-European cultures from the early phases of the colonial age up to the present, is not a science of the other. It has instead been consistently concerned with the relations between selves and others. Or rather with the interactions between and within indigenous, migrant, colonial, and metropolitan populations, since many of the Europeans in these stories – Evangelical missionaries, for example – are not us, whoever we are; they are likely to be othered rather than identified with, by critical and secular scholars in the present. Just as histories are not always susceptible to binary analyses, individual protagonists have often occupied situations that are, so to speak, neither here nor there, whose biographies lie beyond the usefulness of the language of self and other.

The Pacific was once the site for Malinowski's classic evocation of the *kula* exchange system, governed by the gift rather than the commodity, and Margaret

Mead's juxtaposition of Samoan and American sexual mores. Since the mid-1980s anthropologists have been less persuaded by these grand contrasts between cultures that appear unconnected, and interested instead in exchanges and confrontations between indigenous peoples and various outsiders, ranging from European voyagers in the eighteenth century to tourists and southeast Asian logging companies at the end of the twentieth. Work has been done on the cultures of maritime exploration and trade, and on the indigenous political and ritual systems with which explorers and traders interacted; on the narratives introduced by missionaries; on colonial efforts to transform local gender relations, conceptions of sexuality, the body, and work; and on the ways events such as the recent coup in Fiji emerge from distinctive local contentions, rather than the straightforward ethnic conflicts that are apparently and depressingly ubiquitous. Anthropology has sustained its interest in local practices, but developed new concerns, not only with European projects in the Pacific, and with the European ideas – of race, degeneration, conversion, and modernization – that informed successive interventionist projects, but also with the impact of Oceania on Europe, a particular aspect of which I touch upon in this chapter.[4]

Those working in this field acknowledge, or ought to acknowledge, that their comparative and cross-cultural inquiries have often been anticipated by those of the people they study. Questions of cultural, social, and geographic difference, and of translation, were routinely negotiated by travellers and by the peoples they encountered. The experience of the early nineteenth-century Hawaiian who joins the crew of a New England trader and experiences the port towns of the China sea and Australia, and who knew the multicultural ships that were so deftly mythified by Herman Melville, is comparative; as is that of the late nineteenth-century colonial administrator who works in Nigeria, Ceylon, and New Zealand, and tries to codify native custom in each place. We do not interpret cross-cultural interaction, we co-interpret it. To co-interpret is, of course, to interpret the same problem, not necessarily from the same vantage point or with the same ends in view.

Whatever ethnographers once did, theirs has become an endeavour engaged with an array of transactions, relations, and milieux. What they do is no longer reducible to either illuminating or reprehensible efforts to represent the 'other'; nor are they deaf to the stories that have already been told, or those that might be told by others from sites of 'custom', interaction, and cross-cultural history. Consider a practice that is highly charged with exoticism, that has yielded much ethnographic and pseudo-ethnographic representation, representation that is easily characterized as voyeuristic, that indeed overlaps with the overtly pornographic. The tattooed body has long been an object of fascinated inspection; its documentation has commonly entailed the viewing of unclothed native or subaltern bodies – within Europe notably those of criminals and prostitutes – and those bodies have frequently been represented in their tattooed parts rather than as personalized wholes. In some postcolonial writing, colonial ethnology has been too easily demonized as a kind of cultural vivisection, but those who collected and studied tattoos surely came closest to literalizing this operation, through visual representations that detached the buttocks and limbs, and excised areas of the skin, of Pacific Islanders. Most shocking perhaps is the case of H. G. Robley, who based his 1896 study of Maori male tattoos, *moko*, in part on his own collection of Maori heads, reducing an embodied art of empowered warriors to a set of barbaric curiosities.[5]

Is the representation of tattooed skin inherently pernicious? Are scholars, artists and photographers complicit in the colonial headhunting that results in these collections? Are they – am I – refreshing the appetites of a European audience addicted to dehumanizing, exotic spectacle? Obviously, those whose slain body parts are trafficked in, displayed and reproduced are in no sense authors of their own objectifications. We must acknowledge, however, that tattooed people who are, so to speak, caught alive are more or less willing partners of the sideshow voyeur, the image maker, or the viewer. What looks like an objectification may also be an expression of a tattooed person's agency, if that person has commissioned a photograph or produced a self-portrait.

Some indigenous bearers of tattoos appear to have had interests in detaching elements of designs from their own persons; Marquesans could be said to have done this routinely, when they transposed tattoo motifs from their bodies to other art genres, such as tattooed model limbs, like an arm collected by Robert Louis Stevenson in 1888, which constituted an early form of tourist art.[6] Earlier in the nineteenth century, Maori began to make contracts and treaties with Europeans, and often used details or copies of their moko as signatures, and informed Europeans that *moko* were signs of personal identity, analogous to written names.

In making this claim, they were anticipating an interpretation of tattooing that has continually seduced Western interpreters: the notion that the art constituted a species of writing, albeit a typically indecipherable species. This identification had, in a way, been made as early as 1774. Mahine, a young Tahitian who had travelled to New Zealand with Cook, asked the navigator as they were parting company to 'Tattaow some Parou', to tattoo or mark some words on paper, which he might show to future European visitors, that would attest to his good character.[7] Hence, in the 1770s, the Tahitian word 'tattoo' entered the English language through Cook voyage publications; in Tahiti, this same word came to refer to writing as well as tattooing. The business of cross-cultural interpretation was well under way. Of course, Mahine's usage suggests that he was identifying the *act* of tattooing with the *act* of writing, which is not quite the same as equating a finished tattoo with a text. The difference between verb and noun, we might think, is a radical one, between bodily harm and mock discourse, yet tattooing, it seems, is always both.

Te Pehi Kupe, a Maori warrior who visited Liverpool in 1826, hoping to obtain guns to take back to New Zealand, was one of those who advocated this translation; European names, he said, were written with pens, his was written on his forehead. He acquired brief local renown for producing full and accurate transcriptions of his own tattoos without a mirror, and detailed drawings of other's *moko* from memory. For one Dr Traill, who had cared for him while he suffered from measles, he made a sketch of his eldest son's face, which he held up, gazed at 'with a murmur of affectionate delight, kissed it many times, and, as he presented, burst into tears.'[8] The evangelical author from whom I quote may, I suppose, have concocted this, but there is nothing particularly improbable in a Maori – or for that matter anyone else – responding in this fashion to an image of an absent child. My point is that disembodiment is not intrinsically a colonialist operation; body parts and body arts can be objectified and circulated to a variety of effects.

The practice of representing by themselves portions of the tattooed body is manifest in one of the most recent of popular treatments of this subject. The well-known *Vogue* photographer Gian Paolo Barbieri's *Tahiti Tattoos* (published in book, diary and calender form by Taschen) is less ethnological than tastefully homoerotic, and exemplifies a continuing European investment in the noble savage stereotype. The brief prefatory text asserts that the photographs possess an 'archaic power'; 'They portray an exotic world, shot through with a pagan eroticism that has not been seen since Paul Gauguin's paintings of Tahiti created a collective yearning for the freedom and unfettered passion of those primitive people and their island paradise.'[9] It hardly takes critical acuity to identify this silly blurb as a recapitulation of the most vacuous of primitivist images of Polynesia, but it is worth noting exactly what about contemporary Tahitian tattooing is therefore obscured, for Barbieri's viewers. Many Tahitian individuals bear not the traditional designs shown, but a mixture of these, European-style tattoos featuring dragons and the like, and experimental variations on traditional motifs. The tattoos that Barbieri's models bear, and which reflect what is now understood as the 'traditionalist' repertoire in Tahiti, are moreover derived from the powerful full body tattoos of Marquesans, and not from ancient Tahitian practices, which were neither so elaborate, nor so elaborately documented. The Tahitian reinvention of the Marquesan style was facilitated by the Russian explorers who were struck by these characters wrapped in images, as well they might have been, and by the work of a German ethnographer, Karl von den Steinen, who produced an extraordinary visual archive of Marquesan designs and motifs towards the end of the nineteenth century. The Tahitian adaptations of this corpus instance recent cultural borrowings within Polynesia – others are in the domains of music and dance – that have been regarded by some locals as appropriations, and that are consequently contentious. Behind these decorated bodies, then, lie earlier interests in exotic art, earlier projects of representation, and fraught relations among Polynesians in the present. Both the framing of Barbieri's shots and the packaging of his work wilfully if predictably exclude all of this.

To both the tradition of disembodying images and contemporary exoticism, I wish to juxtapose certain photographic treatments of contemporary Samoan tattooing in Auckland, New Zealand – a city to which postwar migration brought a large Polynesian community, among whom Samoans are one of the largest groups. Samoan tattooing is distinctive among contemporary Polynesian forms for its use, not of the electric needle, but of the traditional techniques which were at no stage completely abandoned in Samoa. These require the puncturing of the skin with a comb-like instrument that is dipped into dye and struck repeatedly with a light hammer. This procedure is acutely painful, and the acquisition of the extensive thigh and lower torso designs that constitute the full male tattoo, the *pe'a*, is a prolonged affair entailing a series of gruelling sessions, usually extending over a number of months. The fact that tattooing constituted an ordeal was and is vital to its significance: in the antecedent Samoan context, Alfred Gell has argued, reputation and rank were gained through service, and the initiation-like tattoo constituted a form of 'passive heroism', and entailed both subordination to elders and the empowerment of the youth;[10] in Aotearoa New Zealand today, and for that matter among other Samoan migrants in Australia, California, and elsewhere it carries both this and a powerful expression of ethnic pride.

In what follows, I am concerned with the work of four artists. The first is the pre-eminent Samoan tattooist who worked in Auckland, Sulu'ape Paulo II. He arrived in New Zealand in the mid-1970s and like many Polynesian men, worked in a car assembly factory for a few years, but was then made redundant and began tattooing full time, and for money. His work was known initially only within the Samoan community and among interested outsiders, in the New Zealand art scene, but by the early 1990s he had begun to stage the practice in public. From time to time he tattooed at cultural festivals, and as part of a Samoan play performed in Auckland's main arts centre. Sulu'ape also became known to prominent tattoo artists in California and Europe, and became famous among a global, increasingly Internet-based tattoo community. He attended tattoo conventions in Rome, Barcelona, Madrid, and elsewhere, and executed a number of full traditional *pe'a* in Europe, in spaces such as the Tattoo Museum and Library in Amsterdam; not so long ago he spent some time with the Berlin Hell's Angels; back in New Zealand, he had come to be regarded as one of the major figures of the new cosmopolitan and experimental Polynesian migrant culture that is now so visible there. In November 1999, Sulu'ape was killed at his home in south Auckland.

In occasional public talks, and in a short piece published in 1995, this tattoo artist outlined the symbolic values that he understood to inhere in the design, which he also explicated to those he tattooed, while he applied the motifs to their bodies. He recorded, for example, that the *va'a*, the canoe, 'is a black strip about 20 cm wide which stretches across the back with *fuaulutao* (spears) on both ends, going towards the front under the armpits. It means a vessel, which is understood to be the immediate family – the wearer of the pe'a guards this vessel with spears . . .' He explained that other elements represented the flying fox, 'known for caring for her young under her wings', that *'aso laiti*, "small lines" represented paternal and maternal genealogies, which the bearer of the *pe'a* must know; that the *lausae* motifs 'represent the dark side to any task . . . Do not be afraid – the sea is dark but only some parts are dangerous.'[11]

In these terms, Sulu'ape presented his practice as an encoding of Samoan traditions and values. But his work was notably innovative. He created simpler wrist and upper arm tattoos, which are sported by both young migrant men and women, some of whom see them as signs, not just of Samoan identity, but, as one put it to me, of being 'Kiwi Samoan', a New Zealand Samoan. Less obviously, he experimented, as *tufuga ta tatau* no doubt always had, with the formal organization of the *pe'a*, which is standardized in its overall structure rather than in its details. His most obvious and his contentious innovations lay in his choice of victims. Some years ago, he provided a full *pe'a* to a Samoan woman, who reputedly took the unorthodox view that since there were no men in her generation of her family, it was incumbent upon her to bear the male tattoo. In the aftermath of Sulu'ape's death, some Samoans suggested that the tragedy arose ultimately from this inauspicious decision.

Mark Adams is a New Zealand photographer. Much of his work has dealt with cross-cultural issues, which he has approached through images of monuments, artifacts, sites and environments.[12] In these black-and-white photographs, bodies have not been conspicuous, but they are central to a series of colour works produced during the early 1980s, which documented the practice of Paul Sulu'ape and his brother Petelo. Certain of Adams' close-ups treat the tattoo not as an exotic script, a mysterious form of writing on the body, but as a bloody happening (Figure 13.1). They admit an uncomfortable fascination,

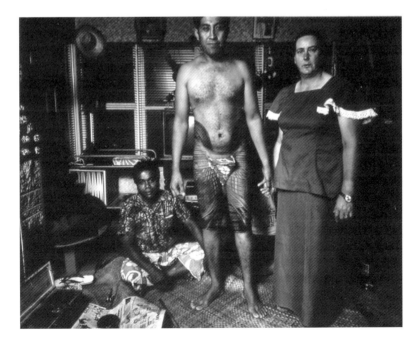

Figure 13.1. Mark Adams, *Farwood Drive, Henderson, Auckland, Su'a Pasino Sefo, Tufuga ta Tatau*, 1982. Cibachrome photograph. Courtesy of the artist.

perhaps, but do not animate so much the arousal of the voyeur, as the unease of a witness, someone inadvertently, perhaps unwillingly in the midst of a scene of careful and restrained but cumulative violence. The sharpness of the photograph and the proximity of skin and stained rag place us directly before a ritualized work of injury, rather than in a calm space in which finished tattoos can be inspected through ink on paper. The implement, evidently mobile, evokes the rhythm of tattooing, a protracted, steady percussion that makes the art a kind of bodily counterpart to a piece of Steve Reich's music. Tattooing has a sound that is heard in one way by those of us who are present, at the scene of this insistent drumming, and in another way altogether by the person whose perforated skin figures as an instrument of this music. No photograph is audible, but some are less removed from aurality than others; some, like this image, alert us to the sounds that are absent.

Adams also produced formally posed photographs, that communicate directly and unambiguously the pride of the bearer of the completed *pe'a*, who faces the viewer in an act of deliberate yet dignified self-exposure (Figure 13.2). Here, the tattooed man may have been a victim of the tattooist, but is also a co-author of the remarkable expression of Samoan art that has become indistinguishable from his body. None of the agency and self-possession that

Figure 13.2. Mark Adams, *Chalfont Crescent, Mangere, Auckland, Su'a Suluape Petelo, Tufuga ta Tatau*, 1985. Cibachrome photograph. Courtesy of the artist.

Figure 13.3. Greg Semu, *O le tatau Samoa. Self portrait with front of pe'a. Basque Road, Newton Gully,* 1995. Gelatin silver print toned with gold and selenium, collection of Auckland Art Gallery Toi o Tamaki. Courtesy of the artist.

is present here can be detected in most older images of Polynesian tattoos, from which the face of the person is often excluded, or presented in oblique profile, in a fashion that permits a man to be regarded as a curiosity.

Yet, as I suggested earlier, this operation of decontextualization, of imaging the body more than the person, does not possess fixed qualities. Nor does it inevitably stigmatize or disempower the bearer of the photographed body. Greg Semu has produced a set of self-portraits, in which he is posed, more-or-less like the subject of a nineteenth-century ethnological photograph (Figure 13.3). The vital difference is that he is close to the camera: the absolute sharpness of the image defines the porosity of his skin; this and the brilliance of the black dye assume an extraordinary tactility, to the extent that the viewer of the prints experiences an illusion of three dimensionality: not only does the body stand before the backdrop but the stain stands before the skin. The hand across the penis is not only an expression of modesty but also an expression of the artist's controlled and limited self-representation, and a sort of stipulation that the viewer's regard ought to be framed by crosscultural awe rather than sexualized curiosity. There is, of course, a marked residual eroticism in these images, that could be seen to renegotiate the stereotypic image of Polynesia as a site of license and voluptuousness.

Semu was brought up by Mormon parents in New Zealand who attached little value to their Samoan heritage; his acquisition of the *pe'a* was a project to recover cultural identity. The vacuity of the studio makes his tattooed skin the object of absolute attention in this set of photographs, and energizes this vindication of the traditional art and his own embodiment of it. Adams, in contrast, has been consistently concerned to situate Sulu'ape's subjects in their environments, and specifically in the suburban state houses that many Polynesians made their homes, from the 1950s and 1960s onwards. The rooms that are partially visible to us are distinctive in their décor; they are unambiguously migrant Polynesian spaces, crowded with woven pandanus mats, family photographs decorated with shell necklaces, plastic floral leis, television, and kava bowl. This setting signals at once a New Zealand welfare regime that was, at the time these photographs were taken, soon to be dramatically attenuated by the 'reforms' of small government and rationalism, and, on the other hand, the absolute but unselfconscious transformation of this kind of space into somewhere that exudes the smell and the feel of islands culture, that is at the same time replete with the artifacts and the detritus of quotidian existence: lighter, ashtray, fags, beer bottle, newspaper. The room just happens to be there, in one sense; in another it conveys a great deal about the position and relocation of a particular set of people. Adams is rigorous about including all this, about what is contingently in the frame, because context in a literal and material sense stands in for context in a succession of other senses. While the ethnological tradition proceeded at odds with twentieth-century anthropological axioms, in so far as tattoos were literally severed from bodies, and tattooed bodies from environments, social relations and meanings, this photographic effort insists on the particular locations in which tattooing takes place and in which the tattooed present themselves. The titles of these works usually take the form of a street name, a suburb, the names of those present, and a date. The personal names are Polynesian; place names like Glen Innes or Otara might be either of British or Maori derivation, reflecting the basic ambiguity of New Zealand's settler-colonial geography. In some cases these titles extend into a succession of notes: 'The guy assisting Sulu'ape is Pio, who first told me of Sulu'ape and his brother Petelo and their cousin Sefo . . .' The caption, in other words, summons up not the static generality of a known custom, that is presumably 'there' rather than 'here', but the accident of acquaintance.

A number of Adams' photographs concern not tattooing internal to the Samoan community, but with Sulu'ape's work on Pakeha (white New Zealanders) and notably on the prominent painter, Tony Fomison (1939–90). Of the various art works I have discussed, these images are most obviously consistent with the project of historical anthropology that I referred to earlier in this chapter: they document the relations between certain indigenous and certain settler actors, at a particular moment. Fomison was a maverick in the modern New Zealand art scene; his work bore few affinities with any of the various trends of the period – which included landscape engaged with the distinctiveness of the New Zealand environment, more internationalist abstract tendencies, pop, and various conceptual practices. His oils on hessian of strange, suffering, sometimes incarcerated figures, clowns, and fools recall early Italian painters such as Masaccio, though these works – described as 'grim, bare and lonely' by one of his Polynesian friends – were also anchored in New Zealand's bicultural landscape. A number illustrate Maori myth or commemorate Maori histories, and Fomison is now cited as a precursor to the postcolonial understanding of the settler nation as a place uncannily marked by indigenous myth, displacement, and cultural exchange.

Though this artist had worked for a few years early in his career as a museum archaeologist, primarily concerned with recording Maori rock art, his subsequent interests in Polynesian cultures and people were manifest not in the documentation of the past, but in what was happening in his present, and in relations he formed with particular people. Though he once travelled to Samoa, and made drawings while he was there, Fomison's orientation was in some respects the inverse of that of the typical European modernist. If the latter incorporated forms derived from tribal art into paintings or sculptures, in the absence of much knowledge of, or contact with, the people who had produced the material, Fomison's interest was more personal. He displayed Pacific artifacts in his studio and house, but refrained from using indigenous forms or designs in his art. What he did do, however, was assimilate a Samoan art form to his own person. Individuals are often tattooed together, and Fomison received his *pe'a* over the same period as Fuimaono Tuiasau, a New Zealand Samoan, an Auckland University student at the time, later a lawyer. Tuiasau wrote more recently:

> I think people misunderstood Tony. When he did get tattooed and he finished his tattoo some months later, people thought that he was trying to be Samoan. And I for one and Sulu'ape, we both knew that he was doing this because of his love of the art of tattooing. He knew he could never be a Samoan, but to have this amazing art on your body and to carry it around was quite a unique thing I think by European standards. The intricacy of the designs, the pain, and the whole cultural aspect of going through getting your body battered blue and black and bloodied – that was something that Tony understood and he wanted to go through that.[12]

Figure 13.4. The umusaga for Fuimaono Tuiasau – The finishing ceremony of his tattoo. Taken at Tuiasau's place, Grotto Road, Onehunga. Next to him is Tony Fomison who shared some of the tattooing sessions with Fui in the shed behind the family home. Su'a Sulu'ape Paulo – Tufuga ta tatau'. Cibachrome photograph by Mark Adams, 9 October 1992. Courtesy of the artist.

These remarks leave an issue open more than they resolve it. But it may be that the question – of whether Fomison's desire was somehow legitimate or somehow misplaced – is not what really needs to be adjudicated. The New Zealand critic, Ian Wedde has observed, in his catalogue of the 1995 Fomison retrospective, that the painter's acquisition of the *pe'a* indeed appears a recapitulation of the longstanding European fantasy to cross the beach and become a member of the tribe; and that Samoans variously tolerated, respected, or objected to this assumption of one of the hallmarks of Samoan manhood, one of the prerequisites of titled status and rank in the Samoan polity. But Wedde reminds us that Fomison was not the only actor in this narrative. Sulu'ape – a *tufuga ta tatau*, a priest and master of the art – made a considered choice to inflict the design on a man he knew. In so doing he was making a decision that was 'personal and controversial', and that was innovative in its context.[13]

It is, in a way, surprising that his tattooing of foreigners should have been censured. From the late eighteenth century onward, tattooists in Tahiti, Hawaii, New Zealand and Samoa among other places had frequently tattooed mariners, deserters, and other travellers; and Samoans regularly tattooed men who travelled from the neighbouring archipelago of Tonga for the purpose. The implications of belonging and Samoan-ness that *tatau* carried were always prone to qualification or suspension, when the objects of the art were connected with, but not of, Samoan society; in many instances, tattoos were only partially reproduced on foreigners. Tattooing appears, then, not as mute exoticism, but as an activity that dealt knowingly with cultural difference; it had long been modified for application to other Polynesians, and had from an early stage in colonial history been made available in a kind of souvenir form to mariners whose bodies carried emblems of their many ports and voyages. Neither the ethnographer's art nor the artist's ethnography discover a 'custom' that is itself innocent of ethnography; we find that the tattooist has got there first, if our object is the marking of alterity.

Adams' images, of Fomison subject to Sulu'ape's practice, and of Fomison present within the family ceremony that marked the completion of Tuiasau's *pe'a*, record what was distinctive about this process, and its awkward but remarkable result (Figure 13.4). The scene is, in a way, like the tattoo itself: what it exhibits is more telling than what it can be said to say.

ACKNOWLEDGEMENTS

I am grateful to Mark Adams for the opportunity to work with him, and to Greg Semu; we all owe a great deal to Sulu'ape Paulo II. I would also like to thank Peter Brunt and Christopher Wright for comments on an earlier version of this chapter, and Annie Coombes for her advice and support.

Notes

Chapter 1 The Challenge of Practice

1. Specialized fields of economic anthropology, kinship studies, and physical or biological anthropology come to mind here. Yet even very technical subjects can ultimately benefit in the visual presentation of their material from a dialogue with the arts. A more conceptual cross-fertilization between 'hard' science (here mathematics), the visual and anthropology is developed by Küchler in this volume.
2. Foster, H., 'The Artist as Ethnographer?' in G. Marcus and F. Myers (eds), *The Traffic in Culture: Refiguring Art and Anthropology*, Berkeley: University of California Press, 1995.
3. For example, Coles, A. (ed.) *De-, Dis-, Ex-: Site-Specificity: The Ethnographic Turn*, London: Blackdog Publications, 2000.
4. Metken, G., *Spurensicherung. Kunst als Anthropologie und Selbsterforschung: Fiktive Wissenschaften in der heutigen Kunst*, Cologne: DuMont, 1977; Metken, G., *Spurensicherung: Eine Revision*, Amsterdam: Fundus, 1996. Lippard, L., *Overlay: Contemporary Art and the Art of Prehistory*, New York: The New Press, 1983. Schneider, A., 'The Art Diviners', *Anthropology Today*, 9(2) (1993), pp. 3-9, and Schneider, A., 'Uneasy Relationships: Contemporary Artists and Anthropology', *Journal of Material Culture*, 1(2), 1996, pp. 183-210.
5. Clifford, J. and Marcus, G. (eds), *Writing Culture: The Politics and Poetics of Ethnography*, Berkeley: University of California Press, 1986.
6. Schneider, A., 'The Art Diviners', *Anthropology Today*, 9 (1993), 2, 3-9, and Schneider, A. 'Uneasy Relationships: Contemporary Artists and Anthropology', *Journal of Material Culture*, 1(2), 1996, pp. 183-210.
7. Wright, C., 'The Third Subject: Perspectives on Visual Anthropology', *Anthropology Today*, 14(4), 1998, pp. 16-22.
8. Grimshaw, A., *The Ethnographer's Eye: Ways of Seeing in Modern Anthropology*, Cambridge: Cambridge University Press, 2001.
9. *Ausbrennen des Landkreises Buchen*. In German 'ausbrennen' has the general sense of 'burning out'; the translation as 'cauterization' is taken from the catalogue, Fuchs, R., Pagé, S., Harten, J., *Anselm Kiefer*, Düsseldorf: Städtische Kunsthalle Düsseldorf, 1984, p. 52.
10. It is useful to consider Kiefer's work in the light of Klaus Theweleit's work on images of earth and blood in German National Socialism (Theweleit,

K., *Male Fantasies* (2 vols), Minneapolis: University of Minnesota Press, 1987), and the extent to which this suggests possible directions for an anthropological approach to his work.

11. Kiefer, A., *A Book by Anselm Kiefer: Transition from Cool to Warm* (introduction by Theodore E. Stebbins and Susan Cragg Ricci), London: Thames & Hudson, 1988.

12. Here again, the status of the object as art work means we are denied access to the pages of the books, many of which have photographs, are partially covered in mud or sand, or have other objects attached to their surface. However, the catalogue that 'accompanied' the work contained reproductions of many of these pages.

13. See Gell, A., *Art and Agency: An Anthropological Theory of Art*, Oxford: Clarendon Press, 1998.

14. See Clifford, J., 'On Ethnographic Self-Fashioning' in his *The Predicament of Culture: Twentieth-Century Ethnography, Literature and Art*, Cambridge MA: Harvard University Press, 1988, pp. 92–113; Stocking, G., 'The Ethnographer's Magic: Fieldwork in British Anthropology from Tylor to Malinowski' in his *Observers Observed: Essays on Ethnographic Fieldwork*, Madison: University of Wisconsin Press, 1983, pp. 70–119.

15. Young, M., *Malinowski's Kiriwina: Fieldwork Photography 1915–1918*, Chicago: University of Chicago Press, 1998. For Jeremy Coote the missed opportunity for collaboration was a loss to anthropology, see his article 'Malinowski the photographer' in *Journal of the Anthropological Society of Oxford* 24 (1) 1993 pp. 66–69.

16. Young, *Malinowski's Kiriwina*, p. 13 Of course Wikiewicz was not a Surrealist – the term was used by Guillaume Appolinaire in 1917 – but it is telling that Young should use this term to differentiate his work from Malinowski's.

17. Young, p. 14.

18. Ibid. p. 13, emphasis in original.

19. See contributions by Jonathan Parry and Alexander Moore in the Society for Visual Anthropology's *SVA Newsletter*, Fall (1988), pp. 1–7 and by Jay Ruby, Radikha Chopra, and Akos Ostor in *SVA Newsletter* Spring (1989), pp. 2–8.

20. Taylor, L., 'Iconophobia: How Anthropology Lost it at the Movies', *Transition* 69 (1996) pp. 64–88.

21. Gell, A., 'The Enchantment of Technology and the Technology of Enchantment' in J. Coote and A. Shelton (eds) *Anthropology, Art and Aesthetics*, Oxford: Oxford University Press, 1992, pp. 40–63. Michael Oppitz has suggested that the low regard for the visual in anthropology results from fear of invasion of the sensual (here images) into the rational world of texts; cf. Oppitz, M., *Die Kunst des Genavigkeit*, Munich: Trickster, 1989, p. 13.

22. Pinney, C., 'The Lexical Spaces of Eye-Spy' in P. Crawford and D. Turton (eds), Film as Ethnography, Manchester: Manchester University Press, 1992, pp. 26–49.

23. Biella, P., *Yanomamö Interactive. The Ax Fight.* CD-Rom. With Napoleon
    A. Chagnon and Gary Seaman. Fort Worth: Harcourt Brace, 1997. Biella,
    P., 'Mama Kone's Possession: Scene from an Interactive Ethnography',
    Visual Anthropology Review, 12(2) (1997), pp. 59– 95.

24. For example Kirsten Hastrup 'Anthropological Visions: some notes on
    visual and textual authority', in Turton and Crawford (eds), *Film as
    Ethnography*, 1992, pp. 8–25. Discussing the visual as 'evidence' Hastrup
    argues (p. 15) that 'while one can take pictures of ritual groves and of the
    participants in the ritual, one cannot capture their secret on celluloid. This
    has to be told.' Belying her reliance on a realist paradigm, she goes on to
    insist that the visual is related metonymically to reality, whereas text is
    related metaphorically. Of course this is only the case if one remains rigidly
    within a realist model. See also Wade, P., (ed.) *In Anthropology Images
    Can Never Have the Last Say*, Manchester: Group for Debates in Anthropo-
    logical Theory (GDAT), Department of Anthropology, University of
    Manchester, 1997. In this instance the audience taking part in the debate
    voted against the motion.

25. MacDougall, D., *Transcultural Cinema*, Princeton: Princeton University
    Press, 1998, p. 63.

26. Personal communication.

27. Mitchell, W.J.T., 'What do Pictures Really Want ?' in *October* 77 (summer)
    (1996), pp. 71–82; Freedberg, D., *The Power of Images*, Chicago: Uni-
    versity of Chicago Press, 1989. Freedberg has argued (p. xx) that bodily
    reactions to images are usually ignored in favour of intellectualized or
    textual responses. Stafford, B.M., *Good Looking: Essays on the Virtues of
    Images*, Cambridge MA: MIT Press, 1996, has argued convincingly for 'an
    imaging field based on transdisciplinary problems' (p. 40).

28. Ruby, J., *Picturing Culture: Explorations of Film and Anthropology*,
    Chicago: University of Chicago Press, 2000. David MacDougall, *Trans-
    cultural Cinema*. Banks, M. and Morphy, H. (eds) *Rethinking Visual
    Anthropology*, New Haven and London: Yale University Press, 1997.
    Grimshaw, A., *The Ethnographer's Eye: Ways of Seeing in Modern
    Anthropology* Cambridge: Cambridge University Press, 2001. Grimshaw,
    A. and Ravetz, A. (eds), *Visualizing Anthropology*, Bristol: Intellect Books,
    2005.

29. Discussing the films selected for an ethnographic film festival in New York
    in the early 1990s, Weinberger laments the fact that 'every film had a
    narrator, many of them still speaking to a room full of slow children:
    Weinberger, E. 'The Camera People', in L. Taylor (ed.) *Visualizing Theory:
    Selected Essays from V.A.R. 1990–1994*, New York: Routledge, 1994, p. 25.

30. *Antony Gormley*, contributions by John Hutchinson, E.H.Gombrich, Lela
    B. Njatin and W.J.T. Mitchell, London: Phaidon, 2000 p. 122. Gormley's
    statement resonates with Martin Heidegger's notion of the 'world picture',
    see his 'Age of the World Picture' in Heidegger, M., *The Question Con-
    cerning Technology and Other Essays*, trans. William Lovitt, New York:

Harper, 1977, pp. 115-54. See also Ingold, T., 'Globes and Spheres: The Topology of Environmentalism' in K. Milton (ed.) *Environmentalism: The View from Anthropology*, London and New York: Routledge, 1993, pp. 31–42 for an intriguing graphic comparison of differing world views.

31. Hutchinson *et al*, *Antony Gormley*, p. 122.

32. Gell, Art and Agency. See also Küchler, S., 'The Art of Ethnography' in Coles, A. (ed.) Site Specificity, pp. 94-114 on the work of Sophie Calle.

33. See George Marcus in this volume. See also Clifford, J. and Marcus, G. (eds) *Writing Culture*, Berkeley: University of California Press, 1988.

34. See Grimshaw, A. and Hart, K., *Anthropology and the Crisis of the Intellectuals*, Prickly Pear Pamphlet No. 1, Cambridge: Prickly Pear Press, 1996, p. 45. Marcus, G., 'Sticking with Ethnography Through Thick and Thin' in his *Ethnography Through Thick and Thin*, Princeton: Princeton University Press, 1998, pp. 231-53.

35. Carpenter, E., *Eskimo Realities*, New York: Holt, Rinehart & Winston 1973.

36. Rothenberg, J. and Rothenberg, D. (eds) *Symposium of the Whole: A Range of Discourses Towards an Ethnopoetics*, Berkeley: University of California Press 1982 p. 139. *Alcheringa* was published between 1970 and 1980 by Boston University and issues came with thin flexible vinyl recordings of, for example, poetry readings in the Zuni language and revivalist church services.

37. McAllester, D. and McAllester, S., *Hogans: Navajo Houses and Songs*, Middletown CT: Wesleyan University Press, 1980. (Second edition 1987.)

38. 'In my translations (and retranslations . . .) I have also tried to retain Navajo word order as much as possible . . . In written English we have been trained to avoid uncertain referents. "He is thinking about it" does not tell us who is thinking about what. The Navajos, on the other hand have been trained to a meticulous respect for privacy. Introductions and namings are felt by them to be intrusive, impolite, and even dangerous. I have kept the Navajo ambiguity in the translation and tried to satisfy the Anglo-European need "to know" with a foot note based on Naat'áanii's [one of McAllester's interviewees] answer when *I* needed to know.' McAllester and McAllester, *Hogans*, pp. 16-17 (their italics).

39. See also Worth, S. and Adair, J., *Through Navajo Eyes: An Exploration in Film Communication and Anthropology*, Bloomington: Indiana University Press, 1972.

40. Tedlock, B., 'Crossing the Sensory Domains in Native American Aesthetics' in C. J. Frisbie (ed.) *Explorations in Ethnomusicology: Essays in Honor of David P. McAllester*, Detroit: Detroit Monographs in Musicology, 1986, p. 188.

41. Liffman, P., 'Comments on Strong's Review of David P.McAllester's and Susan McAllester's *Hogans: Navajo Houses and Songs*', *Chicago Anthropology Exchange* 14(1 and 2) (1981), pp. 182-8.

42. See Stoller, P., *The Taste of Ethnographic Things: The Senses in Anthropology*, Philadelphia: University of Pennsylvania Press, 1989, and *Sensuous Scholarship*, Philadelphia: University of Pennsylvania Press 1997.

43. Washington: Smithsonian Folkways Recordings, 2001. See also Feld, S. *Sound and Sentiment: Birds, Weeping, Poetics, and Song in Kaluli Expression*, Philadelphia: University of Pennsylvania Press, 1982. The inclusion of CDs with anthropological publications is one productive avenue for further experiment, and the potential for productive collaborations between art and anthropology in terms of sound work requires a book in its own right.

44. Stoller, *The Taste of Ethnographic Things*, pp. xv–xvi.

45. See Howes, D. (ed.), *The Varieties of Sensual Experience: A Sourcebook in the Anthropology of the Senses*, Toronto: University of Toronto Press, 1991; and, more recently, Howes, D. (ed.), *Empire of the Senses*, Oxford: Berg, 2004.

46. Münzel, M., 'Zu den Grenzen ethnologischer Kunstbetrachtung' in M. Münzel (ed.) *Die Mythen sehen: Bilder und Zeichen vom Amazonas*, Frankfurt: Museum für Völkerkunde, 1988, pp. 41–3.

47. Taussig, M., *Mimesis and Alterity: A Particular History of the Senses*, London: Routledge, 1994, p. 57.

48. Münzel, *Die Mythen sehen*, p. 42.

49. Howes, D. and Classen, C., 'Conclusion: Sounding Sensory Profiles', in Howes, *The Varieties of Sensual Experience*.

50. Latour, B., 'Visualization and Cognition: Thinking with Eyes and Hands', *Knowledge and Society*, 6 (1986), pp. 1–40, at p. 4.

51. Brody, H., *The Other Side of Eden: Hunter-Gatherers, Farmers, and the Shaping of the World*, London: Faber & Faber, 2001, p. 4–5.

52. Carroll, D., *Paraesthetics: Foucault, Lyotard, Derrida* London: Methuen, 1987.

53. Ibid. p. 27 and pp. 30–1.

54. Ibid. p. 36.

55. Malinowski, B., *A Diary in the Strict Sense of the Term*, trans. Norbert Guterman, London: Routledge 1967.

56. Wagner, R., *Asiwinarong: Ethos, Image and Social Power among the Usen Barok of New Ireland*, Princeton: Princeton University Press, 1986, p. 216.

57. *Documenta X: Short Guide*, Stuttgart: Cantz Verlag, 1997 p. 30. See also catalogue on Baumgarten *AMERICA Invention*, New York: Guggenheim Museum 1993.

58. *Documenta X: Short Guide*, 1997, p. 30.

59. Rosler, M., 'The Bowery in Two Inadequate Representational Systems' in C. de Zegher (ed.), *Positions in the Life World*, Birmingham, Ikon, Generali, MIT Press. Green, R., 'Scenes from a Group Show: Project Unité' in Coles (ed.), *Site Specificity*, pp. 114–35. There are, of course, many other artists who have experimented with fieldwork and ethnography, amongst them Fiona Tan, Sharon Lockhart and Juan Downy, to name but a few.

60. Button, V. and Esche, C., *Intelligence: New British Art 2000*, London: Tate Gallery, 2000, p. 82.

61. 'The collusive relationship she forms with her collaborators is still essentially the primary end product of her art' *Gillian Wearing* Russell

Ferguson, Donna De Salvo, John Slyce, London: Phaidon Press, 1999, p. 83; see also, *Gillian Wearing* London: Serpentine Gallery 2000.

62. Alexander Pühringer (ed.) *Bill Viola*, Salzburg: Salzburger Kunstverein/ Ritter Klagenfurt, 1994, p. 11.

63. Ibid. p. 138.

64. Ibid. p. 140.

65. Ibid. p. 146.

66. Ibid. pp. 154–5. One source of continuing artistic fascination with anthropology is its provision of alternative models for the function of art in culture.

67. Fabian, J., *Remembering the Present: Painting and Popular History in Zaire*, Berkeley: University of California Press, 1996, is a collaboration between Fabian and the Zairian artist Tshibumba Kanda Matulu.

68. Marcus, G. and Myers, F., 'The Traffic in Art and Culture: An Introduction', in G. E. Marcus and F. Myers (eds), *The Traffic in Culture*, 1995, pp. 302 (italics in original), pp. 15–16, and p. 24.

69. Svetlana Alpers is credited with defining the term 'visual culture' in her book *The Art of Describing: Dutch Art in the Seventeenth Century*, Chicago: Chicago University Press, 1983, although the genealogy of the term goes back to Michael Baxandall who developed ideas of visual culture, while not using the term itself, in his book *Painting and Experience in Fifteenth Century Italy: A Primer in the Social History of Pictorial Style*, Oxford: Oxford University Press, 1972.

70. Mitchell, W.J.T., 'What do Pictures *Really* Want?' in *October*, 77 (Summer) (1996), pp. 71–82, at p. 82.

71. 'Visual Culture Questionnaire', in *October* 77 (Summer) (1996).

72. Foster, H., 'The Artist as Ethnographer?' in G. E. Marcus and F. Myers, *The Traffic in Culture*, 1995, pp. 304–5.

73. Kwon, M. 'Experience Vs. Interpretation: Traces of Ethnography in the Works of Lan Tuazon and Nikki S. Lee', in A. Coles (ed.) *Site-Specificity*, p. 86.

74. Foster, H., in Marcus and Myers 1995 op. cit. p.302, his italics.

75. Latour, B., *We Have Never Been Modern*, Englewood Cliffs, NJ: Prentice Hall, 1993.

76. Wardlow, H. 'Bobby Teardrops: A Turkish Video in Papua New Guinea' in *Visual Anthropology Review* 12(1) (1996), pp. 30–46.

77. Grimshaw, A., 'The eye in the door: anthropology, film and the exploration of interior space', in M. Banks and H. Murphy (eds), *Rethinking Visual Anthropology*, New Haven, Yale University Press, 1997, p. 40.

78. Banks, M. and Murphy, H., 'Introduction', *Rethinking Visual Anthropology*, p. 9.

79. David McDougall, 'The Visual in Anthropology', in Banks, M. and Murphy, H., *Rethinking Visual Anthropology*, pp. 292–3.

80. McDougall, D., 'The Visual in Anthropology', p. 285; also McDougall, D., *Transcultural Cinema*, Princeton: Princeton University Press, 1997.

81. Pink, S., 'Renewal of Ethnographic Film: the Future of Visual Anthropology?' in *Anthropology Today* 17(5) (2001), p. 24; see also Pink, S. *Doing Visual Ethnography*, London: Sage, 2001.

82. See Russell, C., *Experimental Ethnography: The Work of Film in the Age of Video* Durham and London: Duke University Press, 1999, p. xi.

83. Ginsburg, F., 'Institutionalizing the Unruly: Charting a Future for Visual Anthropology' in *Ethnos* 63(2) (1998), pp. 173–201.

84. Kosuth, J., *Art After Philosophy and After: Selected Writings*, Cambridge MA: MIT Press, 1993, emphasis in original, p. 117.

85. Kosuth, 1993, p. 117.

86. Kosuth, 1993, p. 119.

87. Hiller, S., 'Editor's Introduction', in S. Hiller (ed.) *The Myth of Primitivism*, London: Routledge, 1991, p. 2.

88. Hiller, S., 'Editor's Introduction', p. 2.

Chapter 2 Appropriations

1. Rubin, W. *'Primitivism' in Twentieth Century Art*, New York: Museum of Modern Art, 1984, pp. 17–20, 239–68. Rhodes, C., *Primitivism and Modern Art*, London: Thames & Hudson, 1994, p. 120. Also, Goldwater, R. J., *Primitivism in Modern Art*, Cambridge MA: Harvard University Press, 1986 (first edition 1938). Connelly, F., *The Sleep of Reason: Primitivism in Modern European Art and Aesthetics, 1725–1907*, University Park PA: Pennsylvania State University Press, 1994. Flam, J. and Deutsch, M. (eds), *Primitivism and Twentieth-Century Art: A Documentary History*, Berkeley: University of California Press, 2003.

2. Rubin, W. *Primitivism*, pp. 17–20; 239–268. Rhodes, *Primitivism and Modern Art*, p. 120.

3. Clifford, J., *The Predicament of Culture: Twentieth-Century Ethnography, Literature, and Art*, Cambridge MA: Harvard University Press, 1988, p. 148.

4. Lucien Lévy-Bruhl, *The 'Soul' of the Primitive*, London: George Allen & Unwin, 1965 (French edition, 1928), pp. 156–57.

5. Here we can only present briefly the exemplary case of Picasso and Cubism in relation to appropriation. On Surrealism and Primitivism, and its close relations with academic anthropology in France in the 1920s and 1930s, see Clifford, *The Predicament of Culture* and Flam and Deutsch, *Primitivism and Twentieth-century Art*. The missed encounters between artists and academic anthropologists in pre-World War Two Germany, Austria and Switzerland, including Ernst Nolde, August Macke, Ernst Klee, all of whom had an interest in anthropology and visited anthropology museums, would merit separate study. On Nolde's and the Expresssionists' primitivism see,

Lloyd, J., 'Emil Nolde's "ethnographic" Still Lifes: Primitivism, Tradition, and Modernity', in S. Hiller (ed.) *The Myth of Primitivism*, London: Routledge, 1991; also Lloyd, J., 'Emil Noldes Kritik am Kolonialismus', *Brücke Archiv*, 20 (2002), pp. 103–15; N'guessan, B.P., *Primitivismus und Afrikanismus: Kunst und Kultur in der deutschen Avantgarde*, Frankfurt: Peter Lang, 2002, pp. 90–128.

6. Paolozzi, E., McLeod, M., Ades, D., Frayling, C., *Lost Magic Kingdoms and Six Paper Moons from Nahuatl*, London: British Museum Publications, 1985, p. 10.

7. See also Schneider, A., 'Uneasy Relationships: Contemporary Artists And anthropology', *Journal of Material Culture*, 1(2) (1996), pp. 183–210.

8. Miller, D., 'Primitive Art and the Necessity of Primitivism to Art', in Hiller (ed.) *The Myth of Primitivism*.

9. Clifford, J., *The Predicament of Culture*, p. 127.

10. Marcus, G. and Myers, F., 'Introduction', in Marcus, G. and Myers, F. (eds), *The Traffic in Culture: Refiguring Art and Anthropology*, Berkeley: University of California Press, 1995, p. 6.

11. Clifford, J., *Predicament of Culture*, p. 190, p. 195, p. 199.

12. Karp, I. and Lavine S.D. (eds), *Exhibiting Cultures: The Poetics and Politics of Museum Display*, Washington DC: Smithsonian Institution, 1991.

13. Schneider, A., 'The art diviners', *Anthropology Today*, 9(2) (1993), pp. 3–9. On museums created as artworks by contemporary artists, see Bronson, A.A. and Gales, P. (eds), *Museums by Artists*. Toronto: Art Metropole, 1983.

14. See notes 1 and 3.

15. Thomas, N., 'Appropriation/Appreciation: Settler Modernism in Australia and New Zealand', in Myers, F.R. (ed.), *The Empire of Things: Regimes of Value and Material Culture*, Santa Fe NM: School of American Research Press, 2001, p. 150.

16. Schneider, A., 'On "appropriation": a critical reappraisal of the concept and its application in global art practices', *Social Anthropology*, 11(2) (2003), pp. 215–29.

17. Al Imfeld, "El Loko - Beuys: Bäume und Pfähle", *Kunstforum International*, 122, 1993, pp. 326-327; my translation.

18. Ibid., p. 330.

19. Kramer, F., *The Red Fez: Art and Spirit Possession in Africa*. London: Verso, 1993 (German edition, 1986). Taussig, M., *Mimesis and Alterity*, London: Routledge, 1993.

20. Bronislaw Malinowski, 'Introduction', in Julian Lips, *The Savage Hits Back*, 1937, p. vii.

21. A famous example is *L.H.O.O.Q.*, by Marcel Duchamp, 1919, where Leonardo's *Mona Lisa* is painted with a moustache. See also note 28. For definitions, see Diamond, D.G. (ed.), *Bullfinch Pocket Pocket Dictionary of Art Terms*, Boston: Little, Brown & Company, 1992.

22. Coombe, R.J., 'The Properties of Culture and the Politics of Possessing Identity: Native Claims in the Cultural Appropriation Controversy',

Canadian Journal of Law and Jurisprudence, VI (2), 1993, pp. 249-85, at p. 257. Coombe, R.J., *The Cultural Life of Intellectual Properties: Authorship, Appropriation and the Law*, Durham: Duke University Press, 1998; Ziff, B. and Rao, P. (eds), *Borrowed Power: Essays on Cultural Appropriation*, New Brunswick NJ: Rutgers University Press, 1997. Brown, M.F., 'Can Culture be Copyrighted?' *Current Anthropology*, 39(2), 1998, pp. 193-222. Harrison, S., 'Cultural Boundaries', *Anthropology Today*, 15(5) (1999), pp. 10-13; Benthall, J., 'The Critique of Intellectual Property', *Anthropology Today*, 15(6), (1999), pp. 1-3.

23. Arnd Schneider 1993.'The Art Diviners', *Anthropology Today*, 9(1) (1993), pp. 3-9.

24. Our discussion, which relates to visual artworks, is concerned with process of copying implying changes of meaning (not those pretending to have the same meaning, i.e. fakes, for which see Phillips, D., *Don't Trust the Label: An Exhibition of Fakes, Imitations and the Real Thing*, London: Arts Council, 1986-7). On how Western art history and museum exhibition practices constructed the 'authenticity' of artworks, see another interesting study by David Phillips, Phillips, D., *Exhibiting Authenticity*, Manchester: Manchester University Press, 1997. On virtually identical copies, or counterfeits with yet different values attributed to them by collectors in the world of rock and popular music, see Jamieson, M., 'The Place of Counterfeits in Regimes of Value: An Anthropological Approach', *Journal of the Royal Anthropological Institute.* (N.S.), 5(1) (1999), pp. 1-11.

25. Krauss, R., 'Retaining the Original? The State of the Question', *Retaining the Original: Multiple Originals, Copies and Reproductions.* Studies in the History of Art, vol. 20.. Hanover: University of New England, 1989, pp. 8-10.

26. Buchloh, B.H.D., 'Allegorical Procedures: Appropriation and Montage in Contemporary Art', *Art Forum.* 21(1) (1982) pp. 43-56.

27. Paternosto, C., *The Stone and the Thread: Andean Roots of Abstract Art*, Austin: University of Texas Press, 1996, p. 192. Kubler, G., *The Shape of Time*, New Haven: Yale University Press, 1962, p. 108.

28. Camnitzer, L., *The New Art of Cuba*, Austin: University of Texas Press, 1994, p. 315. Camnitzer (p. 312) provides the background to this Cuban reappropriation of Leonardo's and Duchamp's Mona Lisas: 'José Angel Toirac . . . discovered a reproduction of the Mona Lisa that was mistakenly printed in mirror image. He promptly drew a moustache an a small beard on it and labeled it "Marcel Duchamp, L.H.O.O.Q. [1919]". His writing, though, in a pun that reached Leonardo himself, was in mirror image as well.' See also note 21.

29. Ziff, B. and Rao, P. *Borrowed Power*, p. 1, citing a resolution passed by the Writers' Union of Canada in 1992.

30. Schneider, A., 'Sites of Amnesia, Non-Sites of Memory: Identity and Other in the Work of Four Uruguayan artists', in Coles, A. (ed.), *Siting Ethnography*, London: Blackdog Publications, 2000.

31. Todd, L., 'Notes on Appropriation', *Parallelogramme*, 16(1) (1990) pp. 24–33, at p. 24.

32. Schneider, A., 'On "Appropriation": a Critical Reappraisal of the Concept and its Application in Global Art Practices', *Social Anthropology*, 2003, 11(2) (2003), pp. 215–29.

33. Rosalind Krauss, 'Giacometti', in Rubin, *Primitivism in Twentieth Century Art*, p. 514. Cooke, L., 'The Resurgence of the Night-mind: Primitivist Revivals in Recent Art', in Hiller (ed.), *The Myth of Primitivism*, pp. 141–2.

34. Whether or not the rescue by the Tartars was fiction is irrelevant, the point is that Beuys established it as an 'origin myth' for his work. See Rosenthal, M., *Joseph Beuys: Actions, Vitrines, Environments*, Houston: Menil Collection/Tate Publishing, 2005, p. 10. When shown the rushes of Michael Oppitz's epic film on Magar Shamanism, *Shamans of the Blind Land* (1981), Beuys exclaimed, 'They literally stole everything from me'; according to Oppitz, the self-irony in this reversal of appropriation was intended; Oppitz, M., *Die Kunst der Genauigkeit*, Munich: Trickster, 1989, p. 84. On Beuys see also, Tisdall, C., *Joseph Beuys*, London: Thames & Hudson, 1979; Harlan, V., Rappmann, R., Schata, P., *Soziale Plastik: Materialien zu Joseph Beuys*, Achberg: Achberger Verlag, 1984. Müller, M., *Wie man dem toten Hasen die Bilder erklärt: Schamanismus und Erkenntnis im Werk von Joseph Beuys*, Alfter (Germany): VDG, 1993.

35. On Maya Deren's work as an artist crossing the boundaries to anthropology see Russel, C., *Experimental Ethnography: The Work of Film in the Age of Video.*Durham, NC: Duke University Press, 1999, pp. 206 –218. Maya Deren, *Divine Horsemen*, London: Thames and Hudson, 1953.

36. Coe, M.D., *Breaking the Maya Code*, London; Thames & Hudson, 1992, p. 202; *Edgewalker: a Conversation with Linda Schele*, a film by Andrew Weeks, Simon Martin, and Lori Conley, Home Life Productions (USA), 1999. Schele, L., *Maya Glyphs: The Verbs*, Austin: University of Texas Press, 1982; Schele, L. and Miller, M.E., *The Blood of Kings*, Fort Worth: Kimbell Art Museum/NewYork: George Braziller, 1986.

37. Carvalho-Neto, P. de (ed.), *Arte Popular del Ecuador: Areas Norte, Sur y Centro*, 2nd edn, Quito: Ediciones Abya-Yala, 1989, pp. XI–XV.

38. See, also Schneider, A., 'Rooting Hybridity: Globalisation and the Challenges of *Mestizaje* and *Crisol de Razas* for Contemporary Artists in Ecuador and Argentina', *Indiana*, 21 (2004), pp. 95–112. On Viteri in the context of modern Ecuadorian art, see Ades, D., *Art in Latin America*, London: Hayward Gallery, 1989, pp. 296–98; Oña, L., 'Ecuador', in Sullivan, E.J. *Latin American Art in the Twentieth Century*, London: Phaidon, 1996, p. 188.

39. Reichek, E., *Tierra del Fuego*, leaflet accompanying the exhibition. Akron OH: Akron Museum, 1992. The original photographs appear in Gusinde, M., *Die Feuerlandindianer*, 3 vols, Vienna-Mödling: Anthropos, 1931–9. See also Schneider, A., 'Uneasy Relationships', p. 186.

40. Jimmy Durham, 'Elaine Reichek: Unravelling the Social Fabric', in Durham, J., *A Certain Lack of Coherence: Writings on Art and Cultural Politics*, London: Kala Press, 1993, p. 235, emphasis in the original.

41. Schechner, R. and Appel, W., (eds), *By Means of Performance: Intercultural Studies of Theatre and Ritual*, Cambridge: Cambridge University Press, 1990. Barba, E., *The Paper Canoe: A Guide to Theatre Anthropology*, London: Routledge, 1995. In this present volume, George Marcus and Fernando Calzadilla discuss the work by Calzadilla and Abdel Hernández, which incorporated ethnography, performance and installation.

42. Tracy, M., Vargas, E., Tarcisio, E., *The River Pierce: Sacrifice II, 13.4.90*, Houston TX: Rice University Press, 1992; see also Arnd Schneider's comments on this project in 'Uneasy Relationships', pp. 189–92.

43. Alfredo Portillos, *Ecumenical Space*, installation at Biennial of São Paulo, 1977 (and Centro Cultural Recoleta, Buenos Aires, 1994 – video sponsored by the Pollock-Krassner Foundation). José Bedia, *De donde vengo*, Philadelphia: Institute of Contemporary Art/University of Pennsylvania, 1994.

44. Esther Pasztory, 'Identity and Difference: The Uses and Meanings of Ethnic Arts', in Barnes, S.J. and Melion, W.S. *Cultural Differentiation and Cultural Identity in the Visual Arts*, Hanover NH: National Gallery of Art/University Press of New England, 1989.

45. Fiadone, A., *El diseño indígena argentino; una aproximación a la iconografía precolumbina*, Buenos Aires: la marca editora, 2001, pp. 20–3.

46. Paternosto, C., *Abstraction: The Amerindian Paradigm*, p. 60.

47. George Kubler, *Esthetic Reognition of Ancient Amerindian Art*, New Haven CT: Yale University Press, 1991; 'Aesthetics Since Amerinidan Art Before Columbus', in Bone, E.H. (ed.) *Collecting the Pre-Columbian Past*, Washington DC: Dumbarton Oaks Research Library and Collection, 1993.

48. Thomas, N., 'Appropriation/Appreciation', p. 139.

49. See note 22.

50. The literature on these subjects is abundant to say the least. One of the best essays is still Clifford, J., 'Identity in Mashpee', *The Predicament of Culture*, Cambridge MA: Harvard University Press.

51. Cecilia Vicuña' lived in London in the early 1970s, studied at the Slade School of Fine Arts, had a show at the ICA in 1973, and formed with Guy Brett, David Medalla and John Dugger the Artist for Democracy movement for which she organized a major Arts Festival for Democracy in Chile at the Royal College of Art in 1974. Lippard, L., 'Spinning the Common Thread'. Cecilia Vicuña' in De Zegher, M.C. (ed.), *The Precarious*, Middletown CT: Wesleyan University Press, 1998, p. 7; De Zegher, M.C., 'Ouvrage', p. 22.

52. Isbell, B.J. and Harrison, R., 'Metaphor Spun: A Conversation with Cecilia Vicuña' (Poetry Reading and Perfomance, Cornell University, Fall 1994). Vicuña, C., *The Precarious*, pp. 50–1, emphasis in the original.

53. Kroeber, T., *Ishi in Two Worlds*, Berkeley: University of California Press, 1961.
54. From a form letter by Claire Pentecost, 1990; courtesy of the artist. An artist's statement, as well as the letter, were exhibited at the show, and provided the following information on the response to the project:

> The letters from Native Americans that are part of the project, were in reply to a query I sent out near the end of March 1990. Most of the names and addresses were furnished to me by the Information Center at the Museum of the American Indian, from the directories of Native American councils, governing bodies and cultural organizations. I'd like to thank Marty DeMontano of the information Center for her help in this process. A few contacts were furnished by friends. I sent them a cover letter, a brief description of the piece and a self addressed stamped envelope. In a few cases where telephone numbers were available, I was able to make follow-up calls. One respondent called me to get a better idea of what I wanted. As of August 1990, 125 letters were sent, 21 returned by the post office for lack of forwarding address, and 22 were answered. A few of my contacts turned out to be people who are not Indians but have lived for some time in a Native American culture. I wish to thank all those who took time from their extremely demanding schedules to answer my letter. A copy of the letter and the initial description are included in the exhibit.

> (Pentecost, C., in Kroeber, *Ishi in Two Worlds*, courtesy of the artist.)

Chapter 3 Moon and Mother: Francesco Clementine's Orient

1. Cf. Bundgaard, H., *Indian Artworlds in Contention: Local, Regional and National Discources on Orissan Patta Painting*, London: Curzon, 1999.
2. Cf. Kramrisch, S., 'Twenty-four Indian Miniatures', in Percy, A. and Foye, R. (eds) *Francesco Clemente: Three Worlds*, Philadelphia PA: Philadelphia Museum of Art, 1990.
3. Foye, R., 'Madras' in Percy, A. and Foye, R. (eds) *Francesco Clemente*, p. 57.
4. Foye, p. 52.
5. Brown, M., 'Can Culture Be Copyrighted?', *Current Anthropology*, 39(2) (1998), p. 194.
6. Kaviraj, S., 'The Imaginary Institution of India', in Chatterjee, P. and Pandey, G. (eds) *Subaltern Studies VII*, Delhi: Oxford University Press, 1992, pp. 1–39.

7. Foye, p. 53.
8. Foye, 1990, p. 110.
9. Inden, R., 'Orientalist Constructions of India', *Modern Asian Studies*, 20(3) (1986), p. 430.
10. Inden, p. 442.
11. Fabian, J., *Time and the Other: How Anthropology Makes its Object*, New York: Columbia University Press, 1983.
12. Foye, p. 50.
13. Foye, p. 52.
14. Bradnock, R. (ed.), *India Handbook*, 4th edn, Bath: Trade and Travel Publications, 1995, p. 830.
15. Foye, p. 55.
16. '. . . it's like going home for me' (Clemente cited in Foye, p. 50).
17. Birdwood, G., *Paris Universal Exhibition of 1878: Handbook to the British Indian Section*, London: Offices of the Royal Commission, 1878.
18. Birdwood, p.2.
19. Birdwood, p.2.
20. Born in Germany, Muller became a naturalized British citizen. He was Professor of Comparative Philology at the University of Oxford and was identified as a romantic champion of India throughout his life.
21. Muller, p.31.
22. Muller, p.29.
23. Muller, p.31.
24. Foye, p. 50.
25. See Heartney, E., 'Hannah Collins at Leo Castelli', *Art in America* February (2001), pp. 136–7, who describes Collins' 'voyeuristic . . . fascination with the exotic'.
26. Formerly the Principal of the Rajahmundry College.
27. Couldrey, O., *South Indian Hours*, London: Hurst & Blackett, 1924, p. 15.
28. Couldrey, pp. 18–19.
29. In 1977 Clemente stayed at the Thesophical Society headquarters in Madras, and in 1979 in the Leadbeater Chambers (Foye, pp. 53 and 56–7), used the Theosophical Society Library extensively, but never attended any meetings.
30. Foye, pp. 58 and 59.
31. Klein, N., *No Logo*, London: Flamingo, 2001, p. 85.
32. Foye, p. 57.

Chapter 4 Where Green Grass Comes to Meet Blue Sky: A Trajectory of Josef Šíma

1. Breton, A., *L'amour fou* in his *Oeuvres complètes*, vol. II, Paris: Gallimard, 1992, p. 780.
2. Serres, M., *The Troubadour of Knowledge*, translated by Sheila Faria Glaser, with William Paulson, Ann Arbor: The University of Michigan Press, 1991, p. 65.

Chapter 5 Encounters with the Work of Susan Hiller

1. In conversation with Susan Hiller, April 1996.
2. Hiller, S., *Thinking About Art*, edited and introduced by Barbara Einzig, Manchester: Manchester University Press, 1996, p. xi.
3. Lippard, L., *Thinking About Art*, p. xiii.
4. Hiller comments that both this work and to some extent *After the Freud Museum* are exceptions to her refusal not to work with materials from other societies. In these instances her work included material from other societies, but with a very important distinction:

   > Fragments uses as basic material, hundreds of broken Pueblo Indian potsherds alongside hundreds of gouache representations of them, plus charts, texts, photos, I determined then never to use materials from societies other than my own and in this instance solely to show how these archaeological materials are categorised and understood in museums in our culture, contrasted with how they are categorised and understood in their culture of origin. The work pivots on contrasting notions of representation – 'our' representation of 'them' and 'their' representation of themselves". (in discussion with Susan Hiller, December 2001.)

5. Hiller, S., *The Myth of Primitivism*, London, Routledge, 1991, reprinted 1992. Also see the highly influential text 'Art and Anthropology/Anthropology and Art', originally presented at the Institute for Social Anthropology, Oxford University, England, 6 May 1977. Published in *Thinking About Art*. See also 'An artist looks at ethnographic exhibitions', in *Thinking About Art*.
6. Hiller, S., introduction, *The Myth of Primitivism*.
7. *Thinking About Art*.
8. Genet, J., 'What remains of a Rembrandt Torn into Four Equal Pieces, and Flushed down the Toilet . . .': *Rembrandt*, New York: Hanuman Books, 1988, p. 9.

9. Susan Hiller, quoted in the preface by Lucy Lippard in *Thinking about Art*, p. X1.

10. Susan Hiller, *Witness* catalogue, 2001, unpaginated.

11. Ronell, A., *Crack Wars*, Lincoln NE: University of Nebraska Press, 1992, p. 155.

12. D. Vase quoted by R. Durand, The Disposition of the Voice', in M. Benamon and C. Caramello (eds), *Performance in Postmodern Culture*, Milwaukee WI: Uni. Wisconsin, 1977, p. 99.

13. Durand, p. 100.

14. Ronell, A., p. 155.

15. Durand, R., p. 100.

16. 'Clinic' was exhibited as part of the exhibition 'Susan Hiller: Recall – Selected Works 1969–2004' held at BALTIC Center for Contemporary Art. It was a work commissioned specifically for BALTIC.

17. Jean Fisher, quoting Susan Hiller (interviewed by Rozika Parker) in catalogue, Matts Gallery, London, 1990, unpaginated.

18. Benjamin, W., 'Edward Fuchs, Collector and Historian', *One Way Street and Other Writings*, trans. Edmund Jephcott, Kingsley Shorter, London: Verso, 1979, p. 351.

19. *After the Freud Museum* publ. Bookworks, 1995 (unpaginated)

20. Extended versions have since been exhibited in many museum contexts, including her retrospective at the Tate, Liverpool in 1996, 'Material Culture' at the Hayward Gallery in 1998, 'The Muse in the Museum' at the Museum of Modern Art, New York, Tate Modern, London in 2002 and BALTIC Center for the Arts in 2004.

21. Susan Hiller, *Thinking About Art*, 'Art and Anthropology/Anthropology and Art', p. 23.

22. Ibid.

23. Rex Butler catalogue essay, 'The tip of the Iceberg' on the work of Janet Burchill and Jennifer McCamley, University Art Museum, University of Queensland, 2001, p. 63.

24. Hiller, S., 'Art and Anthropology/Anthropology and Art', ibid p. 23.

25. Foucault, M., *Language, Counter Memory, Practice*, ed. D.F. Bouchard, Ithaca: Cornell University Press, 1977, p. 160.

26. Taussig, M., *The Magic of the State*, London: Routledge, p. 197.

27. Ibid., p. 198.

28. From Hiller's notes on *Wild Talents*:

> in the years leading up to World War II, he became famous for using his extraordinary talents to locate lost objects and persons, to participate in numerous scientific experiments in England, Poland and elsewhere, and to collaborate with archeologists in locating and explaining human artifacts from Neolithic and Paleolithic times. Later, during the Nazi regime, he worked surreptitiously in Warsaw using his abilities to locate people in concentration camps, until eventually he was arrested and never seen again.

29. Zizek, S., ibid, p. 217.
30. Taussig, M., ibid., p. 121.
31. Taussig, M., ibid., p. 121.
32. Zizek, S., ibid., p. 217.
33. Taussig, M., ibid., p. 198.

Chapter 6 Reflections on Art and Agency: Knot-sculpture between Mathematics and Art

1. Friedman, N. and Barrallo, J. (eds), *Isama 99: The International Society of the Arts, Mathematics and Architecture*, Bilbao: The University of the Basque Country, 1999.
2. The complex and manifold interchange between artists and mathematicians is outlined in the extremely useful edited volume by Emmer, M. (ed.), *The Visual Mind: Art and Mathematics*, Cambridge MA: MIT Press, 1993.
3. In the realm of mathematics, such surfaces are found where at every point the positive and negative curvatures exactly balance, locally minimizing the surface area needed to span and close off a given opening (see Sequin, C., 'Computer Augmented Inspirations', in Friedman and Barrallo, p. 420).
4. Http://www.bangor.ac.uk/SculMath/.
5. This point has been exquisitely developed by Gell, A., 1998 *Art and Agency: An Anthropological Theory*, Oxford: Oxford University Press, 1998.
6. Ibid., p. 9.
7. Ibid., p. 82. See also pp. 84–6.
8. Ibid., p. 83.
9. Eglash, R., *African Fractals: Modern Computing and Indigenous Design*, New Brunswick: Rutgers University Press, 1999.
10. Gell, p. 216.
11. Kemp, M., *The Science of Art: Optical Themes in Western Art from Brunelleschi to Seurat*, New Haven: Yale University Press, 1990.
12. Baxandall, M., *Painting and Experience in Fifteenth-century Italy*, Harmondsworth: Penguin, 1975.
13. Kline, M., *Mathematics in Western Culture*, Harmondsworth: Penguin, 1953.
14. Alpers, S., *The Art of Describing*, Chicago: Chicago University Press, 1983.
15. Ginzburg, C., 'Morelli, Freud, and Sherlock Holmes: Clues and Scientific Method', in Eco, U. and Sebeok, T., *The Sign of Three*, Bloomington: Indiana University Press, 1983, p. 94.
16. Bois, Y.A., *Painting as Model*, Cambridge MA: MIT Press.
17. Gell.

18. Brisson, D. (ed.), *Hypergraphics: Visualizing Complex relationships in Art, Science and Technology*, Boulder CO: Westview Press, 1978.
19. Banchoff , T., *Beyond the Third Dimension*, New York: Freeman, 1990.
20. Barrow, J., *Pie in the Sky: Counting, Thinking and Being*, Oxford: Oxford University Press, 1992.
21. Bill, M., 'The Mathematical Way of Thinking in the Visual Arts of Our Time', in Emmer, M., *The Visual Mind: Art and Mathematics*, Cambridge MA: MIT Press, 1949 reprinted 1993.
22. Ibid., p. 8.
23. The most important studies to date are by Ascher, M., 1991 *Ethnomathematics: A Multicultural View of Mathematical Ideas*, Pacific Grove CA: Brooks Publishing Co., 1991, Zaslavsky, C. 'Ethnomathematics and Multicultural Mathematics Education', *Teaching Children Mathematics*, 4(9) (1998): pp. 502–8, as well as her *Africa Counts: Number and Pattern and African Culture*, Brooklyn: Lawrence Hill Press, 1973. Eglash, R., *African Fractals*, New Brunswick: Rutgers University Press, 1997.
24. Levinson, S., 1992. 'Primer for the Field Investigation of Spatial Description and Conception', Pragmatics 2(1) (1992): pp. 5–47. Washburn, D. and Crowe, D.W., *Symmetries of Culture*, Seattle: University of Washington Press. Silverman, E., 'Traditional Cartography in Papua New Guinea', in Woodward, D. and Lewis G.M. (eds), *Cartography in the Traditional African, American, Arctic, Australian, and Pacific Societies* ed. D. Woodward and G.M. Chicago and London: University of Chicago Press.
25. Cf. Wassman, J., 'The Yupno as Post-Newtonian Scientists: The Question of What is "Natural" in Spatial Descriptions', *Man* (N.S.) 29(3) (1994): pp. 645–7. Mackenzie, M., *Androgynous Objects: Stringbags and Gender in the Pacific*, Berlin: Harwood Press, 1991.
26. Bateson, G., 'Style, Grace, and Information in Primitive Art', *Steps to an Ecology of Mind*, New York: Ballantine Books, 1972, pp. 28–152.
27. Gell, A., 'Traps as Artworks, Artworks as Traps', *Journal of Material Culture*, 1(1) (1996): p. 36.
28. Vogel, S., 'Artifact and Art', in *Art/Artefact: African Art in Anthropological Collections*, exhibition catalogue, New York, Center for African Art and Prestel Verlag, 1988.
29. The knot served as metaphor of such topologies in numerous publications. Cf. Serres, M., *Conversations on Science, Culture and Time*, with Bruno Latour, translated by Roxanne Lapidus, Ann Arbor: University of Michigan Press, 1995.
30. Strohecker, C., n.d. 'Why Knot?' Ph.D. Dissertation. Epistemology and Learning Group. Media Arts and Sciences, Massachusetts Institute of Technology, p. 31.
31. Stringham, I., 'Regular Figures in n-dimensional Space', *American Journal of Mathematics*. See also Henderson, L. *The Fourth Dimension and Non-Euclidean Geometry in Modern Art*, Princeton: Princeton University Press, 1983, pp. 278–92, and Brisson, D. (ed.), 1978. *Hypergraphics: Visualizing*

Complex relationships in Art, Science and Technology, Boulder CO: Westview Press, 1978.

32. Diehl, G. *Vasareli*. Naefels: Bonfini Press Corporation. Translated from French by Eileen B. Hennessy.
33. Denari, N., *Interrupted Projections: Another Global Surface or Territorial Re-codings on the World Sheet*, Tokyo: Atsushi Sato.
34. ibid, p. 47.
35. Ho, M., The New Age of the Organism. *Architectural Design*, 129 (1998): pp. 44–51.
36. Wassmann, J., 'The Yupno as Post-Newtonian Scientists: the question of what is "Natural" in Spatial Descriptions', *Man* (N.S.), 29(3) (1994): pp. 645–67 at p. 646.
37. Ibid.
38. See Peterson, I., 'Equations in Stone', *Science News*, 138(10) (1990): 352–60.
39. Sequin, C., 'Computer-augmented Inspiration', in Friedman and Barrallo, pp. 419–29. Francis, with Collins, B., 'On Knot-Spanning Surfaces: An Illustrated Essay on Topological Art', in Emmer, M. (ed.), *The Visual Mind* Cambridge MA: MIT, 1995, pp. 57–65.
40. Sequin, p. 421.
41. Francis, p. 59.
42. This point was made by N. Thomas in Thomas, N. and Lousche, D. (eds), *Double Vision*, Cambridge: Cambridge University Press, 1999, p. 4.
43. See Eglash, R., *African Fractals: Modern Computing and Indigenous Design*, New Brunswick: Rutgers University Press.
44. See Brown, R., 'John Robinson's Symbolic Sculptures, Knots and Mathematics', in Friedman and Barrallo, pp. 75–81.
45. Robinson, J., *Symbolic Sculptures*, catalogue for the exhibition at the Pop Maths Roadshow, Leeds University, 1989, published by Mathematics and Knots.
46. //www.bangor.ac.uk/SculMath/, see also www.bangor.ac.uk/cpm.

Chapter 7 Artists in the Field

1. Clifford, J. and Marcus, G. (eds), *Writing Culture: the Poetics and Politics of Ethnography*, Berkeley: University of California Press, 1986.
2. Marcus, G., *Ethnography Through Thick and Thin*, Princeton: Princeton University Press, 1998; and Marcus, G. (ed.), *Critical Anthropology Now*, Santa Fe: School of American Research Press, 1999.
3. For example, Taussig, M., *Mimesis and Alterity*, New York: Routledge, 1993; and Taylor, J., *Paper Tangos*, Durham: Duke University Press, 1998.

4. The following is a brief account, provided to me by Abdel Hernández, of the earlier projects in Cuba created by Abdel and his circle that have similarities to the experiments of the *Artists In Trance* workshop:

Their first project in Cuba occurred in 1987 and was called *Performance in Communities*. It consisted of an ensemble of performances created in a collective expedition to rural communities of the eastern province of Holguin. The artists included Nilo Castillo, Alejandro Lopez, and Hernández. Staying three or four days each in different communities, eliciting participation and reactions from villagers, they conceived performances as forms of mediation, where representation loses its mimetic associations, functioning more as re-presentation, the artist presenting culture. The performances were preceded by interviews and exchanges, and were, in a sense, the artists' responses to these initial interactions. These performances were reminiscent of body art, but without its mainly self-referential character. Movements of the body were intended to explore the social dynamics of self-other relations. For example, an abstract dance performance entitled *Yo Vinatero* used movement to enact the culture of *artisanal* winemakers.

Their second project occurred in 1988 and 1989, and merged art practices with social science investigation. It was called *Pilón*. Lazaro Saavedra, Alejandro Lopez, Alejandro Frometa, Huber Moreno, and Hernández created installations derived from residence in the community of Pilón in the region south of the Sierra Maestra for a period of one year. This project thrust itself into a common kind of anthropological fieldwork – the community study – with the motivation of creating a different sort of milieu for their art than that of the cosmopolitan art world. Ethnographic fieldwork created the context for both the production and the reception of the art works, but with the intention of eventually exposing this project in Pilón to the Havana art world.

The Pilón project practised a kind of montage as a mode of fieldwork, allowing the juxtaposition of the villagers' perspectives within an installation or *mise-en-scène*. Instead of presenting content didactically, for example, they left relationships among sequenced photographs open, so that histories, regional narratives, and typifications could be filled in through commentaries and reactions. The artists' role consisted in repeatedly shuffling the photographs in alternative sequences as a result of the responses and comments of the villagers. While this art in the field followed tendencies to move from art institutions towards natural or social spaces, the Pilón project was not limited to taking informed, high art to the community as a simple documentation of experiences on site. The process moved from interactions with popular culture to the creation of montages, writings, and discourses that were returned to the Havana art world so as to re-enter cosmopolitan debates.

Their third project occurred in 1990 and 1991 (prior to Hernández's departure from Cuba), and was called *Hacer*. The importance of this project was as an alternative form of artistic production that took shape as a laboratory workshop emphasizing the exploration of intersubjective communication. Conceived as a critical pedagogy, performances and happenings were used as triggers in cultural elicitation throughout Havana's urban spaces. Artists David Palacios, Julio Fowler, Carlos Michel Fuentes, two social psychologists, ten art students and dancers, and Hernández introduced different types of evocation: ecological, therapeutic, cultural, sociological. *Hacer* was constituted as a workshop with a common meeting site in a classroom where discussions took place about the diverse performances produced in urban public spaces. Hernández, for instance, worked among subcultures of street musicians. The works emerging from this project employed several modalities from simple interviews to therapeutic techniques.

5. Hernández's interest in evocation engages in anthropology primarily with Stephen Tyler's contributions to the Writing Culture initiative. See Tyler, S., *The Unspeakable*, Madison: University of Wisconsin Press, 1987.

6. As Fernando Calzadilla explains the naming of the market installation: 'The name we gave to the installation, *El Mercado de Acá* (*The Market From Here*) makes a reference to working in our own culture, therefore the dichotomy modern/primitive is broken, the idea of the primitive is gone. A reference to the anthropological gaze looking at its own culture, a disruption with the "other" because there is no other, there is no "over there". The Market is from here.'

7. For example, Frake, C., 'How to Ask for a Drink in Subanun', *American Anthropologist*, 76 (1966): 273-90, 1966.

8. Up until now, at least in Venezuela, at least for me, theatre has been oriented towards representation, narrative, the enclosing and the construction of subjects in a physical and psychological space, the domain of codified structures and symbolism. In my making of scenography, a scaffold, a division, a colour extension intuits the movement of bodies in space. I create a reality where the illusory is not present, but suggested. Each tying, each fabric, each joint, shows with ease its irreverence towards what is mimetic and representational. It is in this sense that scenography achieves the crystallization of the staging: by synchronizing all scenic elements as significant affects. I produce a reality that is distinctive and autonomous from its socio-political referent, one that produces emotions, sinaesthetic relations among the participants. These sinaesthetic relations trigger a social transformation in the spectator through the pondering on an experienced reality. The spectator watches what is being lived and thus identifies with what he sees; an anthropological reading in which the audience fills in the blanks with its own sounds, with its own memories.

By deconstructing theatrical competence, its codes and structures, although I start with its own material, I break meaning and representational relationships to allow the free flow of experience and desire. There is nothing to be trapped, projected, or introjected, except for flows, networks, and systems. All the rest appears and disappears as a galaxy of transitory objects representing only the failure of representation. In my theatrical design I concentrate in creating significants that can trigger in the spectators a collective imaginary, entities in which to identify processes, ethnographic evocations that could lead them to ponder through emotion, and this emotion, in turn, could lead them to social transformation, which is the ulterior aim in the creation of theatrical event.

9. *El Mercado de Coche* had to be set aside because a major reform was taking place at the time with heavy-handed political and economic interests at stake that had interrupted its continuity and normal flow of interaction.

10. In Benjamin, W., *Illuminations*, New York: Schoken Books, 1969.

11. Kosuth, J., *Art After Philosophy and After*, Cambridge: MIT Press. 1991, p. 107.

12. Although social structures, which are part of the dominant culture, generally become the basis of the dominant ideology, it is pertinent to emphasize the fact that subcultures, which are often subordinate and in opposition to the dominant one, generate their own social structures and ideologies. The market as social institution is inscribed in the dominant culture and confroms to its social structure, but the inner arrangement of illegal street vendors, herb 'doctors,' cooked food vendors, working children, and so forth, which defies the socio-spatial normativity of the dominant culture, is the ideology I am referring to and the one we didn't want to betray in our observation.

13. Clifford, J., *The Predicament of Culture*, Cambridge: Harvard University Press, 1988.

14. Johannes Fabian, *Time and the Other*, New York: Columbia University Press, 1983, p. 109.

15. In Brennan, T. and Jay, M. (eds), *Vision in Context*, New York: Routledge, 1996, p. 19.

16. Fuenteovejuna, like Lope de Vega's play, was the name of the house where I lived and had a studio. It was an old mansion in a run-down upper-class neighbourhood that awaited demolition while we made use of its generous spaces.

17. According to the Oxford English Dictionary, proxemics is the study of socially conditioned spatial factors in ordinary human relations. Space is used to encode social meanings that govern relationships among subjects, subjects and objects, and among objects. An important part of the study is how the gaze constructs a relationship between the object presented and the position of the spectator, and since spectators are always looking, they are most of the time constructing a 'frame of representation' in the act of looking. How we positioned ourselves in the installation and how the objects were positioned conformed to what we considered had encoded spatial factors that manipulate the frame of representation constructed by the spectators' gaze.

18. To explore these questions briefly, I will follow Pierre Bourdieu and James Clifford in how cultural goods transit different social realms. In *The Field*

of Cultural Production, New York: Columbia University Press, 1993, Bourdieu distinguishes two fields of cultural production; field one corresponds to the producers of cultural goods, and field two, to the non-producers of cultural goods. Field one is a closed system regulated by the laws of its own criteria for evaluation and recognition. The exchange is between cultural producers on one side, and peers, competitors, patrons, and cultural institutions on the other. We can call this the field of high culture. Below is field two, an open system where large-scale media producers exchange with the public at large regimented by the laws of competition. For Bourdieu the exchange between peers in field one is horizontal while the exchange in field two is vertical, from large scale producers to the public at large. Large scale producers draw from field one for their supply of manpower and innovations while (in my opinion) cultural producers in field one draw from the bottom of the pool of field two although this is not clear in Bourdieu's presentation. Bourdieu's schema is stagnant and leaves little room for transformation.

If we place Bourdieu's position in relation to James Clifford's objects moving from art to not-art, from culture to not-culture, and back and forth from art to culture, the diagram is different. For Clifford, there can be no movement from zone 4 to zone 1. (See diagram in Clifford, *The Predicament of Culture*, p. 22.)

What is interesting for art critics, sociologists, and anthropologists is that TMFH breaks both Bourdieu's and Clifford's schema of symbolic goods and objects moving across the boundaries of ethnographic fields and high art, or from large-scale non-producers of cultural goods to the closed system of cultural producers. While we where doing an ethnographic 'reading' of our relation with the markets visited, the materials used in the installation were transformed from large scale produced by not-cultural producers to high art. A movement that, although coming from different angles, both Clifford and Bourdieu deny. Every single thing that entered the exhibit was touched, rubbed, handled, and designed so it would not be a 'ready-made', or an ethnographic exhibit of folklore or natural science museums. The spatial text, the manner in which the material intersected the space had an exactness that related to the closed system of a work of art, and obliquely to sociological and anthropological issues. Altar pieces, bags, ties and knots, herbs, saints and perfume jars, dresses and gifts, fruits and shoes, were all treated separately and in a way that followed the same line that we transited while doing the ethnographic fieldwork: trance in the fold, sliding in the light refracted through the plastic, sinking in the betweenness of art and the rest, of art and ourselves; immersed in the 'tetrahedronic' relationship of word, image, dialogue, and evocation.

The resulting product of this relationship is definitely akin to a work of art. For the Frankfurt School, the association of the work of art with a commodity has had terrible consequences: 'that art renounces its own autonomy and proudly takes its place among consumption goods constitutes the charm of novelty . . . Pure works of art which deny the commodity society by the very fact that they obey their own law were always wares all the same' (Adorno, T. and Horkheimer, M., *Dialectic of Enlightenment*, New York: Herder and Herder, 1972). Ironically, in TMFH we are talking about wares in the strict sense of the word. Ironically, the 'wares' did not enter the art market economy or resort to novelty to become a commodity. There was no product to sell or exchange, to preserve or enter the consumer art market. The ephemerality of the work was emphasized by its participation in a course/event as a specific project for a specific moment, like the market that does not exist except in the passing of hands, in the relation of goods and not in the goods themselves. Just as a scenography doesn't exist in the absence of the performer. For this reason, TMFH regains the autonomy denied by Adorno and Horkheimer. For this reason, it can transit spaces denied by Clifford and Bourdieu.

19. For a concept of becoming see Deleuze, G. and Guattari, F., *A Thousand Plateaus*, Minneapolis: University of Minnesota Press, 1987, Plateau #10.
20. Schechner, R., *By Means of Performance*, Cambridge: Cambridge University Press, 1990, p. 37.
21. Cited in Schechner, p. 39.
22. Videotaped interview, Calzadilla's translation.
23. 'Installation as a hybrid discipline, is made up of multiple histories; it includes architecture and Performance Art in its parentage, and the many directions within contemporary visual arts have also exerted their influence. By crossing the frontiers between different disciplines, installation is able to question their individual autonomy, authority and, ultimately, their history and relevance to the contemporary context.' De Oliveira, N., Oxley, N., Petry, M., *Installation Art*, Washington DC: Smithsonian Institution Press, 1994, p. 7.

Chapter 9 Dialogues

1. See 'Dave Lewis', monograph by Rohini Malik, London: Autograph (the Association of Black Photographers), 1997.
2. See Hall, S. and Sealy, M. (eds), *Different*, Phaidon and Autograph, 2001.
3. See 'The Impossible Science of Being: Dialogues between Anthropology and Photography', Exhibition at Photographers Gallery, London, 1995 See also Interview with Dave Lewis, 'Kricky Positions: Dave Lewis and Chris Wright', *Anthropology Today*, 12(2) 1996, pp. 12–17.
4. See Dave Lewis, *Royal Anthropological Institute 1995*, in *Anthropology Today,* 12(2) (1996) p. 14.
5. Jayne Ifekwunigwe was Reader in Anthropology at the University of East London, and is now a Visiting Scholar in the Department of Cultural Anthropology, Duke University, NC, USA.

6. Wittenborn, R. and Biegert, C., *James Bay Project – A River Drowned By Water*, Montreal: Montreal Museum of Fine Art, 1981. See also, Schneider, A., 'Uneasy Relationships: Contemporary Artists and Anthropology', *Journal of Material Culture*, 1 (1996): pp. 183–210. Wittenborn and other artists, such as Nikolaus Lang (see this section), but also Chrisitian Boltanksi, Paul-Armand Gette, and Anne and Patrick Poirier have been associated with concerns in 1960s and 1970s art to track or secure evidence (or 'Spurensicherung' in German) and work on factual and fictive traces of human activity; see, Metken, G., *Spurensicherung. Kunst als Anthropologie und Selbsterforschung: Fiktive Wissenschaften in der heutigen Kunst*, Cologne: DuMont, 1977; also Heinrichs, H.J., *Wilde Künstler: Über Primitivismus, art brut und die Trugbilder der Realität*, Hamburg: Europäische Verlagsanstalt, 1995, pp. 77–80; Metken, G., *Spurensicherung: Eine Revision*, Amsterdam: Fundus, 1996. Metken makes some reference to Claude Lévi-Strauss and structuralism, but a history focusing on the specific relation to anthropology remains to be written. More recently, Mark Dion has also carried out work on botanical collections, archives, and museums; see Coles, A., 'Fieldwork and the Natural History Museum: Mark Dion Interview', in Coles, A. (ed.), *The Optic of Walter Benjamin*, Vol. 3 , de- dis- ex-, London: Blackdog Publications, 1999.
7. Wittenborn and Biegert, *James Bay Project*, p. 268.
8. Ibid., p. 269.
9. Ibid., p. 11.
10. Ibid., p. 25.
11. Ibid., pp. 33–4.
12. Latour, B. *We Have Never Been Modern*, Cambridge MA: Harvard University Press, 1993.
13. Rainer Wittenborn in collaboration with Claus Biegert *Amazon of the North - James Bay Revisited* Ezra and Cecile Zilkha Gallery, Center for the Arts, Wesleyan University, Connecticut, 1997.
14. On Nikolaus Lang's work and his relation to 'Spurensicherung' (securing evidence of factual and fictive traces), see Metken, G., *Spurensicherung. Kunst als Anthropologie und Selbsterforschung: Fiktive Wissenschaften in der heutigen Kunst*, Cologne: DuMont, 1977; Metken, G., *Spurensicherung: Eine Revision*, Amsterdam: Fundus, 1996; Arnd Schneider, 'The Art Diviners', *Anthropology Today*, 9(2), 1993. pp. 3 –9.
15. Lang, N., *Nunga und Goonya*, Munich: Kunstraum München, 1991.
16. Ibid., p. 36.
17. Murphy, B., 'New Voyages Under Different Stars', in Lang, *Nunga and Goonya*, pp. 95–6.
18. Ibid., p. 106.
19. Ibid., p. 114.
20. On Rimer Cardillo, see Schneider, A., 'Acts of Empathy', *Rimer Cardillo Retrospective*, Samuel Dorsky Museum, State University of New York at New Paltz, 2004 (catalogue); Schneider, A., 'Sites of Amnesia, Non-Sites of

Memory: Identity and Other in the work of four Uruguayan artists', in Coles, A., *Siting Ethnography*, London: Blackdog Publications, 2000; also Haber, A., 'Uruguay', in Sullivan, E. (ed.), *Latin American Art in the Twentieth Century*, London: Phaidon, 1996.
21. In an interview with Alicia Haber, 'The Scenario of Memory', in *Charrúas y Montes Criollos: A los Quinientos Anos de la Conquista Europea*, exhibition catalogue by Rimer Cardillo, Montevideo: Ed. Galería Latina, 1991.
22. Rimer Cardillo, *Araucaria*, Bronx Museum of the Arts, New York, 1998, catalogue with essays by Marysol Nieves, Lucy Lippard, and Patricia Phillips; Uruguay: *Rimer Cardillo*, XLIX Biennale di Venezia, catalogue, 2001 with essays by Clever Lara, Angel Kalenberg and Lucy Lippard.

Chapter 10 Travels in a New World – A Work around a Diasporic Theme by Mohini Chandra

1. An earlier version of this chapter appeared in conjunction with Chandra's exhibition *Travels in a New World* at Bluecoat Gallery, Liverpool in 1997. I am grateful to Mohini Chandra for discussing her work with me at length.
2. D'Ozouville, B., 'Reflexions sur le dualisme dans la représentation photographique d'une societé coloniale, iles Fidji 1879–1916', *Journal des Anthropologues*, 80–81 (2000): p. 239; Avtar, B., *Cartographies of Diaspora: Contesting Identities*, London, Routledge, 1996, p. 3.
3. D'Ozouville, p. 218.
4. In recent years important historical studies in the Fiji-Indian community have emerged, notably in the work of scholars such as Brij Lal and Vijay Mishra. The publication of one of the few first hand accounts of Indian experience of indentured labour in Fiji by Totaram Sanadhya (Sanadhya, T., *My Twenty-one years in Fiji*, Suva: Fiji Museum, 1991) also increased awareness of this hitherto largely neglected topic.
5. Gupta, A. and Ferguson, J. (eds), *Anthropological Locations: Boundaries and Grounds of Field Science*, Berkeley: University of California Press, 1997, pp. 12–13.
6. The title is a reference to Enoch Powell's infamous 'rivers of blood' speech of 1968 on non-White immigration and racial integration.
7. Chandra originally studied sociology and was not a stranger to the academic debates of the social sciences in general.
8. Clifford, J., *The Predicament of Culture*, Cambridge MA, Harvard University Press, 1988, p. 3.

9. Edwards, E., 'Beyond the Boundary: A Consideration of the Expressive in Photography and Anthropology', in Banks, M. and Morphy, H. (eds), *Rethinking Visual Anthropology*, London: Yale University Press, 1997; Schneider, A., 'Uneasy relationships: Contemporary Artists and Anthropology', *Journal of Material Culture*, 1(2) (1996): pp. 184-5.

10. Marcus, G. and Myers, F. (eds), *The Traffic in Culture: Refiguring Art and Anthropology*, Berkeley: University of California Press, 1995, pp. 19-10.

11. Benjamin, W., 'The Task of the Translator', in Arendt, H. *Illuminations*, London: Fontana, 1992, pp. 72-7.

12. Chandra, M., 'Pacific Album: Vernacular Photography of the Fiji Indian Diaspora', *History of Photography*, 24(2) (2000): pp. 1-7.

13. Schneider, A., 'Uneasy relationships', p. 184.

14. Chandra, M., Pacific Album: Vernacular Photography of the Fiji Indian Diaspora, London: Royal College of Art, unpublished Ph.D. thesis, 1999, p. 2.

15. Dening, G., *Islands and Beaches: discourse on a silent land, Marqueses 1774-1880*, Honolulu, University of Hawaii, 1980, pp. 31-2.

16. Avtar, B., *Cartographies of Diaspora*, London: Routledge, pp. 182-3.

17. Chandra, M., *Pacific Album*, 1999, p. 232.

18. Indeed recent work in neurophysiology positions memory as a form of creativity or imagination.

19. Chandra, M., 'Visible Fragments: Photography and Diaspora,' *Creative Camera*, 361 (1999): pp. 32-5. See also Pinney, C., *Camera Indica: The Social Life of Indian Photographs*, London: Reaktion, 1997, for an important and detailed analysis of the formative inflections of Indian popular photographic practices. In Fiji local photographers were responsible for printing and disseminating film-star publicity stills and had the opportunity to examine their visual language close to as practitioners, not simply as consumers (Chandra, *Pacific Album*, pp. 2-3).

20. This work has now been published, see Chandra, M., *Album Pacifica*, London: Autograph, 2001.

21. For a consideration of the materiality of photographs as objects of memory, see Edwards, E., 'Photographs as Objects of Memory', in Kwint, M., Aynesley, J. and Breward, C. (eds), *Material Memories: Design and Evocation*, Oxford: Berg, 1999, and Edwards, E. and Hart, J. (eds), *Photographs Objects Histories*, London: Routledge, 2004.

22. Chandra 'Visible Fragments', p. 35; 'Pacific Album', *History of Photography*, p. 5.

Chapter 11 No Borders: The Ancient American Roots of Abstraction

1. The most recent tendency among scholars is to stop using the denomination 'pre-Columbian', replacing it with 'pre-Hispanic', therefore stressing the fact that the aboriginal cultures did not suddenly disappear with the arrival of Columbus but that it was a gradual process that originated with colonization. Now, as this new usage is not yet widely established – important texts keep appearng under the 'pre-Columbian' rubric – I have indistinctly kept both denominations.

2. One of these works, *Pintura*, dating from 1961–2, is illustrated in Florencia Bassano Nelson's essay 'Joaquín Torres-García and the Tradition of Construct- ive Art', in Rasmussen, W. (ed.), *Latin American Artists of the Twentieth Century*, New York: The Museum of Modern Art, 1993, p. 82.

3. Later on I remembered that in his *Graphic Tectonics* series of prints of the 1940s, Josef Albers had developed bidimensional reductions of the tectonics of the ancient pyramids at Monte Albán in Mexico.

4. See his 'The Painting of Tamayo and Gottlieb' in O'Neill, J.P. *Barnett Newman: Selected Writing and Interviews,* New York: Knopf, 1990.

5. George Kubler, *The Art and Architecture of Ancient America*, New York: Penguin, 1975, p. 334.

6. To this day, however, most of the reviewers of my *The Stone and The Thread: Andean Roots of Abstract Art*, Austin: University of Texas Press, 1996, consider that I am writing on 'Inca architecture'.

7. In point of fact, the first evaluation of the arts in American antiquity started in the nineteenth century with the general history of the arts, *Handbuch der Kunstgeschichte*, written by the German historian Franz Kugler in 1842, in which he affirmed its autonomy before the European arts, although he was somehow repelled by the 'infidelity' of the Aztec sculpture to the Classical standards. Around the same time, Stephens and Catherwood started the graphic record of the Mayan ruins while the former defined them as 'works of art' (some of the plates were used by Kugler as illustrations in his book). In Captain Dupaix's *Expediciones* of the early nineteenth century there is a fine perception of the Mesoamerican ruins as unprecedented works of art. In this line, Spinden's path-breaking evaluation of Mayan art of the 1920s; Pijoan's general art history, and in Mexico, Covarrubias, Paul Westheim, Justino Fernández and Salvador Toscano extended the aesthetic apreciation of the pre-Columbian arts, yet relying largely on the Meso- american manifestations. (See the comprehensive narrative of this process by Kubler, G., *Esthetic Recognition of Ancient Amerindian Art*, New Haven: Yale University Press, 1991.)

8. *Piedra abstracta, La escultura inca: una visión contemporánea*, Buenos Aires: Fondo de Cultura Económica, 1989.

9. Cited by Rowe, J., 'Two Pucara Statues', in Rowe, J. and Menzel, D. (eds), *Peruvian Archaeology, Selected Readings*, Palo Alto CA: Peek Publications, 1967.

10. For a more detailed argumentation of this point see my *The Stone and Thread*, Chapter 9. I know of only one, and remarkable, history of the art in Latin America that begins with an assessment of the pre-European period. It is Castedo, L., *Historia del arte y la arquitectura colonial – Desde la época precolombina hasta hoy*, Santiago de Chile: Editorial Pomaire, 1970.

11. For an updated and remarkable evaluation of the Andean arts, see Pasztory, E., 'Andean Aesthetics', in *The Spirit of Ancient Peru: Treasures from the Museo Arqueológico Rafael Larco Herrera*, New York; Thames & Hudson, 1997. Equally notable is her treatment of the subject in her recent *Pre-Columbian Art*, Cambridge University Press, 1998.

12. See, in this sense, my essay 'Josef und Anni Albers: die Begegnung mit der frühen Kunst Altamerikas', in *Josef und Anni Albers: Europa und Amerika*, Bern: Kunstmuseum Bern, 1998 (in German).

13. In my *The Stone and the Thread* (Chapter 11) I specifically used the term a 'lesson in abstraction' to refer to the sequence of Wari textiles in which the winged anthropo-, zoo-morphic figures appearing on the 'Sun Gate' frieze at Tiwanaku, in the Bolivian highlands, are gradually geometricized until in one outstanding example (known as the 'Lima Tapestry', in the National Museum of Anthropolgy in Lima, Peru) the original natural forms appear as a mere arrangement of rectangular forms, leaving only a syntactic relationship with the original model. The grouping and detailed study of these textiles – although it is not known whether they responded to an actual chronological evolution, was first done by Alan R. Sawyer in *Tiahuanaco Tapestry Design*, New York: Museum of Primitive Art, 1963.

14. For a more detailed treatment of this subject see my *The Stone and the Thread*, Chapter 7.

15. Cited by James Clifford in *The Predicament of Culture: Twentieth Century Ethnography, Literature and Art*, Cambridge MA: Harvard University Press, 1988, p. 239.

16. In 'Pre-Columbian Stone Sculpture', the preface for an exhibition that he curated in 1944 for the Wakefield Gallery, whose director was Betty Parsons. He later expanded the preface for an article published in *La Revista Belga;* reprinted in O'Neill, J.P. *Barnett Newman: Selected Writings and Interviews*, New York: Alfred Knopf, 1990, p. 62.

17. I discerned the emergence of an abstraction of the Americas in 'North and South Connected: An Abstraction of the Americas', an essay in the accompanying catalogue of the exhibition of the same title, which I curated for the Cecilia de Torres Gallery in New York, in November of 1998. It featured ancient Andean textiles and works by Joaquín Torres-García, Josef and Anni Albers, Adolph Gottlieb, Alfred Jensen, Louise Nevelson, Lenore Tawney, Gonzalo Fonseca, Francisco Matto, E.Ramírez Villamizar, Alejandro

Puente, Cecilia Vicuña and myself. Later I curated a larger version of this show, *Abstraction: The Amerindian Paradigm*, which not only presented an expanded number of aboriginal art objects of the Americas, but also included works by Paul Klee, Tony Smith and Helmut Federle as well. The exhibition opened in the summer of 2001 at the Palais des Beaux Arts in Brussels and travelled later to the IVAM (Instituto Valenciano de Arte Moderno) in Valencia, Spain, where it closed on early January 2002. See also Braun, B., *Pre-Columbian Art and the Post-Columbian World-Ancient American Sources of Modern Art*, New York: Abrams, 1993.

18. One of these works, *Cruz del Sur (Southern Cross)*, from 1992, is illustrated in Braun, p. 305.

Chapter 12 Carlos Capelán: Our Modernity not Theirs

1. Derrida, J. *L'écriture et la différence*, Paris: Seuil, 1967, and Derrida, J., 'Structure, Sign and Play in the Discourse of the Human Sciences' in Macksey, R. and Donato, E. (eds), *The Languages of Criticism and the Sciences of Man*, Baltimore: Johns Hopkins University Press, pp. 246-72

2. Diffusionism refers to a kind of analysis of culture, common in the early part of the twentieth century, in which origins are central, in which the understanding of culture is sought in the geneaology of its elements creating a mapping of cultural movements over time. This approach has returned in some forms of globalization discourse and is the logical basis of notions such as hybridity. Cf. Hannerz, U., 'On some reports from a free space', in Meyer, B. and Geschiere, P. (eds), *Globalization and Identity*, Oxford: Blackwell, 1999, pp. 325-9.

3. Clifford, J., *Routes: Travel and Translation in the late Twentieth Century*, Cambridge MA: Harvard University Press, 1997.

4. This was an unpublished interview that I made with him in October 1995.

5. Augé, M., *Théorie des pouvoirs et idéologie*, Paris: Plon, 1975 and *Pouvoirs de vie pouvoirs de mort*, Paris: Flammarion, 1977. Ekholm Friedman, K., *Catastrophe and creation: The Transformation of an African Culture*, London: Harwood, 1992.

6. This discussion is clearly and intentionally an oversimplification of the great variety of cultural forms and life forms in the world. The intention is to stress the kinds of differences as families of differences that I take to exist in reality.

7. Sahlins, M., 'Goodbye to Tristes Tropes: Ethnography in the Context of Modern World History', *Journal of Modern History*, 65 (1993): 1-25.

Chapter 13 The Case of Tattooing

1. This project is drawn from work in progress; a much fuller range of illustration and citation will appear in an expanded publication in due course.
2. Foster, H., 'The artist as ethnographer', in Marcus, G.E. and Myers, F.R., *The Traffic in Culture: Refiguring Art and Anthropology*, Berkeley: University of California Press, 1995, pp. 302-9; the essay appears in a somewhat different form in Foster, H., *The Return of the Real*, Cambridge MA: MIT Press, 1996.
3. Foster, 'The artist as ethnographer', p. 307.
4. Key earlier texts in the historical anthropology of Oceania include Dening, *Islands and Beaches*, Melbourne: Melbourne University Press, 1980, and Sahlins, M., *Historical Metaphors and Mythical Realities*, Lanham: University Press of America, 1981. For broader reflections on the field, see Douglas, B., *Across the Great Divide*, Chur: Harwood Academic Publishers, 1998, and Thomas, N., *In Oceania*, Durham: Duke University Press, 1997.
5. Robley, H.G., *Moko*, London: Chapman & Hall, 1896.
6. See reproduction in Thomas, N., *Oceanic Art*, London: Thames & Hudson, 1995, Figure 93.
7. Cook, J., *The Journals of Captain James Cook, Volume II: The Voyage of the* Resolution *and* Adventure *1772-1775*, ed. J. C. Beaglehole, Cambridge: Hakluyt Society, 1961, p. 426.
8. Craik, J.L., *The New Zealanders*, London: George Lillie, 1830, pp. 332-3.
9. Barbieri, G.P., *Tahiti Tattoos* (diary), Cologne: Taschen, 2000.
10. Gell, A. *Wrapping in Images: Tattooing in Polynesia*, Oxford: Clarendon Press, 1993, Chapter 2, summarized at pp. 120-1.
11. Sulu'ape Paulo II, 'Samoan Tattooing' in Wedde, I. (ed.), *Fomison: What Shall We Tell Them?* Wellington: City Gallery, 1993.
12. See, e.g., Adams, M. and Thomas, N., *Cook's Sites: Revisiting History*, Dunedin: Otago University Press, 1999.
13. In Wedde, ed. *Fomison*.
14. Ibid.

Index